In Other Words

Pierre Bourdieu

In Memory of my Father

In Other Words

Essays Towards a Reflexive Sociology

Pierre Bourdieu

Translated by Matthew Adamson

Stanford University Press
Stanford, California
1990

Stanford University Press
Stanford, California
© Chapters 1, 2, 3, 4, 5, 6, 8, 9, 10, 11, 12, Les Editions de Minuit
   1987; Chapter 7, Pierre Bourdieu; Chapter 13, Les Editions de Minuit
   1982; Bibliography, Yvette Delsaut
English translation (except Chapter 7 and Bibliography) © 1990
   Polity Press, Cambridge; English translation of Chapter 7 © 1990
   Loic J. D. Wacquant with Matthew Lawson
Originating publisher of English edition:
   Polity Press, Cambridge, in association with
   Basil Blackwell, Oxford
First published in the U.S.A. by
   Stanford University Press, 1990
Printed in Great Britain
Cloth ISBN 0–8047–1557–2
Paper ISBN 0–8047–1725–7
LC 88–63436

Contents

Preface   page   vii

Part I *Pathways*

1   'Fieldwork in philosophy'   3
2   Landmarks   34

Part II *Confrontations*

3   From rules to strategies   59
4   Codification   76
5   The interest of the sociologist   87
6   Reading, readers, the literate, literature   94
7   A reply to some objections   106

Part III *New Directions*

8   Social space and symbolic power   123
9   The intellectual field: a world apart   140
10   The uses of the 'people'   150
11   Programme for a sociology of sport   156
12   Opinion polls: a 'science' without a scientist   168

Part IV *Conclusion*

13   A lecture on the lecture   177

Bibliography of the works of Pierre Bourdieu, 1958–1988   199
    (*compiled by Yvette Delsaut*)

Index   219

Preface

The spirit of the castle is in its drawbridge.

René Char

I have spoken often enough about the particular difficulties of sociological writing, and perhaps the texts the reader will find here refer to them only too frequently. But they justify, I believe, the publication of these transcriptions – relieved of the most flagrant repetitions and clumsy turns of phrase – of talks, interviews and papers. Written discourse is a strange product, which is created in a pure confrontation between the writer and 'what he or she has to say', outside any direct experience of a social relation, and outside the constraints and temptations of an immediately perceptible demand, which takes the form of a variety of signs of resistance or approval. I do not need to mention the irreplaceable advantages of being thus closed in on oneself: it is clear that, among other effects, this closure founds the autonomy of a text from which the author has as far as possible withdrawn, merely removing the rhetorical effects meant to display his intervention and involvement in his discourse (even if this goes no further than the use of the first person), as if to leave the reader's liberty intact.

But the presence of a listener, and especially an audience, has effects which are not all negative, especially when you have to convey an analysis and an experience at the same time, and to overcome obstacles to communication which very often have to do less with problems of understanding than with a disposition of the will: if the urgency and the linear nature of spoken discourse entail simplifications and repetitions (encouraged in addition by the fact that the same questions tend to recur), the facility of the spoken word, which enables you to go very quickly from one point to another, cutting the corners that a rigorous argument must negotiate one by one, means you can make compressions, abbreviations and

vii

comparisons which convey an idea of the complex totalities that writing unfolds and develops in the interminable succession of paragraphs and chapters. The concern to communicate feelings or ideas that is imposed by the direct presence of attentive interlocutors prompts you to go from abstraction to example and back again, and encourages you to look for metaphors or analogies which, when you can point out their limits at the very moment you use them, enable you to give people a first approximate insight into the most complex models and thus to introduce your listeners to a more rigorous presentation. But above all, the juxtaposition of remarks that are very varied in circumstance and topic may, by demonstrating how the same theme is treated in different contexts, or the same model applied to different domains, show in action a mode of thought that the finished nature of the written work can convey only imperfectly, when it does not conceal it completely.

The logic of the interview which, in more cases than one, becomes a genuine dialogue, has the effect of removing one of the main forms of censorship which the fact of belonging to a scientific field can impose, one that may be so deeply internalized that its presence is not even suspected: that which prevents you from answering, in writing itself, questions which, from the professional's point of view, can only appear trivial or unacceptable. Furthermore, when a well-intentioned interlocutor puts forward, in all good faith, his reservations or resistances, or when he acts as the devil's advocate by voicing objections or criticisms he has read or heard, he can give you an opportunity either to state quite fundamental propositions that the elliptical style of academic dignity or the proprieties of scientific etiquette lead you to conceal, or to give explanations, denials or refutations that the disdain or the disgust aroused by the self-destructive over-simplifications of incomprehension and incompetence or by the stupid or base accusations of bad faith tempt you to reject. (I will not here indulge in the – somewhat narcissistic – cruelty of presenting an anthology of the criticisms made of me, in the form of political slogans and denunciations – determinism, totalitarianism, pessimism, etc. – and which shock me above all by their hypocrisy: it is so easy and so profitable to pose as the defender of fine feelings and good causes – art, freedom, virtue, disinterestedness – against someone who can be accused with impunity of hating them because he unveils, without even appearing to deplore the fact, all that it is a point of honour for the believer to conceal.) The fact of being questioned, which creates a certain demand, authorizes and encourages you to explain your theoretical intentions, and all the ways in which they differ from other competing views, and to set out in greater detail the empirical operations, and the difficulties (often undetectable in the final record) they have had to overcome – all the information, in other words, which the perhaps exaggerated refusal to be indulgent and to spell things out as simply as possible often leads you to censor.

But the major advantage of an oral exchange is linked above all to the very content of the sociological message and to the resistances that it arouses. Many of the remarks presented here assume their full significance only if you refer to the circumstances in which they were pronounced and the audience to which they were addressed. Part of their effectiveness probably results from the effort of persuasion aimed at overcoming the extraordinary tension sometimes created by the clarification of a rejected or repressed truth. Gershom Scholem said to me one day: I don't talk about Jewish problems in the same way when I am talking to Jews in New York, Jews in Paris and Jews in Jerusalem. Likewise, the reply I can give to the questions I am most frequently asked varies with the interlocutors – sociologists or non-sociologists, French sociologists or foreign sociologists, specialists from other fields or ordinary laymen and women, and so on. This does not mean that there is not one true answer to each of these questions and that this truth does not always need to be stated. But when, like me, you feel that you owe it to yourself to concentrate in each case on the point where you expect the maximum resistance, which is the exact opposite of having any demagogic intentions, and to tell each audience, without being provocative but also without making any concessions, the aspect of the truth which it will find most difficult to accept, in other words what you think its truth to be, making use of the knowledge you think you have of its expectations so as not to flatter and manipulate it, but to 'get across', as they say, what it will find most difficult to accept or to swallow – in other words what disturbs its most trusted investments – you know that you always run the risk of seeing socio-analysis turn into a socio-drama.

The uncertainties and imprecisions of this deliberately foolhardy discourse thus have their counterpart in the quavering of the voice which is the mark of risks shared in any honest exchange of ideas and which, if it can still be heard, however faintly, through its written transcription, seems to me to justify its publication.

Part I

Pathways

1

'Fieldwork in philosophy'

Q. What was the intellectual situation like when you were a student
– Marxism, phenomenology and so on?

A. When I was a student in the fifties, phenomenology, in its
existentialist variety, was at its peak, and I had read *Being and
Nothingness*[1] very early on, and then Merleau-Ponty and Husserl;
Marxism didn't really exist as an intellectual position, even if people
like Tran-Duc-Thao managed to give it a certain profile by raising
the question of its relation with phenomenology. However, I did
read Marx at that time for academic reasons; I was especially
interested in the young Marx, and I had been fascinated by the
'Theses on Feuerbach'. But this was the period of Stalinist ascend-
ancy. Many of my fellow students who these days have become
violently anti-communist were then in the Communist Party. The
pressure exerted by Stalinism was so exasperating that, around 1951,
we had founded at the École normale (with Bianco, Comte, Marin,
Derrida, Pariente and others) a Committee for the Defence of
Freedom, which Le Roy Ladurie denounced in the communist cell at
the École . . .
Philosophy as taught in the University was not very inspiring –
even if there were some very competent people, like Henri Gouhier,
under whose supervision I wrote a dissertation (a translation and
commentary of the *Animadversiones* of Leibniz), Gaston Bachelard
and Georges Canguilhem. Outside the Sorbonne, and especially at
the École des hautes études and the Collège de France, there were
Éric Weil, Alexandre Koyré, and Martial Guéroult, whose classes I

Interview with A. Honneth, H. Kocyba and B. Scwibs, given at Paris in April
1985 and published in German under the title 'Der Kampf um die symbolische
Ordnung', in *Ästhetik und Kommunikation*, 16, nos 61–62 (1986).
1   J.-P. Sartre, *Being and Nothingness*, tr. H. E. Barnes (New York, 1956).

3

followed once I was at the École normale. All these people were outside the usual syllabus, but it's pretty much thanks to them and to what they represented – a tradition of the history of the sciences and of rigorous philosophy (and thanks also to my reading of Husserl, who was still little translated in those days) – that I tried, together with those people who, like me, were a little tired of existentialism, to go beyond merely reading the classical authors and to give some meaning to philosophy. I studied mathematics and the history of the sciences. Men like Georges Canguilhem, and also Jules Vuillemin, were for me, and for a few others, real 'exemplary prophets' in Weber's sense. In the phenomenologico-existentialist period, when they weren't very well known, they seemed to point to the possibility of a new path, a new way of fulfilling the philosopher's role, quite different from just vaguely holding forth about the big problems. There was also the review *Critique*, then in the middle of its best years, with Alexandre Koyré, Éric Weil and others writing for it; in it, you could come across both wide-ranging and precise information on work being done in France and, especially, abroad. I was, doubtless for sociological reasons, less attracted than other people (for instance, Foucault) to the Bataille–Blanchot side of *Critique*. The desire for a clean break, rather than for some 'transgression', was in my case directed against institutional power, and especially against the institution of the university and all the violence, imposture and sanctified stupidity that it concealed – and, behind that institution, against the social order. This may have been because I didn't have any accounts to settle with the bourgeois family, as did others, and so I was less inclined to the symbolic breaks dealt with in *The Inheritors*.[2] But I think that the concern to *nicht mitmachen*, as Adorno put it – the refusal to compromise with institutions, beginning with intellectual institutions – has never left me.

Many of the intellectual leanings that I share with the 'structuralist' generation (especially Althusser and Foucault) – which I do not consider myself to be part of, firstly because I am separated from them by an academic generation (I went to their lectures) and also because I rejected what seemed to me to be a fad – can be explained by the need to react against what existentialism had represented for them: the flabby 'humanism' that was in the air, the complacent

---

2 P. Bourdieu and J. C. Passeron, *Les héritiers, les étudiants et la culture* (Paris, 1964); trans. as *The Inheritors: French Students and their Relation to Culture*, tr. R. Nice (Chicago, 1979).

appeal to 'lived experience' and that sort of political moralism that lives on today in *Esprit*.[3]

Q.   Were you never interested in existentialism?

A.   I read Heidegger, I read him a lot and with a certain fascination, especially the analyses in *Sein und Zeit* of public time, history and so on, which, together with Husserl's analyses in *Ideen II*,[4] helped me a great deal – as was later the case with Schütz – in my efforts to analyse the ordinary experience of the social. But I never really got into the existentialist mood. Merleau-Ponty was something different, at least in my view. He was interested in the human sciences and in biology, and he gave you an idea of what thinking about immediate present-day concerns can be like when it doesn't fall into the sectarian over-simplifications of political discussion – in for instance his writings on history, on the Communist Party, on the Moscow Trials. He seemed to represent one potential way out of the philosophical babble found in academic institutions . . .

Q.   But at that time, wasn't philosophy dominated by a sociologist?[5]

A.   No – that was just the effect of institutional authority. And our contempt for sociology was intensified by the fact that a sociologist could be president of the board of examiners of the competitive 'agrégation' exam in philosophy and force us to attend his lectures – which we thought were lousy – on Plato or Rousseau. This contempt for the social sciences lasted among philosophy students at the École normale – who represented the 'elite', and therefore the dominant model – at least until the sixties. At that time, the only sociology was mediocre and empirical, without any theoretical or indeed empirical inspiration behind it. And this conviction on the part of philosophers from the École normale was reinforced by the fact that the sociologists of the twenties and thirties, Jean Stoetzel or even Georges Friedmann, who had written a rather poor book on Leibniz and Spinoza, struck them as being the products of a negative vocation. This was even more pronounced for the first sociologists of the

---

3   *Esprit*: political and literary review (broadly Christian and left-wing) founded in the 1930s; became a forum for Resistance writing in the Second World War.
4   E. Husserl, *Ideas: General Introduction to Pure Phenomenology*, tr. W. R. B. Gibson (London, 1931).
5   Georges Davy, the last survivor of the Durkheimian school.

post-war years who, with a few exceptions, had not followed the royal road – École normale and agrégation – and who, in the opinion of some people, had even had to fall back on sociology because of their failure in philosophy.

Q. But how did the change that happened in the sixties come about?

A. Structuralism was very important. For the first time, a social science imposed itself as a respectable, indeed dominant discipline. Lévi-Strauss, who baptized his science anthropology, instead of ethnology, thus bringing together the Anglo-Saxon meaning and the old German philosophical meaning – at about the same time Foucault was translating Kant's *Anthropologie*[6] – ennobled the human science that was thus established, by drawing on Saussure and linguistics, and turned it into a royal science, to which even philosophers were obliged to pay heed. That was when the full force of what I call the '-ology effect' – in allusion to all those nouns that use that suffix, archaeology, grammatology, semiology, etc. – was felt; it was a clear expression of the effort philosophers were making to break down the frontier between science and philosophy. I never had much liking for these half-hearted changes of label which enable one to draw freely on the profits of scientificity and the profits associated with the status of philosopher. I think that just at that time what was necessary was to question the status of philosopher and all its prestige so as to carry out a true conversion into science. And, speaking for myself, although I made an attempt in my work to put into operation the structural or relational way of thinking in sociology, I resisted with all my might the merely fashionable forms of structuralism. And I was even less inclined to show any indulgence for the mechanical transference of Saussure or Jakobson into anthropology or semiology that was common practice in the sixties, since my philosophical work had brought me very early on to read Saussure closely: in 1958–9 I lectured on Durkheim and Saussure, trying to establish the limits of attempts to produce 'pure theories'.

Q. But you became an ethnologist to begin with?

A. I had undertaken research into the 'phenomenology of

6 I. Kant, *Anthropologie du point de vue pragmatique*, tr. M. Foucault (Paris, 1964).

emotional life', or more exactly into the temporal structures of emotional experience. To reconcile my need for rigour with philosophical research, I wanted to study biology and so on. I thought of myself as a philosopher and it took me a very long time to admit to myself that I had become an ethnologist. The new prestige that Lévi-Strauss had given that science probably helped me greatly. . . . I undertook both research that could be called ethnological – on kinship, ritual and the pre-capitalist economy – and research that could be described as sociological, especially statistical surveys that I carried out with my friends from the INSEE,[7] Darbel, Rivet and Seibel, from whom I learned a great deal. For instance, I wanted to establish the principle (one that had never been clearly determined in the theoretical tradition) behind the difference between proletariat and sub-proletariat; and, by analysing the economic and social conditions of the appearance of economic calculation, in the field of economics but also that of fertility and so on, I tried to show that the principle behind this difference can be traced to the domain of the economic conditions enabling the emergence of types of rational *forecasting*, of which revolutionary aspirations are one dimension.

Q. But this theoretical project was inseparable from a methodology . . .

A. Yes. I re-read, of course, all of Marx's works – and many others – on the question (this was probably the period when I read Marx most, and even Lenin's survey of Russia). I was also working on the Marxist notion of relative autonomy in relation to the research that I was starting to carry out into art (a short book, *Proudhon, Marx, Picasso*,[8] written in French between the wars by a German émigré called Max Raphael, had been of great use to me). All of this was before the triumphant return of structuralist Marxism. But above all I wanted to get away from speculation – at that time, the works of Frantz Fanon, especially *The Wretched of the Earth*,[9] were the latest fashion, and they struck me as being both false and dangerous.

---

7 The National Institute of Statistics and Economic Studies.
8 M. Raphael, *Proudhon, Marx, Picasso: Three Studies in the Sociology of Art*, tr. I. Marcuse (London, 1980).
9 F. Fanon, *The Wretched of the Earth*, tr. C. Farrington (Harmondsworth, 1967).

Q.   At the same time you were engaged in anthropological research.

A.   Yes. And the two were closely linked. This was because I also
wanted to understand, through my analyses of temporal consciousness, the conditions of the acquisition of the 'capitalist' economic
habitus among people brought up in a pre-capitalist world. And
there too, I wanted to do it by observation and measurement, and
not by second-hand thinking based on second-hand material. I also
wanted to resolve purely anthropological problems, especially those
that the structuralist approach raised for my work. I have related, in
the introduction to my *The Logic of Practice*,[10] how I was stupefied
to discover, by the use of statistics – something that was very rarely
done in ethnology – that the type of marriage considered to be
typical in Arabo-Berber societies, namely marriage with the parallel
girl cousin, accounted for about 3 to 4 per cent of cases, and 5 to 6
per cent in Marabout families, that are stricter and more orthodox.
This forced me to think about the notion of kinship, rule, and rules
of kinship, which led me to the antipodes of the structuralist
tradition. And the same thing happened to me with ritual: although
it was coherent and, up to a certain point, logical, the system of the
oppositions constitutive of ritual logic turned out to be incapable of
integrating all the data gathered. But it was a very long time before I
really broke with some of the fundamental presuppositions of
structuralism (which I made use of simultaneously in sociology when
I imagined the social world as a space of objective relations that
transcends the agents and is irreducible to interactions between
individuals). I first had to discover, by returning to observe a more
familiar terrain, on the one hand the society of Béarn, where I come
from, and on the other hand the academic world, and the objectivist
presuppositions – such as the privilege of the observer with respect to
the native, who is bound to remain ignorant of his situation – that are
part and parcel of the structuralist approach. And then it was, I
think, necessary for me to leave ethnology as a social world, by
becoming a sociologist, so that the raising of certain unthinkable
questions could become possible. I'm not telling my life story here: I
am trying to make a contribution to the sociology of science.
Belonging to a professional group brings into play an effect of
censorship which goes far beyond institutional or personal constraints: there are questions that you don't ask, and that you can't

---

10   P. Bourdieu, *Le sens pratique* (Paris, 1980); trans. as *The Logic of Practice*,
tr. R. Nice (Cambridge, 1989).

8

ask, because they have to do with the fundamental beliefs that are at the root of science, and of the way things function in the scientific domain. This is what Wittgenstein says when he points out that radical doubt is so deeply identified with the philosophical stance that a well-trained philosopher does not so much as dream of casting doubt on this doubt.

Q. You often quote Wittgenstein – why is that?

A. Wittgenstein is probably the philosopher who has helped me most at moments of difficulty. He's a kind of saviour for times of great intellectual distress – as when you have to question such evident things as 'obeying a rule'. Or when you have to describe such simple (and, by the same token, practically ineffable) things as putting a practice into practice.

Q. What was the principle behind your doubt about structuralism?

A. I wanted, so to speak, to reintroduce agents that Lévi-Strauss and the structuralists, among others Althusser, tended to abolish, making them into simple epiphenoma of structure. And I mean agents, not subjects. Action is not the mere carrying out of a rule, or obedience to a rule. Social agents, in archaic societies as well as in ours, are not automata regulated like clocks, in accordance with laws which they do not understand. In the most complex games, matrimonial exchange for instance, or ritual practices, they put into action the incorporated principles of a generative habitus: this system of dispositions can be imagined by analogy with Chomsky's generative grammar – with this difference: I am talking about dispositions *acquired through experience*, thus variable from place to place and time to time. This 'feel for the game', as we call it, is what enables an infinite number of 'moves' to be made, adapted to the infinite number of possible situations which no rule, however complex, can foresee. And so, I replaced the rules of kinship with matrimonial strategies. Where everyone used to talk of 'rules', 'model' or 'structure', somewhat indiscriminately, and putting themselves in the objectivist position, that of God the Father watching the social actors like puppets controlled by the strings of structure, everyone now-adays talks of matrimonial strategies (which means they put them-selves in the place of the agents, without however making them into rational calculators). This word, strategies, evidently has to be stripped of its naively teleological connotations: types of behaviour

9

can be directed towards certain ends without being consciously directed to these ends, or determined by them. The notion of habitus was invented, if I may say so, in order to account for this paradox. Likewise, the fact that ritual practices are the product of a 'practical sense', and not of a sort of unconscious calculation or of obedience to a rule, explains that the rites are coherent, but that their coherence is the partial and never total coherence that we associate with practical constructions.

Q. Didn't this breaking away from the structuralist paradigm risk throwing you back on the 'individualist' paradigm of rational calculation?

A. In retrospect – although in fact things never happen this way in the context of real research – the use of the notion of *habitus*, an old Aristotelian and Thomist concept that I completely rethought, can be understood as a way of escaping from the choice between a structuralism without subject and the philosophy of the subject. There too, certain phenomenologists, including Husserl himself who gives a role to the notion of habitus in the analysis of antepredicative experience, or Merleau-Ponty, and also Heidegger, opened the way for a non-intellectualist, non-mechanistic analysis of the relations between agent and world. Unfortunately, people apply to my analyses – and this is the principal source of misunderstanding – the very alternatives that the notion of habitus is meant to exclude, those of consciousness and the unconscious, of explanation by determining causes or by final causes. Thus Lévi-Strauss sees in the theory of matrimonial strategies a form of spontaneism and a return to the philosophy of the subject. Others, on the contrary, will see in it the extreme form of what they reject in the sociological way of thinking: determinism and the abolition of the subject. But it's probably Jon Elster who presents us with the most perverse example of incomprehension. Instead of claiming, as does everyone else, that I advocate one of the terms of the alternative so that he can emphasize the importance of the other, he charges me with a sort of oscillation between the one and the other and he can thus accuse me of contradiction or, more subtly, of piling up mutually exclusive explanations. His position is all the more astonishing in that, probably as a result of the polemical situation, he has been led to take into account what is at the very basis of my representation of action, the way in which dispositions are adjusted in accordance with one's position, and expectations in accordance with opportunities:

10

the *sour grapes* factor. Since the habitus, the virtue mad
necessity, is a product of the incorporation of objective necessi'
produces strategies which, even if they are not produced by consciously aiming at explicitly formulated goals on the basis of an
adequate knowledge of objective conditions, nor by the mechanical
determination exercised by causes, turn out to be objectively adjusted to the situation. Action guided by a 'feel for the game' has all
the appearances of the rational action that an impartial observer,
endowed with all the necessary information and capable of mastering
it rationally, would deduce. And yet it is not based on reason. You
need only think of the impulsive decision made by the tennis player
who runs up to the net, to understand that it has nothing in common
with the learned construction that the coach, after analysis, draws up
in order to explain it and deduce communicable lessons from it. The
conditions of rational calculation are practically never given in
practice: time is limited, information is restricted, etc. And yet
agents *do* do, much more often than if they were behaving randomly,
'the only thing to do'. This is because, following the intuitions of a
'logic of practice' which is the product of a lasting exposure to
conditions similar to those in which they are placed, they anticipate
the necessity immanent in the way of the world. One would have to
re-examine in the perspective of this logic the analysis of distinction,
one of the paradoxical modes of behaviour which fascinate Elster
because they are a challenge to the distinction between consciousness and the unconscious. Let me say for now – though it's actually
much more complicated – that the dominant agents appear distinguished only because, being so to speak born into a position that is
distinguished positively, their habitus, their socially constituted
nature, is immediately adjusted to the immanent demands of the
game, and they can thus assert their difference without needing to
want to, that is, with the unselfconsciousness that is the mark of
so-called 'natural' distinction: they merely need to be what they are
in order to be what they have to be, that is, naturally distinguished
from those who are obliged to strive for distinction. Far from being
identifiable with distinguished behaviour, as Veblen thinks (and
Elster equates me wrongly with him), to strive for distinction is the
opposite of distinction: firstly because it involves recognition of a
lack and the avowal of a self-seeking aspiration, and secondly
because, as can easily be seen in the *petit bourgeois*, consciousness
and reflexivity are both cause and symptom of the failure of
immediate adaptation to the situation which defines the virtuoso.
The habitus entertains with the social world which has produced it a

11

real ontological complicity, the source of cognition without consciousness, intentionality without intention, and a practical mastery of the world's regularities which allows one to anticipate the future without even needing to posit it as such. We here find the foundations of the difference established by Husserl, in *Ideen I*, between protension as the practical aiming at a yet-to-come inscribed in the present, thus apprehended as already there and endowed with the doxic modality of the present, and the project as the position of a futurity constituted as such, that is, as capable of happening or of not happening; and it is because he did not understand this difference, and especially the theory of the agent (as opposed to the 'subject') that founds it, that Sartre, in his theory of action, and above all in his theory of the emotions, came up against difficulties absolutely identical to those that Elster, whose anthropology is very close to his, tries to solve by a sort of new philosophical casuistry: how can I freely free myself from freedom, freely give the world the power to determine me, as in fear, etc? But I dealt with all that in great detail in *The Logic of Practice*.

Q.   Why did you pick up this notion of habitus?

A.   The notion of habitus has been used innumerable times in the past, by authors as different as Hegel, Husserl, Weber, Durkheim and Mauss, all of whom used it in a more or less methodical way. However, it seems to me that, in all these cases, those who used the notion did so with the same theoretical intention in mind, or at least pointed to the same line of research – whether, as in Hegel (who also uses, with the same function, notions like *hexis*, *ethos*, etc.), there is an attempt to break with Kantian dualism and to reintroduce the permanent dispositions that are constitutive of realized morality (*Sittlichkeit*), as opposed to the moralism of duty; or whether, as in Husserl, the notion of habitus and different concepts akin to it, such as *Habitualität*, show an attempt to escape from the philosophy of consciousness; or whether, as in Mauss, there is an attempt to account for the systematic functioning of the socialized body. By developing the notion of habitus, with reference to Panofsky who, in *Gothic Architecture and Scholasticism*,[11] himself developed a pre-existing concept to account for the effect of scholastic thought, I wanted to rescue Panofsky from the Neo-Kantian tradition in which he was still imprisoned (this is even clearer in *Meaning in the Visual*

---

11   E. Panofsky, *Gothic Architecture and Scholasticism* (New York, 1957).

Arts[12]), by turning to good account the altogether accidental, and in any case unique, use he had made of this notion (Lucien Goldmann had seen this clearly: he had criticized me sharply for reclaiming for materialism a thinker who, in his opinion, had always refused to go in that direction for reasons of 'political prudence' – that was the way he saw things . . .). Above all, I wanted to react against the mechanistic tendencies of Saussure (who, as I showed in *The Logic of Practice*, conceives practice as simple *execution*) and those of structuralism. In that respect I was very close to Chomsky, in whom I found the same concern to give to practice an active, inventive intention (he has appeared to certain defenders of personalism as a bulwark of liberty against structuralist determinism): I wanted to insist on the *generative capacities* of dispositions, it being understood that these are acquired, socially constituted dispositions. It is easy to see how absurd is the cataloguing which leads people to subsume under structuralism, which destroys the subject, a body of work which has been guided by the desire to reintroduce the agent's practice, his or her capacity for invention and improvisation.

But I wanted to emphasize that this 'creative', active, inventive capacity was not that of a transcendental subject in the idealist tradition, but that of an acting agent. At the risk of seeing myself aligned with the most vulgar forms of thought, I wanted to insist on the 'primacy of practical reason' that Fichte spoke of, and to clarify the specific categories of this reason (I tried to carry out this task in *The Logic of Practice*). I made much use, less for thinking than as a way of giving me the courage to express my thoughts, of the celebrated 'Theses on Feuerbach': 'The chief defect of all hitherto existing materialism (that of Feuerbach included) is that the thing is conceived only in the form of the object of contemplation, but not as human activity, practice.' It was necessary to take back from idealism the 'active side' of practical knowledge which the materialist tradition, notably with the theory of 'reflection', had abandoned to it. Constructing the notion of habitus as a system of acquired dispositions functioning on the practical level as categories of perception and assessment or as classificatory principles as well as being the organizing principles of action meant constituting the social agent in his true role as the practical operator of the construction of objects.

Q. All of your work, and especially the criticisms you make of the

---

12   E. Panofsky, *Meaning in the Visual Arts* (Harmondsworth, 1970).

ideology of the gift or, in the theoretical field, of the deeply antigenetic tendency of structuralism, draws its inspiration from the concern to reintroduce the genesis of dispositions, the history of the individual.

A.   In this sense, if I liked the games with labels that people have enjoyed playing in the intellectual field ever since certain philosophers introduced into it the modes and models of the artistic field, I would say that I am trying to develop a *genetic structuralism*: the analysis of objective structures – those of different *fields* – is inseparable from the analysis of the genesis, within biological individuals, of the mental structures which are to some extent the product of the incorporation of social structures; inseparable, too, from the analysis of the genesis of these social structures themselves: the social space, and the groups that occupy it, are the product of historical struggles (in which agents participate in accordance with their position in the social space and with the mental structures through which they apprehend this space).

Q.   All this seems very far from the rigid determinism and the dogmatic sociologism which is sometimes ascribed to you.

A.   I can't recognize myself in that image and I can't help finding an explanation for it in a certain resistance to analysis. In any case, I find it quite ridiculous that sociologists or historians, who aren't always the best equipped to enter these philosophical discussions, are now reviving that debate indulged in by ageing scholars of the Belle Époque who wanted to save spiritual values from the threat of science. The fact that they can't find anything to set against a scientific construction except a metaphysical thesis strikes me as a clear sign of weakness. The discussion must be situated on the terrain of science, if we want to avoid falling into debates for schoolchildren and cultural weekly magazines, in which night all philosophical cats are black. Sociology's misfortune is that it discovers the arbitrary and the contingent where we like to see necessity, or nature (the gift, for instance, which, as has been known since Plato's myth of Er, is not easy to reconcile with a theory of liberty); and that it discovers necessity, social constraints, where we would like to see choice and free will. The habitus is that unchosen principle of so many choices that drives our humanists to such despair. It would be easy to establish – though I am doubtless rather overstating the challenge – that the choice of this philosophy of free

14

choice isn't randomly distributed ... The essential thing about historical realities is that one can always establish that things could have been otherwise, indeed, *are* otherwise in other places and other conditions. This means that, by historicizing, sociology denaturalizes, defatalizes. But it is then accused of encouraging a cynical disenchantment. The question of knowing whether what the sociologist presents as an objective report and not a thesis – for instance, the fact that the consumption of food or the uses of the body vary depending on the position one occupies in the social space – is true or false, and of showing how one can explain these variations, is thus avoided, on a terrain in which this question would stand some chance of being solved. But in other respects, driving to despair those whom we have to call absolutists, whether enlightened or not, who criticize his disenchanting relativism, the sociologist discovers the necessity, the constraint of social conditions and conditionings, right in the very heart of the 'subject', in the form of what I have called the habitus. In short, he reduces the absolutist humanist to the depths of despair by showing him necessity in contingency, by revealing the system of social conditions which have made a particular way of being or doing possible, a way that is thus necessitated without, for all that, being necessary. Wretchedness of man without God or any hope of grace – a wretchedness that the sociologist merely reveals and brings to light, and for which he is made responsible, like all prophets of evil tidings. But you can kill the messenger: what he says is still true, and has still been heard.

This being the case, how can it escape notice that by expressing the social determinants of different forms of practice, especially intellectual practice, the sociologist gives us the chance of acquiring a certain freedom from these determinants? It is through the illusion of freedom from social determinants (an illusion which I have said a hundred times is the specific determination of intellectuals) that social determinations win the freedom to exercise their full power. Those who walk into the debate with their eyes closed and a little nineteenth-century philosophical baggage would do well to think about this if they don't want to lay themselves open to the easiest forms of objectification in the future. And so, paradoxically, sociology frees us by freeing us from the illusion of freedom, or, more exactly, from the misplaced belief in illusory freedoms. Freedom is not something given: it is something you conquer – collectively. And I regret that in the name of a petty narcissistic libido, encouraged by an immature denial of the realities, people can deprive themselves of an instrument that allows one truly to constitute oneself – a little more than before, at any rate – as a free subject, by making an effort of reappropriation. Let's take a very simple example: through one of my friends, I had obtained the dossiers that a philosophy teacher in the preparatory classes had compiled on his pupils; there was a photo, the parents' occupation, and appraisals of written work. Here is a simple document: a teacher (of freedom) wrote of one of his pupils that she had a servile relationship to philosophy; it so happens that this pupil was the daughter of a housewife (and she was the only one of her kind in this sample). The example – a real one – is evidently somewhat facile, but the elementary act which consists of writing on a piece of schoolwork 'dull', 'servile', 'brilliant', 'thought-ful', etc., is the implementation of socially constituted taxonomies which are in general the interiorization of oppositions existing in the university in the form of divisions into disciplines and departments, and also in the social field overall. The analysis of mental structures is an instrument of liberation: thanks to the instruments of sociology, we can realize one of the eternal ambitions of philosophy – discovering cognitive structures (in this particular case, the categories of understanding of the teacher) and at the same time uncovering some of the best-concealed limits of thought. I could give hundreds of examples of social dichotomies relayed by the education system which, becoming categories of perception, hinder or imprison thought. The sociology of knowledge, in the case of the professionals of knowledge, is the instrument of knowledge *par excellence*, the instrument of knowledge of the instruments of knowledge. I can't see how we can do without it. Let no one pretend that I think it's the *only* instrument. It's one instrument among others, which I think I have made more powerful than it was before, and which can be made even more powerful. Every time the social history of philosophy, the social history of literature, the social history of painting, etc., is written, this instrument will be developed further: I can't see what objections anyone, except perhaps a mere obscurantist, could make to it. I think that enlightenment is on the side of those who turn their spotlight on our blinkers . . .

Paradoxically, this critical and reflexive disposition is not at all self-evident, especially for philosophers, who are often led, by the social definition of their function, and by the logic of competition with the social sciences, to refuse as something scandalous the historicization of their concepts or their theoretical inheritance. I will take (since it allows one to reason *a fortiori*) the example of Marxist philosophers who are led by their concern for 'a grand theoretical design', for instance, to perpetuate 'fighting concepts' such as

16

spontaneism, centralism, voluntarism (one could think of others), and to treat them as philosophical – in other words transhistorical – concepts. For instance, in France they have just published a *Dictionnaire critique du marxisme*[13] in which three-quarters (at least) of the entries are of this type (the few words which do not belong to this category were made up by Marx himself). These concepts are very frequently insults, words of abuse produced in the course of different struggles and for the needs of those struggles. Many 'Marxist' philosophers perpetuate them, wrest them out of their historical context and discuss them independently of their original use.

Why is this example interesting? Because you can see that the constraints, interests or dispositions associated with belonging to the philosophical field weigh more heavily on Marxist philosophers than does Marxist philosophy. If there is one thing that Marxist philosophy should make necessary, it is close attention to the history (and the historicity) of the concepts that we use to think about history. But the feeling that philosophy is somehow aristocratic leads one to forget to submit to historical criticism concepts that are visibly marked by the historical circumstances of their production and use (the Althusserians excelled in this way). Marxism, in the reality of its social use, ends up by being a mode of thought completely immune to historical criticism, which is a paradox, given the potentialities and indeed the demands inherent in Marx's thought. Marx laid down the bases of a sociolinguistic pragmatics, in particular in *The German Ideology*[14] (I referred to it in my sociological analysis of the style and rhetoric of Althusser). These directions have remained a dead letter, because the Marxist tradition has never had much time for reflexive ✓ criticism. In the Marxists' defence, I will say that, although one can derive from Marx's work the principles of a critical sociology of sociology and of the theoretical instruments that sociology, especially that of the Marxist variety, uses in order to think of the social world, Marx himself never made much use of historical criticism against Marxism itself . . .

Q. I remember that in Frankfurt we tried to discuss certain aspects of *Distinction*:[15] would you say that symbolic structures are a

---

13 G. Labica and G. Bensussan, *Dictionnaire critique du marxisme* (Paris, 1985).
14 K. Marx and F. Engels, *The German Ideology* (Moscow, 1964).
15 P. Bourdieu, *La distinction. Critique sociale du jugement* (Paris, 1979); trans. as *Distinction. A Social Critique of the Judgement of Taste*, tr. R. Nice (Cambridge, Mass., 1984).

representation of the fundamental articulations of social reality, or would you say that these structures are to a certain extent autonomous or produced by a universal mind?

A. I have always been uncomfortable with the hierarchical representation of stratified levels (infrastructure/superstructure) which is inseparable from the question of the relations between symbolic structures and economic structures which dominated the debate between structuralists and Marxists in the 1960s. I am starting to wonder more and more whether today's social structures aren't yesterday's symbolic structures and whether for instance class as it is observed is not to some extent the product of the theoretical effect of Marx's work. Of course, I won't go so far as to say that it's the symbolic structures that produce the social structures: the theoretical effect is exerted all the more powerfully in that there pre-exist, *in potentia*, 'in outline', in reality, as one of the possible principles of division (which isn't necessarily the one that's most evident to common perception), those divisions which theory, as an explicit principle of vision and division, brings into visible existence. What is sure is that, within certain limits, symbolic structures have an altogether extraordinary power of *constitution* (in the sense of philosophy and political theory) which has been greatly underestimated. But these structures, even if they no doubt owe much to the specific capacities of the human mind, like the very power to symbolize, to anticipate the future, etc., seem to me defined in their specificity by the historical conditions of their genesis.

Q. So the desire to break away from structuralism has always been very strong in you, at the same time as the intention of transferring to the domain of sociology the experience of structuralism – an intention that you set out in your 1968 article, 'Structuralism and Theory of Sociological Knowledge', which appeared in *Social Research*.[16]

A. The retrospective analysis of the genesis of my concepts that you invite me to make is necessarily an artificial exercise, which risks making me fall into what Bergson called the 'retrospective fallacy'. The different theoretical choices were no doubt more negative than positive, to begin with, and it's probable that they also arose from

---

16 P. Bourdieu, 'Structuralism and Theory of Sociological Knowledge', *Social Research*, 35, no. 4 (Winter 1968), pp. 681–706.

the quest for solutions to problems that one could call personal, like the concern to apprehend in a rigorous way politically burning problems which doubtless guided the choices I made, from my work on Algeria up to *Homo academicus*,[17] by way of *The Inheritors*, or else those kinds of deep and only episodically conscious drives that lead one to feel an affinity for or an aversion to this or that way of living the intellectual life, and thus to support or combat this or that philosophical or scientific position. I think, too, that I have always been strongly motivated in my choices by a resistance to the phenomena of fashion and to the dispositions, which I perceived as frivolous or even dishonest, of those who connived with them: for instance, many of my research strategies draw their inspiration from a concern to refuse the totalizing ambition that is usually identified with philosophy. In the same way, I've always had a pretty ambivalent relationship with the Frankfurt School: the affinities between us are clear, and yet I felt a certain irritation when faced with the aristocratic demeanour of that totalizing critique which retained all the features of grand theory, doubtless so as not to get its hands dirty in the kitchens of empirical research. The same goes for the Althusserians, and for those interventions, both simplistic and peremptory, that philosophical arrogance enables people to make.

WooF

It was the concern to react against the pretensions of grand criticism that led me to 'dissolve' the big questions by applying them to objects that from a social point of view were minor or indeed insignificant and, in any case, closely defined, and thus capable of being empirically apprehended, such as photographic practices. But I was reacting no less against the microphrenic empiricism of Lazarsfeld and his European epigones, whose false technological perfection concealed an absence of any real theoretical problematic – an absence that generated empirical errors, sometimes of a completely elementary sort. (In parenthesis, I'd say that it would be granting far too much to the so-called 'hard' current of American sociology if one were to accord it the empirical rigour it claims for itself, as opposed to the more 'theoretical' traditions, often identified with Europe. One needs to take into account the whole effect of domination exercised by American science, and also the more or less apologetic or unconscious adherence to a positivist philosophy of science, to explain how the inadequacies and technical mistakes caused by the positivist conception of science, on all levels of

---

17 P. Bourdieu, *Homo academicus* (Paris, 1984); trans. as *Homo academicus*, tr. P. Collier (Cambridge, 1988).

research, from sampling to the statistical analysis of data, can pass unnoticed. One soon loses count of the number of cases in which segments of experience aping experimental rigour conceal the total absence of a real sociologically constructed object.)

Q. And, in the case of structuralism, how did your practical attitude to this particular trend develop?

A. On this point too, to be completely honest, I think I was guided by a sort of theoretical sense, but also and perhaps above all by a rejection – quite a deep-seated one – of the ethical position implied by structuralist anthropology, the haughty and distant relationship established between the researcher and the object of his research, namely ordinary people, thanks to the theory of practice, explicit in the case of the Althusserians, who made the agent into a mere 'bearer' (*Träger*) of the structure (the notion of the unconscious fulfilled the same role in Lévi-Strauss). In this way, breaking away from Lévi-Strauss's analysis of native 'rationalizations', which are quite incapable of enlightening the anthropologist about the real causes or the real reasons behind modes of practice, I insisted on asking informants the question why. This obliged me to discover, with reference to marriages for instance, that the reasons for contracting the same category of marriage – in this case, marriage with the parallel cousin on the father's side – could vary considerably depending on the agents and also on the circumstances. I was on the track of the notion of strategy ... And at the same time, I was beginning to suspect that the privilege granted to scientific and objectivist analysis (genealogical research, for example), in dealing with the natives' vision of things, was perhaps an ideology inherent in the profession. In short, I wanted to abandon the cavalier point of view of the anthropologist who draws up plans, maps, diagrams and genealogies. That is all very well, and inevitable, as *one moment*, that of objectivism, in the anthropologist's procedures. But you shouldn't forget the other possible relation to the social world, that of agents really engaged in the market, for example – the level that I am interested in mapping out. One must thus draw up a theory of this non-theoretical, partial, somewhat down-to-earth relationship with the social world that is the relation of ordinary experience. And one must also establish a theory of the theoretical relationship, a theory of all the implications, starting with the breaking off of practical belonging and immediate investment, and its transformation into the distant, detached relationship that defines the scientist's position.

This vision of things, that I am presenting in its 'theoretical' form, probably started out from an intuition of the irreducibility of social existence to the models that can be made of it or, to put it naively, of 'life's profusion', of the gap between real practices and experiences and the abstractions of the mental world. But far from making this the foundation and justification of irrationalism or of a condemnation of scientific ambition, I tried to convert this 'fundamental intuition' into a theoretical principle, which must be seen as a factor in everything that science can say about the social world. For instance, you have the whole set of ideas, which I'm dealing with at present, about *scholè*, leisure and school, as the principle of what Austin called the *scholastic view*, and of the errors that it systematically creates.

Science can't do anything by paying lip-service to the rich inexhaustibility of life: that is merely a feeling, a mood without interest, except for the person expressing it, who in this way puts on the airs of an emancipated lover of life (in opposition to the frigid and austere scientist). This acute feeling for what Weber called the *Vielseitigkeit*, the manysidedness, of social reality, its resistance to the venture of knowledge, was doubtless the basis of the thinking that I have been constantly engaged in on the limits of scientific knowledge. And the work that I am preparing on the theory of fields – and which could be called 'the plurality of worlds' – will end with a consideration of the plurality of logics corresponding to different worlds, that is, to different fields as places in which different kinds of common sense, different commonplace ideas and different systems of topics, all irreducible to each other, are constructed.

It is clear that all this was rooted in a particular social experience: a relationship, which was not experienced as either natural or self-evident, with the theoretical position. This difficulty in adopting a cavalier point of view, from a position of superiority, on Kabyle peasants, their marriages or their rituals, doubtless stemmed from the fact that I had known very similar peasants, who had a similar way of talking about honour and shame, etc., and that I could sense the artificiality both of the vision that I sometimes had by observing things from a strictly objectivist point of view – that of genealogy, for example – and indeed of the vision that informants proposed to me when, in their concern to play the game, to be equal to the situation created by the theoretical questioning, they turned themselves as it were into the spontaneous theoreticians of their practice. In a word, my critical relation to intellectualism in all its forms (and especially in its structuralist form) is without any doubt linked to the particular place I originally occupied in the social world and to the particular relation to the intellectual world that this form favoured, and that sociological work has only reinforced, by neutralizing the sanctions and repressions linked to learning at school – which, for their part, by giving me the means to overcome the repressions of scientific language, doubtless made it possible for me to say a number of things that scientific language excluded.

Q. By working within a structuralist logic, albeit in an unorthodox way, you drew people's attention to the concept of honour and domination, of strategies for acquiring honour; you also emphasized the category of *praxis*.

A. I really must point out that I have never used the concept of praxis which, at least in French, tends to create the impression of something pompously theoretical – which is pretty paradoxical – and makes one think of trendy Marxism, the young Marx, the Frankfurt School, Yugoslav Marxism . . . I've always talked, quite simply, of practice. That being said, the big theoretical intentions, those condensed in the concepts of habitus, strategy and so on, were present in my work, in a half-explicit and relatively undeveloped way, right from the start (the concept of *field* is much more recent: it emerged from the encounter between research into the sociology of art that I was starting to undertake, in my seminar at the École normale, around 1960, and the beginning of the chapter devoted to religious sociology in *Wirtschaft und Gesellschaft*). For instance, in my earliest analyses of honour (I've since reformulated them several times . . .), you find all the problems that I am still tackling today: the idea that struggles for recognition are a fundamental dimension of social life and that what is at stake in them is the accumulation of a particular form of capital, honour in the sense of reputation and prestige, and that there is, therefore, a specific logic behind the accumulation of symbolic capital, as capital founded on cognition [*connaissance*] and recognition [*reconnaissance*]; the idea of strategy, as a way of directing practice that is neither conscious and calculated, nor mechanically determined, but is the product of the sense of honour as a feel for that particular game, the game of honour; and the idea that there is a logic of practice, whose specificity lies above all in its temporal structure. I would refer here to the critique I wrote of the analysis of the exchange of gifts in Lévi-Strauss: the model which shows the interdependence of gift and counter-gift destroys the practical logic of exchange, which can only function if the objective model (every gift requires a counter-gift) is not experienced as such. And this misconstrual of the model is possible because the temporal structure of exchange (the counter-gift is not only different, but *deferred*) masks or contradicts the objective structure of exchange. I think these analyses included, potentially, the essentials of what I have since developed. That is why I was able to pass imperceptibly and quite naturally from the analysis of Berber culture to the analysis of school culture (in any case, I got these two activities to coexist in practical terms between 1965 and 1975, since I was working simultaneously on what would lead on the one hand to *Distinction* and on the other to *The Logic of Practice*, two complementary books which summarize that whole period): most of the concepts around which I organized the work on the sociology of education and culture that I carried out or directed at the Centre for European Sociology came into being on the basis of a generalization of the results of the ethnological and sociological work that I had done in Algeria (that is particularly easy to see in the preface that I wrote for the collective book on photography, *Un art moyen*[18]). I am thinking in particular of the relationship between subjective hopes and objective opportunities that I had observed in the economic, demographic and political behaviour of Algerian workers, and that I could also observe in French students or their families. But the transfer is even more evident in the interest I took in the cognitive structures, taxonomies and classificatory activities of social agents.

Q.   And is the development of your empirical interest in the way education is directed (*The Inheritors*) linked to your position in the intellectual field?

A.   It's clear that my vision of culture and the education system owes a great deal to the position I occupy in the university, and especially to the path that led me there (which doesn't mean that it is relativized by this fact) and to the relationship with the school institution – I've described it several times – that was favoured by this path. But it also goes without saying that, as I have just shown, the analysis of schools – and this is something which is misunder-

---

18   P. Bourdieu, L. Boltanski, R. Castel and J. C. Chamboredon, *Un art moyen, essai sur les usages sociaux de la photographie* (Paris, 1970).

stood by the superficial commentators who treat my work more or less as if it could be reduced to a stance inspired by the SNES, the higher education trade union, or, at best, to the efforts made by a classical philologist to resist the ravages of 'egalitarianism' – was located within a theoretical problematic or, more simply, within a specific tradition, peculiar to the human sciences, and at least partly irreducible to investigations into 'universities today' or political events. To start with, I had the intention of carrying out a social critique of culture. I wrote an article called 'Systems of Education and Systems of Thought',[19] in which I wanted to show that mental structures, in societies where writing is of primary importance, are inculcated by the school system; that the divisions of educational organization are the basis of the forms of classification.

Q. You were developing once more Durkheim's project of writing a sociology of the structures of the mind analysed by Kant. But you also introduced a new interest in social domination.

A. An American historian of sociology named Vogt has written that doing for his own society, as I am trying to do, what Durkheim had done for primitive societies, presupposed a considerable change in point of view, linked to the disappearance of the effect of neutralization that goes with studying a distant, exotic society. The minute one raises for our own society, for our education system for instance, the gnoseological problems raised by Durkheim for primitive religions, they become political problems; it's impossible not to see that the forms of classification are forms of domination, that the sociology of knowledge or cognition [*connaissance*] is inseparably a sociology of recognition [*reconnaissance*] and miscognition [*méconnaissance*], that is, of symbolic domination. (In reality, this is true even in societies which are not very highly differentiated, such as Kabyle society: the classificatory structures which organize the whole vision of the world refer, in the final analysis, to the sexual division of labour.) The fact of asking of our own societies traditional ethnological questions, and of destroying the traditional frontier between ethnology and sociology, was already a political act. (Concretely, that is expressed by the reactions that the two forms of work arouse: while my analysis of the mental structures that are

---

19 P. Bourdieu, 'Systèmes d'enseignement et systèmes de pensée', trans. as 'Systems of Education and Systems of Thought', *International Social Science Journal*, 19, no. 3 (1967), pp. 338–58.

objectified in the space of the Kabyle house arouse only approval, or indeed admiration, the analyses I managed to carry out of the 'categories of professional understanding', basing my work on the way upper-sixth-form teachers judged their pupils, or on the obituaries in the yearbook of former students at the École normale supérieure, seem gross transgressions showing a lack of respect for the proprieties.) Classificatory schemes, systems of classification, the fundamental oppositions of thought, masculine/feminine, right/left, east/west, but also theory/practice, are political categories: the critical theory of culture leads quite naturally to a theory of politics. And the reference to Kant, instead of being a way of transcending the Hegelian tradition by saving the universal, as in certain German thinkers, is a means of radicalizing the critique by raising in all cases the question of the social conditions of possibility – including the social conditions of possibility of critique itself. This sociologically armed *Selbstreflexion* leads to a sociological critique of the theoretical critique, thus to a radicalization and a rationalization of the critique. For example, the critical science of classifications (and of the notion of class) represents one of the few chances we have of really moving beyond the limits inscribed in a historical tradition (a conceptual tradition, for instance) – those limits that the absolute thinker realizes by ignoring them. It is in discovering its historicity that reason gives itself the means of escaping from history.

Q.   What is interesting is seeing, in the development of your theory, a theoretical investigation into your reactions to your environment.

A.   I took the decision to tell the story of the path I have followed from this point of view, that is, by trying to supply the elements of a sociological analysis of the development of my work. If I have done so, it is also because this sort of self-analysis is part, I think, of the preconditions of the way my thinking has developed. If I can say what I do say, today, it's probably because I have not stopped using sociology against my determinations and my social limits; and above all, in order to transform the intellectual moods, likes and dislikes that are, I believe, so important in intellectual choices into conscious and explicit propositions.

But the position that your questioning is forcing me to adopt, that of intellectual autobiography, means that I am inclined to select certain aspects of my history, which are not necessarily the most important, or the most interesting, even intellectually (I have in mind, for instance, what I told you about my experience as a student and about the École normale). But, above all, it inclines me to rationalize, so to speak, both the way events happened and the meaning they had for me – even if only as a sort of professional point of honour. I don't have to tell you that many things that have played a determining part in my 'intellectual path' happened by chance. My own contribution, doubtless linked to my habitus, consisted essentially in making the most of them, to the best of my abilities (I think, for example, that I seized on a great number of opportunities that many people would have let go by).

Furthermore, the strategic vision that your questions impose on me, by inviting me to situate myself in relation to other work, should not hide the fact that the real basis, at least on the level of experience, of my headlong, rather crazy commitment to science, is the pleasure of playing, and playing one of the most extraordinary games that one can play, that of research, in the form it takes in sociology. For me, intellectual life is closer to the artist's life than to the routines of an academic existence. I cannot say, like Proust, 'I often went to bed early . . .' But those working meetings which often didn't finish until impossibly late, mostly because we were having such a good time, are among the best moments in my life. And I would have to include too the pleasures of those interviews which start at ten in the morning and last all day; and the extreme diversity of a job in which you can, in the course of one week, interview a manager or a bishop, analyse a series of statistical tables, consult historical documents, observe a conversation in a café, read theoretical articles, have discussions with other researchers, and so on. I wouldn't have liked to go and clock in at the Bibliothèque nationale every day. I think that what lies behind the cohesion of the group that I have been leading for some years is what one might call 'communicative enthusiasm', which transcends the distinction between seriousness and frivolity, between the modest devotion to 'humble, easy tasks', which the University often identifies with seriousness, and the more or less grandiose ambition which leads people to flirt with the great topics of the day. How shall I put it? You don't have to choose between the iconoclastic and inspired liberty of the great intellectual games and the methodical rigour of positive or indeed positivist research (between Nietzsche and Wilamowitz, if you like), between a total absorption in fundamental questions and the critical distance associated with a great store of positive information (Heidegger versus Cassirer, for instance). But there's no point in going that far for an example: the sociologist's job is probably, of all intellectual jobs, the one that I could both be happy doing and successful at – at least, I hope so. This does not exclude – on the contrary – a very strong feeling of responsibility (or even guilt), due to a feeling of being privileged, of having unpaid debts. But I don't know whether I ought to be saying these things . . .

Q. Does this ability to talk about such things depend on the position you occupy today?

A. Definitely. Sociology confers on you an extraordinary autonomy, especially when you don't use it as a weapon against others, or as an instrument of defence, but rather as a weapon against yourself, an instrument of vigilance. But at the same time, in order to be capable of taking sociology as far as it will go, without being over-protective towards yourself, you probably have to be in a social position such that objectification isn't intolerable . . . ?

Q. You have given a report on the sociogenesis of your concepts, and that has given us an overall view of the development of the theory which tries to study symbolic struggles in society, from archaic societies up to those of today. Can you say now what was the role played by Marx and Weber in the intellectual genesis of your concepts? Do you feel Marxist when you are talking about symbolic struggle, or do you feel Weberian?

A. I've never thought in those terms. And I tend to object to those questions. Firstly because, when they are usually asked – I know this isn't true in your case – it's almost always with a polemical, classificatory intention behind it, in order to catalogue you – *katègorein* means to accuse in public: 'Bourdieu, basically, is a Durkheimian.' From the point of view of the speaker, this is pejorative; it means: he isn't a Marxist, and that's bad. Or else 'Bourdieu is a Marxist', and *that* is bad. It's almost always a way of reducing, or destroying, you. It's like when these days people wonder about my relations with Gramsci – in whom they discover, probably because they have read me, a great number of things that I was able to find in his work only *because* I hadn't read him . . . (The most interesting thing about Gramsci, who, in fact, I did only read quite recently, is the way he provides us with the bases for a sociology of the party apparatchik and the Communist leaders of his period – all of which is far from the ideology of the 'organic intellectual' for which he is best known.) At any rate, the answer to the question whether an author is Marxist, Durkheimian or Weberian gives us practically no information about that author.

I even think that one of the obstacles to the progress of research is this classificatory mode of functioning of academic and political thought, which often hamstrings intellectual inventiveness by making it impossible to surpass false antinomies and false divisions. The logic of the classificatory label is very exactly that of racism, which stigmatizes its victims by imprisoning them in a negative essence. In any case, it constitutes, in my view, the principal obstacle to what strikes me as the proper relationship one ought to have with the texts and authors of the past. As far as I'm concerned, I have very pragmatic relationships with authors: I turn to them as I would to fellows and craft-masters, in the sense those words had in the mediaeval guild – people you can ask to give you a hand in difficult situations.

Q. That reminds me of the word 'bricolage', which Lévi-Strauss used to use: you have a problem and you use all the tools that you consider to be useful and usable.

A. If you like. But the conceptual *realpolitik* I practise isn't without a theoretical direction which enables me to avoid pure and simple eclecticism. I think that you cannot develop a really productive way of thinking without giving yourself the means of having a really *re*productive way of thinking. It seems to me that this is partly what Wittgenstein wanted to suggest when, in the *Vermischte Bemerkungen*,[20] he said that he had never invented anything and that he had got everything from someone else – Boltzmann, Herz, Frege, Russell, Kraus, Loos, and so on. I could produce a similar list, probably a longer one. Philosophers are much more present in my work than I can say, often for fear of seeming to be offering up sacrifice to the philosophical ritual of having to declare my genealogical allegiances . . . Sociological research as I conceive it is also a good area in which to carry out what Austin called *fieldwork in philosophy*.

In this respect, I would like to take this opportunity to correct the impression I may have given of attacking Austin in my work on language. In fact, if people read Austin properly, and he is probably

---

20 L. Wittgenstein, *Vermischte Bemerkungen*, trans. as *Culture and Value*, tr. P. Winch (Oxford, 1980).

one of the philosophers I most admire, they would notice that the essential aspects of what I tried to reintroduce into the debate on the performative were already said, or suggested, there. My criticisms were in fact aimed at the formalist readings which have reduced Austin's socio-logical indications (in my opinion, he went as far as he could) to analyses of pure logic; these readings, as often in the linguistic tradition, could not rest before emptying the linguistic debate of everything external, as Saussure had done – but in his case it was done in full awareness.

Q. How do these bright ideas come about? What makes you look at one author rather than another?

A. 'You get what you can where you can', as common sense says, but of course, you don't go asking for just anything from just anybody . . . It's the role of culture to point out those authors in whom you have some hope of finding help. There is a philosophical sense which is rather like the political sense . . . Culture is that sort of freely available and all-purpose knowledge that you acquire in general at an age when you don't yet have any questions to ask. You can spend your life increasing it, cultivating it for its own sake. Or else, you can use it as a sort of more or less inexhaustible toolbox. Intellectuals are prepared by the whole logic of their education to treat works inherited from the past as a culture, in other words, as a treasure that they contemplate, venerate, celebrate, by the same token giving themselves added prestige by that very fact – in short, as accumulated wealth destined to be exhibited and to produce symbolic dividends, or mere narcissistic gratifications, and not as a productive capital that you invest in research, in order to produce effects. This 'pragmatic' view may appear shocking, since culture is so closely associated with the idea of gratuity, of purposiveness without purpose. And it was probably necessary to have a rather barbaric relationship to culture – at once more 'serious', more 'self-interested' and less fascinated, less religious – so as to be able to treat it in this way, especially when it came to culture *par excellence*, namely philosophy. This non-fetishistic relationship to authors and texts has only been reinforced by the sociological analysis of culture – which had probably been made possible by that relationship . . . In fact, it is doubtless inseparable from a representation of intellectual work which is uncommon among intellectuals, and consists of considering the job of being an intellectual as a job like any other, eliminating everything that most aspiring intellectuals feel it neces-

29

sary to do in order to feel intellectual. There are in every activity two relatively independent dimensions, the technical dimension properly speaking and the symbolic dimension, a sort of practical metadiscourse by which the person acting – as is the case with the hairdresser's white apron – shows and indeed shows off certain remarkable properties of his or her action. This is also true in the intellectual professions. Reducing the proportion of time and energy devoted to this show means increasing considerably the technical output; but, in a world in which the social definition of practice involves a proportion of show, of *epideixis*, as the Pre-Socratics called it – and they were well acquainted with it – also means exposing oneself to the possible loss of the symbolic profits of recognition which are associated with the normal exercise of intellectual activity. And this involves the complementary fact that making concessions, even of the most limited and controlled kind, to the show business that is becoming more and more part of the intellectual's job, exposes one to all sorts of risk.

That being said, I would like to come back to the initial question about the relationship I have to canonical authors, and to try and answer it by reformulating it in a form in which it seems perfectly acceptable, in other words, in the form of the fundamental question of the theoretical space in which an author consciously and unconsciously situates himself or herself. The main function of a theoretical education (which can't be measured by the number of footnotes accompanying books and articles) is that it enables one explicitly to take into account this theoretical space, that is, the universe of scientifically pertinent positions at any given state of scientific development. This space of scientific (and epistemological) stances always imposes its order on modes of practice, and in any case on their social meaning, whether this fact is realized or not – and all the more brutally, no doubt, the less it is realized. And becoming aware of this space, that is, of the scientific problematic as a space of possibilities, is one of the main conditions for a self-aware and thus controlled scientific practice. Authors – Marx, Durkheim, Weber, and so on – represent landmarks which structure our theoretical space and our perception of this space. The difficulty of sociological writing stems from the fact that you have to struggle against the constraints inscribed in the theoretical space at a given moment – and especially, in my case, against the false incompatibilities that they tend to produce; and this has to happen in full awareness of the fact that the product of this labour of breaking away will be perceived through categories of perception which, being adjusted to the transformed space, will tend to reduce the construction proposed to one or other of the terms of the opposition that it transcends.

Q. Because they are what is at stake . . .

A. Absolutely. Any attempt to work through and beyond canonical oppositions (between Durkheim and Marx, for instance, or between Marx and Weber) is liable to pedagogical or political regression (one of the main stakes clearly being the political use of emblematic concepts or authors). The most typical example is the scientifically quite absurd opposition between individual and society, which the notion of habitus, as social life incorporated, and thus individuated, is meant to transcend. Whatever we do, political logic will always ask the same question: all that's needed, in fact, is to introduce politics into the intellectual field for an opposition to be created, one which has only a political reality, between supporters of the individual ('methodological individualism') and supporters of 'society' (labelled as 'totalitarian'). This regressive pressure is so strong that the more sociology advances, the more difficult it will be to live up to the scientific inheritance, to draw concurrently on the collective results of the social sciences.

Q. In your work, you have no room for universal norms, unlike Habermas, for example.

A. I have a tendency to ask the problem of reason or of norms in a resolutely historicist way. Instead of wondering about the existence of 'universal interests', I will ask: who has an interest in the universal? Or rather: what are the social conditions that have to be fulfilled for certain agents to have an interest in the universal? How are fields created such that agents, in satisfying their particular interests, contribute thereby to producing the universal (I have in mind the scientific field)? Or fields in which agents feel obliged to set themselves up as defenders of the universal (such as the intellectual field in certain national traditions – for example, in France today)? In short, in certain fields, at a certain moment and for a certain time (that is, in a non-irreversible way), there are agents who have an interest in the universal. I think historicism must be pushed to its limit, by a sort of radical doubt, to see what can really be saved. You can, of course, start off with universal reason. I think it is better to call universal reason itself into question, resolutely accepting the fact that reason is a historical product whose existence and durability are the product of a determinate type of historical conditions, and

31

determining historically what those conditions are. There is a history of reason; that doesn't mean that reason can be reduced to its history, but that there are historical conditions for the appearance of social forms of communication that make the production of truth possible. Truth is the stake in a series of struggles in every field. The scientific field, which has reached a high degree of autonomy, has this peculiarity: you have a chance of success in it only if you conform to the immanent laws of the field, that is, if you recognize truth practically as a *value* and respect the methodological principles and canons defining *rationality* at the moment under consideration, at the same time as bringing into battle in the competitive struggles all the specific instruments that have been accumulated in the course of prior struggles. The scientific field is a game in which you have to arm yourself with reason in order to win. Without producing or requiring supermen inspired by motivations radically different from those of ordinary people, it produces and encourages, by its own logic, and outside any normative imposition, particular forms of communication, such as competitive discussion, critical dialogue and so on, which tend in fact to favour the accumulation and control of knowledge. To say that there are social conditions for the production of truth is to say that there is a politics of truth, an action constantly exercised in order to defend and improve the functioning of the social universes in which rational principles are applied and truth comes into being.

Q.   In the German tradition, there is a concern to justify, to found – this need to justify one's critique, as in Habermas; is there a stable point, a foundation, which justifies all my thoughts, and which everyone has to recognize?

A.   One can ask this question once and for all, at the outset. Then consider that it's been answered. As far as I'm concerned, I think it has to be asked empirically, historically. Doubtless, it's a little disappointing, because it's less 'radical' . . . Identifying yourself with reason is a very tempting position for any thinker. In fact, one has to risk one's very position as a universal thinker to have a chance of thinking in a rather less particular way. When, in my last book, I claim to objectify the University, a universe of which I am part and which is a source of all claims of universality, I expose myself more than ever to the question of the foundation, of the legitimacy of this attempt at objectification. This question – that nobody ever asks me when I talk about the Kabyles, the Béarnais, or industrial managers

– is asked of me the minute I claim to objectify the professionals of objectification. I am trying to ask the question of the foundation in almost positivist terms: what are the particular difficulties you come up against when you want to objectify a space in which you are included, and what are the particular conditions you have to fulfil in order to have a chance of surmounting them? And I discover that the interest you can have in objectifying a universe of which you are part is an absolute ambition, an ambition to exploit an absolute and non-relativistic viewpoint. This is the very thing that the thinker laying claim to a self-founding thought used to grant himself or herself. I discover that one becomes a sociologist, a theoretician, so as to have an absolute point of view, a *theoria*; and that, for as long as it is unrecognized, this kingly, divine ambition is a tremendous cause of error. So much so that, to escape even a little from the relative, one absolutely has to abdicate from the claim to absolute knowledge, uncrown the philosopher-king. And I discover too that in a field at a certain moment, the logic of the game is such that certain agents have an *interest* in the universal. And, I have to say, I think this is true in my case. But the fact of knowing it, of knowing that I am investing personal impulses, linked with my whole life story, in my research, gives me some small chance of knowing the limits of my vision. In short, the problem of foundations cannot be raised in absolute terms: it's a question of degree and one can construct instruments to disentangle oneself, at least partly, from the relative. The most important of these instruments is self-analysis, understood as knowledge not just from the point of view of the scientist, but also of his instruments of knowledge in their historically determinate aspects. The analysis of the University in its structure and its history is also the most fertile of explorations of the unconscious. I consider that I will have properly fulfilled my contract of 'civil servant to humanity', as Husserl put it, if I manage to reinforce the weapons of reflexive critique which every thinker must bear against himself or herself in order to have any chance of being rational. But, as you can see, I always tend to transform philosophical problems into practical problems of scientific politics: and in this way I confirm the opposition that Marx established, in the *Communist Manifesto*, between French thinkers who always think politically and German thinkers who ask universal, abstract questions 'on ways of realizing human nature' . . .

2

Landmarks

Q. In today's sociology, several 'schools' coexist, with different paradigms and methods; their supporters sometimes quarrel violently. In your work, you try to go beyond these oppositions. Can it be said that what is at stake in your research is the development of a synthesis that will lead to a new sociology?

A. Today's sociology is full of false oppositions, which my work often leads me to transcend – even if I don't set out deliberately to do so. These oppositions are real divisions in the sociological field; they have a social foundation, but they have no scientific foundation. Let us take the most evident, such as the opposition between theorists and empiricists, or that between subjectivists and objectivists, or that between structuralism and certain forms of phenomenology. All these oppositions (and there are many others) seem to me to be completely fictitious and at the same time dangerous, because they lead to mutilations. The most typical example is the opposition between an approach that can be called structuralist, which aims at grasping objective relations that are independent of individual minds and wills, as Marx said, and a phenomenological, interactionist or ethnomethodological procedure which aims at grasping what agents actually experience of interactions and social contacts, and the contribution they make to the mental and practical construction of social realities. A good many of these oppositions owe their existence partly to an effort to constitute in theoretical terms positions linked to the possession of different forms of cultural capital. Sociology, as it is in its present state, is a science with broad ambitions, and the legitimate ways of practising it are extremely varied. One can bring together under the name of sociologist people

Interview with J. Heilbron and B. Maso, published in Dutch in the *Sociologisch Tijdschrift*, 10, no. 2 (October 1983).

who carry out statistical analyses, others who develop mathematical models, others who describe concrete situations, and so on. All these types of competence are rarely found together in one and the same person, and one of the reasons for the divisions that tend to be set up as theoretical oppositions is the fact that sociologists expect to impose as the sole legitimate way of practising sociology the one that they find most accessible. Almost inevitably 'partial', they try to impose a partial definition of their science: I have in mind those censorious characters who use the reference to empirical facts in a repressive or castrating way (even though they don't themselves carry out empirical research) and who, under the appearance of underlining the importance of modest caution as against the theorists' audacities, ask the epistemology of resentment which lies behind positivist methodology to justify itself, so that they can prohibit others from doing what they themselves are unable to do, and so that they can impose their own limits on others. In other words, I think that a good number of so-called 'theoretical' or 'methodological' works are merely the justificatory ideologies of a particular form of scientific competence. And an analysis of the field of sociology would probably show that there is a high correlation between the type of cultural capital which different researchers have at their disposal and the form of sociology that they defend as the only legitimate one.

Q. Is that what you mean when you say that the sociology of sociology is one of the first conditions of sociology?

A. Yes, but the sociology of sociology has other virtues too. For instance, the simple principle according to which every holder of a position is well advised to note the limits of the holders of other positions allows one to make the most of criticisms to which one may be subjected. If, for example, you take the relations between Weber and Marx, which are always studied academically, you can view them in another way and ask how and why one thinker enables you to see the truth of the other and vice versa. The opposition between Marx, Weber and Durkheim, as it is ritually invoked in lectures and papers, conceals the fact that the unity of sociology is perhaps to be found in that space of possible positions whose antagonism, apprehended as such, suggests the possibility of its own transcendence. It is evident, for instance, that Weber saw something that Marx did not, but also that Weber could see what Marx hadn't because Marx had seen what he had. One of the major difficulties in sociology lies in the fact that, very often, you have to include in science that against which you began by constructing scientific truth. Against the illusion of the arbitrary state, Marx constructed the notion of the state as an instrument of domination. But, against the disenchantment effected by the Marxist critique, you have to ask, with Weber, how the state, being what it is, manages to impose the recognition of its domination, and whether it isn't necessary to include in the model that against which you constructed the model, namely the spontaneous representation of the state as legitimate. And you can integrate apparently antagonistic writers on religion in the same way. It isn't out of any love of paradox that I would say that Weber carried out the Marxist intention (in the best sense of the term) in areas where Marx had not managed to do so. I'm thinking in particular of religious sociology, which is far from being Marx's forte. Weber built up a veritable political economy of religion; more precisely, he brought out the full potential of the materialist analysis of religion without destroying the properly symbolic character of the phenomenon. When he states, for example, that the Church is defined by the monopoly of the legitimate manipulation of the machinery of salvation, far from proceeding to one of those purely metaphorical transfers of economic language that have been frequent in France in the last few years, he produces an extraordinary leap forward in understanding. This kind of exercise can be carried out in regard to the past, but also in regard to present oppositions. As I've just said, every sociologist would do well to listen to his adversaries as it is in their interest to see what he cannot see, to observe the limits of his vision, which by definition are invisible to him.

Q. For several years, 'the crisis of sociology' has been a privileged theme among sociologists. Just recently, people have talked of the 'break-up of the sociological world'. To what extent has this 'crisis' been a scientific crisis?

A. It seems to me that the present situation, which as you say is often described as a crisis situation, is entirely favourable to scientific progress. I think that the social sciences, out of a desire for respectability, so as to appear, even in their own eyes, as sciences like all the other sciences, had built up a false 'paradigm'. In other words, the type of strategic alliance between Columbia and Harvard, the Parsons–Merton–Lazarsfeld triangle, on which for several years the illusion of a unified social science rested, was a sort of intellectual holding company which led an almost conscious strategy of ideo-logical domination until it finally collapsed – which, I think, marked a considerable progress. To verify this opinion, you would merely need to look at who is bandying around the word 'crisis'. In my view, it's all the people who benefited from that monopolistic structure. That means that in every field – in the sociological field as in all the others – there is a struggle for a monopoly over legitimacy. A book like the one by Thomas Kuhn on scientific revolutions had the effect of an epistemological revolution in the eyes of certain American sociologists (though in my opinion it wasn't that at all) because it was used as a weapon against that false paradigm that a certain number of people, placed in an intellectually dominant position because of the economic and political dominance of their nation and their position in the academic world, had managed to impose quite widely throughout the world.

You would need to analyse in detail the division of the labour of domination that had been established. On the one hand you had an eclectic theory founded on a selective reinterpretation of the Euro-pean inheritance, and destined to work in such a way that the history of the social sciences begins in the United States. In some ways, Parsons was to the European sociological tradition what Cicero had been to Greek philosophy; he takes the original authors, and retranslates them into a rather limp language, producing a syncretic message, an academic combination of Weber, Durkheim and Pareto – but, of course, not Marx. On the other hand, you had the Viennese empirical bias of Lazarsfeld, a sort of short-sighted neo-positivism, relatively blind to the theoretical side. As for Merton, somewhere between the two, he offered us minor academic treatises, clear and simple little syntheses, in the shape of his 'medium-range theories'. You had a real sharing out of competences, in the juridical sense of the word. And all this formed a *socially* very powerful unity, which could give you the impression that there was a 'paradigm' as in the natural sciences. This is where what I call the 'Gerschenkron effect' comes in: Gerschenkron explains that capitalism in Russia has never had the form that it took in other countries for the simple reason that it didn't get going until quite late. The social sciences owe a great number of their characteristics and their difficulties to the fact that they too only got going a lot later than the others, so that, for example, they can use consciously or unconsciously the model of more advanced sciences in order to simulate scientific rigour.

In the years 1950–60, what was mimicked was the unity of science, as if there were science only when there is unity. Sociology was criticized for being dispersed and torn by conflict. And sociologists were so insistently forced to swallow the idea that they are not scientific because they are in conflict, or controversial, that they have a certain longing for this unification, whether it is true or false. In fact, the false paradigm of the east coast of the United States was a sort of orthodoxy . . . It mimicked the *communis doctorum opinio* that is appropriate not to science, especially when it is only just beginning, but more to the mediaeval Church or to a juridical institution. In many cases, the sociological language of the fifties carried off the amazing feat of talking about the social world as if it wasn't talking about it at all. It was a language of denial, in Freud's sense of the word, responding to the fundamental demand those in power make of any discourse on the social world – a demand that it be kept at arm's length and neutralized. You need only read American reviews of the fifties: half the articles were devoted to anomie, to empirical or theoretical variations on Durkheim's fundamental concepts, and so on. It was a sort of empty academic rambling about the social world, with very little empirical material. What struck me in particular, in very different writers, was the use of concepts that were neither concrete nor abstract, concepts that are only understandable if you have some idea of the concrete referent in the mind of the people using these concepts. They thought 'jet-setting sociologist' and they said 'universalist professor'. The unreality of the language used reached new peaks. Fortunately there were exceptions, such as the Chicago School, which talked about slums and about the street-corner society, which described gangs or homosexual circles, in short, real circles and real people . . . But in the little Parsons–Lazarsfeld–Merton triangle, they couldn't see any of this.

So for me, the 'crisis' people talk about these days is the crisis of an orthodoxy, and the proliferation of heresies marks in my opinion progress towards scientific rigour. It's no coincidence that the scientific imagination has been liberated thereby, if all the opportunities offered by sociology are once more available. We are now dealing with a field that has its own struggles, which have some chance of becoming once again scientific struggles, in other words, confrontations that are settled in such a way that you have to be scientific if you're going to win: you won't any longer be able to win just by rabbiting vaguely on about ascription/achievement and anomie, or by presenting statistical tables on the 'alienation' of the workers that are theoretically – and thus empirically – badly constructed.

Q. In sociology, there is a tendency towards a very high, sometimes excessive, degree of specialization. Is that an aspect of the Gerschenkron effect that you have just mentioned?

A. Absolutely. People want to imitate the advanced sciences in which you have very precise and very narrow objects of research. It's this excessive specialization that is glorified by the positivist model, by a kind of suspicion of all ambitions of a general kind, which are perceived as a remnant of philosophy's ambition to encompass all knowledge. In fact, we are still in a phase in which it is absurd to separate, for example, the sociology of education and the sociology of culture. How can you carry out the sociology of literature or the sociology of science without reference to the sociology of the education system? For instance, when people write a social history of intellectuals, they almost always forget to take into account the structural evolution of the education system, whose effects can include an 'overproduction' of graduates, immediately translated back into the intellectual field, both in terms of production – with, for instance, the appearance of a socially and intellectually subversive 'bohème' – and in terms of consumption – with the quantitative and qualitative transformation of the literate public. Clearly, this specialization also corresponds to people's interests. It's a well-known fact: for instance, in an article on the evolution of law in Italy in the Middle Ages, Gerschenkron shows that, as soon as jurists won their independence from princes, each one began to carve up the speciality so as to be a big fish in a little stream rather than a little fish in a big stream. The two effects together meant that people specialized excessively, and any relatively general form of research was ruled out of court: they forgot that in the natural sciences, up to Leibniz, even up to Poincaré, the great scientists were simultaneously philosophers, mathematicians and physicists.

Q. Like many sociologists, you're not particularly kindly disposed to philosophers. And yet, you often refer to philosophers such as Cassirer or Bachelard, who in general are neglected by sociologists.

A. As you say, I often have a dig at philosophers, because I expect a great deal from philosophy. The social sciences are at one and the same time new ways of thinking, sometimes in direct competition with philosophy (I have in mind here theories of the state, political science, and so on), and also objects of thought that philosophy could profitably reflect on. One of the functions of philosophers of science could be to provide sociologists with weapons which they could use to defend themselves against the imposition of a positivist epistemology which is one aspect of the Gerschenkron effect. For example, when Cassirer describes the genesis of the new way of thinking, of the new concepts that are brought into play by modern mathematics or physics, he completely refutes the positivist view by showing that the most highly developed sciences were only able to come into being, at a very recent date, by treating relationships between entities as more important than entities themselves (like the forces of classical physics). He thereby shows that what people offer us in the guise of scientific methodology is only an ideological representation of the legitimate way of doing science which corresponds to nothing real in scientific practice.

Here's another example. Especially in the Anglo-Saxon tradition, people criticize the researcher for using concepts that function as signposts pointing to phenomena that are worth examining but that often remain obscure and vague, even if they are suggestive and evocative. I think some of my concepts (I have in mind, for instance, recognition or miscognition) fall into this category. In my defence, I could mention all those 'thinkers', so clear, so transparent, so reassuring, who have talked about symbolism, communication, culture, the relationships between culture and ideology, and all that was confused, hidden or repressed by this 'dark clarity'. But I could also and above all appeal to those who, like Wittgenstein, have said how heuristically powerful open concepts are and who have denounced the 'closure' of notions that were too well-constructed, of 'preliminary definitions' and the other false rigours of positivist methodology. Once again, a really rigorous epistemology could free researchers from the methodological tradition that weighs down on research – a tradition often appealed to by the most mediocre researchers in order to 'pare the lion cubs' claws', as Plato put it – in other words, to disparage and reduce the creations and innovations of the scientific imagination. So I think one may have the impression of a certain vagueness in some of the notions I coined, when they are considered as the product of a conceptual labour, whereas what I was after was to make them work in empirical analyses instead of leaving them to 'run in neutral': every one of them (the notion of field, for instance) is, in a condensed form, a research programme and a principle by which one can avoid a whole set of mistakes. Concepts can – and, to some extent, must – remain open and provisional, which doesn't mean vague, approximate or confused: any real thinking about scientific practice attests that this *openness* of concepts, which gives them their 'suggestive' character, and thus their capacity to produce scientific effects (by showing things that have never been seen before, by suggesting research that needs to be done, and not just commentaries), is the essence of any scientific thought *in statu nascendi*, in opposition to that completed science that provides mental pabulum for methodologists and all those who invent, once the dust of battle has settled, rules and methods that are more harmful than useful. A researcher's contribution can consist, in more than one case, in drawing attention to a problem, to something which nobody saw because it was too evident, too clear, because, as we say, it was 'staring them in the face'. For example, the concepts of recognition and miscognition were introduced, to start with, in order to name something which is absent from the theories of power, or else designated only in a very rough-and-ready way (power comes from below, etc.). They actually do designate a line of research. It's in this way that I envisage my work on the form taken by power in the University as a contribution to the analysis of the objective and subjective mechanisms through which the effects of symbolic imposition are exercised, of recognition and miscognition. One of my intentions, in the use I make of these concepts, is to abolish the academic distinction between conflict and consensus which makes it impossible to analyse all the real situations in which consensual submission is accomplished in and through conflict. How could a philosophy of consensus be attributed to me? I know full well that those who are dominated, even in the education system, oppose and resist this domination (I introduced the works of Willis into France). But, at a certain period, the struggles of the dominated were so romanticized (to such an extent that 'in struggle' had ended up by working as a sort of Homeric epithet, liable to be stuck on anything that moved – women, students, the dominated, workers, and so on) that people finally forgot something that everyone who has seen it from close up knows perfectly well: the dominated are dominated in their brains too. That is what I want to suggest when I use notions such as recognition and miscognition.

Q. You insist on the fact that social reality is historical through and through. Where do you locate yourself with respect to historical studies, and why do you hardly ever see things in a long-term perspective?

A. In social science as it is at the moment, long-term history is, I think, one of the privileged places of social philosophy. Among sociologists, this fact frequently gives rise to general considerations on bureaucratization, on the process of rationalization, modernization and so on, which bring a great number of social benefits to their authors, but few scientific benefits. In fact, to practise sociology in the way I envisage it, these benefits had to be relinquished. The history I would need for my work very often doesn't exist. For example, at the moment I have set myself the problem of the modern artist or intellectual. How do the artist and the intellectual gradually acquire their independence, and win their freedom? To answer this question rigorously, you have to do some extremely difficult work. The historical work which should enable you to understand the genesis of structures as they can be observed at a given moment in one or other field is very difficult to carry out, since you can't be satisfied either with vague generalizations founded on a few documents selected haphazardly, or with patient documentary or statistical compilations which often leave blanks where they should be giving us essential information. So a full and complete sociology should clearly include a history of the structures that are the product at a given moment of the whole historical process. And that runs the risk of naturalizing structures and passing off, for instance, a state of the distribution of goods or services between agents (I am thinking, for example, of sporting activities, but the same would be true of people's preferences for different films) as the direct and, if I may put it like this, 'natural' expression of dispositions associated with different positions in the social space (this is done by those people who want to establish a necessary relation between a 'class' and a pictorial style or a sport). It is necessary to write a structural history which finds in each state of the structure both the product of previous struggles to transform or conserve the structure, and, through the contradictions, tensions and power relations that constitute that structure, the source of its subsequent transformations. That is more or less what I have done in order to account for the transformations that have been happening in the educational system for several years. I refer you to the chapter of *Distinction*[1] entitled 'Classes and Classifications', in which I analyse the social effects of changes in relations between the educational field and the social field. Schools constitute a field which, more than any other, tends to reproduce itself, because of the fact that, among

1 P. Bourdieu, *La distinction. Critique sociale du jugement* (Paris, 1979); trans. as *Distinction. A Social Critique of the Judgement of Taste*, tr. R. Nice (Cambridge, Mass., 1984).

other reasons, agents have control over their own reproduction. That being said, the educational field is in the thrall of external forces. Among the most powerful factors of transformation of the educational field (and more generally, of all the fields of cultural production), you have what the Durkheimians called morphological effects: the influx of more numerous (and also culturally much poorer) clienteles, which entails all sorts of change at every level. But in reality, to understand the effects of morphological changes, you have to take into account the whole logic of the field, the struggles internal to the professional body, the struggles between faculties (Kant's conflict of faculties), struggles within each faculty, between different academic positions and different levels of the teaching hierarchy, and also the struggles between different disciplines. These struggles acquire a much greater transformative effectiveness when they come up against external processes: for instance, in France as in many countries, the social sciences, sociology, semiology, linguistics and so on, which in themselves introduce a form of subversion of the old tradition of 'the classics', of literary history, philology or even philosophy, found reinforcements in the massive number of students who were attracted to them, this influx of students entailing in turn an increase in the number of junior and senior lecturers, and so on, and, leading thereby to conflicts within the institution, of which the May '68 uprisings were partly an expression. You can see how the permanent sources of change, internal struggles, are effective when the internal demands of the lower clergy (the junior lecturers), always inclined to demand the right to a universal vocation, come up against the external demands of the laity (the students), demands which are often themselves linked, in the case of the educational system, with a surplus of products in the educational system, with an 'overproduction' of graduates. In short, you mustn't grant a kind of mechanical effectiveness to morphological factors: apart from the fact that these often gain their specific effectiveness from the very structure of the field in which they operate, the increase in numbers is itself linked to profound changes in the way agents, according to their dispositions, perceive different products (establishments, specialities, degrees, etc.) offered by the educational establishment and, by the same token, to changes in educational demands, etc. So, to take an extreme example, everything suggests that workers who, in France, hardly made any use of secondary education, began to do so in the 1960s, at first, of course, for legal reasons, because the school-leaving age was raised to sixteen and so on, but also because, in order to maintain their position, which is not the lowest, and to avoid falling into the sub-proletariat, they had to possess a minimum education. I think that the relation to immigrants is a factor in the relation to the education system; and, step by step, so is the whole social structure. In short, changes that have occurred in the educational field are defined by the relation between the structure of the educational field and the external changes which have determined decisive transformations in the relation between families and schools. Here too, to avoid vague language about the influence of 'economic factors', you have to understand how economic changes are translated back into changes in the social uses that the families affected by these changes can put education to – for instance, the crisis among small shop-owners, small craftsmen and small agricultural workers. So one completely new phenomenon is the fact that the social categories such as peasants, craftsmen or small shop-owners, who made little use of the educational system to reproduce themselves, started to make use of it because of the redeployment forced on them by economic changes, that is to say, when they had to face up to the prospect of leaving conditions in which they had complete control over their social reproduction – by the direct transmission of skills: for example, in technical education, you find a very high proportion of shopkeepers' and craftsmen's sons who are seeking in the educational establishment a base for redeployment. Nowadays, this sort of intensification of the way education is used by categories that never used to use it very much causes problems for the categories that were previously great users of education and who, in order to keep their distance, have had to intensify the time and money they invest in education. So there will be a counter-attack in the form of an intensification of demand in all categories that expect their reproduction to take place through education; anxiety concerning the education system is going to increase (we have hundreds of signs of it, the most significant being the new way private education is being used). There are chain reactions, and a kind of dialectic in the way the stakes are raised in the use made of education. It's all terribly closely tied up together. That's what makes analysis difficult. We are dealing with a network of relationships that get reduced to linear processes. For those who, in the preceding generation, held a monopoly over the highest levels, in higher education, the *grandes écoles* and so on, this sort of generalized intensification in the way the educational establishment is used raises all kinds of difficult problems, forcing one to invent all sorts of strategies – to such an extent that these contradictions are an extraordinary factor of innovation. The educational mode of reproduction is a statistical mode of reproduction. What is reproduced is a relatively constant fraction of the class (in the logical sense of the term). But the factors determining who will sink and who will swim no longer depend on the family alone. But the family *is* interested in specific individuals. If you tell them: overall, 90 per cent will swim, but none of them will come from *your* family, they're not at all pleased. So there is a contradiction between the specific interests of the family as a body and 'collective class interests' (in quotes, for the sake of brevity). As a consequence, the interests proper to the family, the interests of parents who do not want to see their children fall below their level, the interests of children who do not want to fall down a social class, and who will respond to failure with more or less resignation or rebellion depending on their origin, will lead to extremely varied and extraordinarily inventive strategies, whose aim is to maintain their position. That is what is shown by my analysis of the May '68 movement: the places where you can observe the greatest rebelliousness in '68 are those places in which the gap between the statutory aspirations linked to high social origin and educational success is at a maximum. This is the case, for example, in a discipline such as sociology which was one of the citadels of rebellion (the first explanation of this is to say that sociology as a science is subversive). But this gap between aspirations and performances, which is a subversive factor, is inseparably a factor of innovation. It's no coincidence if a number of the May '68 leaders were great innovators in intellectual life and elsewhere. Social structures don't run like clockwork. For example, the people who don't get the job that was so to speak statutorily assigned to them – the ones people call 'failures' – will work at changing the job so that the difference between the job they had expected to get and the job they actually get disappears. All the phenomena associated with the 'overproduction of graduates' and 'devaluation of degrees' (we have to use these words with some care) are major factors of renewal because the contradictions which stem from them lead to change. That being said, movements of rebellion on the part of the privileged are extraordinarily ambiguous: these people are terribly contradictory and, in their very subversion of the institution, seek to preserve the advantages associated with a previous state of the institution. Throughout the history of Nazism, the racist and imbecile tendencies of the small shopkeeper have been constantly emphasized. But I think that those whom Weber called 'proletaroid intellectuals', who are very unhappy and very dangerous people, have played a very important and terribly disastrous part in all periods of violence throughout history – the Chinese Cultural Revolution, the mediaeval heresies, the pre-Nazi and Nazi movements, or even the French Revolution (as Robert Darnton has shown in the case of Marat, for instance). Likewise, there were terrible ambiguities in the movement of May '68, and the funny, intelligent, rather carnivalesque side of it, incarnated by Daniel Cohn-Bendit, masked another, far less amusing and likeable side of the movement: resentment is always ready to leap head first into the first breach that opens up before it . . . As you can see, I've taken my time over this one, and I have replied to a 'theoretical' question by referring to a concrete analysis. This wasn't entirely intentional, but I'll accept it as it is – for two reasons. I have been able in this way to show that my conception of history, in particular the history of the educational organization, has nothing in common with the mutilated, absurd, 'sloganized' image that is sometimes given of it, based, I suppose, on nothing more than the knowledge of the word 'reproduction': on the contrary, I think that the specific contradictions of the mode of reproduction that has an educational component are one of the most important factors of change in modern societies. In the second place, I wanted to give a concrete intuition of the fact that, as all good historians know, the discursive alternatives, structure and history, reproduction and change, or, on another level, structural conditions and agents' individual motivations, prevent one from constructing reality in all its complexity. I would say in particular that the model I am putting forward of the relation between habitus and field supplies us with the only rigorous way of reintroducing individual agents and their individual actions without falling back into the amorphous anecdotes of factual history.

Q. In the relations between the social sciences, economics occupies a central position. What are, in your opinion, the most important aspects of the relations between sociology and economics?

A. Yes, economics is one of the major reference points for sociology. First and foremost because economics is already a part of sociology, largely due to the work of Weber, who transferred numerous models of thought borrowed from economics into the area of religion among others. But not all sociologists have the vigilance and theoretical competence of Max Weber and economics is one of the mediations through which the Gerschenkron effect works: indeed, economics is the first victim of that effect, especially because of an often altogether unrealistic use of mathematical models.

In order for mathematics to work as an instrument of generaliz-ation, which enables you, by being highly formalized, to free yourself from particular cases, you have to begin by constructing the object in accordance with the specific logic of the universe in question. This presupposes a break with the deductivist thought which is often rife these days in the social sciences. The opposition between the paradigm of the Rational Action Theory (RAT), as its defenders call it, and the one I am putting forward in the form of the theory of the habitus, is reminiscent of the opposition established by Cassirer, in *The Philosophy of the Enlightenment*,[2] between the Cartesian tradition which conceives the rational method as a process leading from principles to facts, via demonstration and rigorous deduction, and the Newtonian tradition of the *Regulae philosophan-di* which recommends the abandoning of pure deduction in favour of an analysis based on the phenomena and returning to first principles and to the mathematical formula which will be capable of giving a complete description of the facts. All economists would no doubt reject the idea of constructing an economic theory *a priori*. And yet, this epidemic of what the philosophers of the Cambridge School called *morbus mathematicus* wreaks havoc even in areas far removed from economics. It makes you want to appeal, against this Anglo-Saxon deductivism, which can go hand in hand with a certain positivism, to the 'strictly historical method', as the Locke of the *Essay Concerning Human Understanding*[3] put it, which Anglo-Saxon empiricism set up in opposition to Descartes. The deductivists, among whom one could also classify Chomskyan linguists, often create the impression of playing with formal models taken from games theory, for example, or from the physical sciences, without any great concern for the reality of different kinds of practice or for the real principles of their production. It even happens that, playing with mathematical competence as others play with literary or artistic culture, they seem to be desperately in search of the concrete object to which this or that formal model might be applied. Doubtless the models of simulation can have a heuristic function, by allowing you to imagine possible modes of functioning. But the people who construct them often abandon themselves to the dogmatic tempta-tion that Kant was already denouncing in mathematicians, and which

---

2 E. Cassirer, *The Philosophy of the Enlightenment*, tr. F. C. Koelin and J. P. Pettegrove (Princeton, NJ, 1969).
3 J. Locke, *An Essay Concerning Human Understanding* (Oxford, 1975).

means you move from the model of reality to the reality of the model. Forgetting the abstractions that they have had to bring into operation in order to produce their theoretical artefact, they give it as a complete and adequate explanation; or else they claim that the action whose model they have constructed has this model as its base. More generally, they seek to impose universally the philosophy which implicitly haunts all economic thought.

That is why I think that you can't appropriate some of the scientific knowledge represented by economics for your own work without submitting it to a complete reinterpretation, as I have done for the notions of supply and demand, and without breaking away from the subjectivist and intellectualist philosophy of economic action which is part and parcel of it and which is the real principle of the social success of Rational Action Theory or of the 'methodological individualism' which is its Frenchified version. That is the case, for example, with the notion of interest that I introduced into my work, among other reasons in order to break away from the narcissistic view according to which only certain activities – artistic, literary, religious, philosophical and other activities, in short all the forms of practice for which and from which intellectuals live (you would have to add militant activities, in politics or elsewhere) – would lie beyond all self-interested determination. Unlike the natural, ahistorical or generic interest referred to by economists, interest, in my view, is an investment in a game, any game, an investment which is the condition of entry into this game and which is simultaneously created and reinforced by the game. There are thus as many forms of interest as there are fields. This explains that the investments that certain people make in certain games, in the artistic field for example, appear disinterested when they are perceived by someone whose investments and interests are placed in another field, in the economic field for instance (and these economic interests can appear as uninteresting to those who have placed their investments in the artistic field). You have to determine empirically in each case the social conditions of production of this interest, its specific content, etc.

Q.   At a certain time, around 1968, you were criticized for not being a Marxist. Today you are criticized – often by the same people – for still being a Marxist or too Marxist. Could you specify or define your relation to the Marxist tradition and to Marx's work, especially as far as the problem of social classes is concerned?

A.   I have often pointed out, especially with regard to my relation to Max Weber, that you can think with a thinker against that thinker. For example, I constructed the notion of field both *against* Weber and *with* Weber, by thinking about the analysis he proposes of the relations between priest, prophet and sorcerer. To say that you can think at the same time with and against a thinker means radically contradicting the classificatory logic in accordance with which people are accustomed – almost everywhere, alas, but especially in France – to think of the relation you have with the thought of the past. *For* Marx, as Althusser said, or *against* Marx. I think you can think with Marx against Marx or with Durkheim against Durkheim, and also, of course, with Marx and Durkheim against Weber, and vice versa. That's the way science works.

As a consequence, to be or not to be a Marxist is a religious alternative and not at all scientific. In religious terms, either you're a Moslem or you aren't, either you make the profession of faith, the *shahada*, or you don't. Sartre's statement, according to which Marxism is the impassable philosophy of our time, is doubtless not the most intelligent thing this otherwise highly intelligent man said. There may be impassable philosophies, but there is no impassable science. By definition, science is there to be surpassed. And since Marx went to such lengths to claim the title of scientist, the only fitting homage to pay him is to use what he did, and what others have done with what he did, so as to surpass what he thought he did.

If you take the problem as settled, the particular case of social classes is clearly particularly important. It is certain that if we talk about class, it's essentially thanks to Marx. And you could even say that if there is something like classes in reality, it's to a large extent thanks to Marx, or more exactly to the theoretical effect exercised by Marx's work. That being said, I still won't go as far as to say that Marx's theory of classes satisfies me. Otherwise my work would have no meaning. If I had recited the *Diamat*, or developed some form or other of that 'basic Marxism' which was all the rage in France, and throughout the world (E. P. Thompson called it 'French flu') in the seventies, at a time when I was criticized rather for being a Weberian or a Durkheimian, it's probable I would have had a great deal of success in universities, because it's easier to be a commentator, but I think that my work would not have been, in my eyes at least, worth an hour's trouble. As far as classes are concerned, I wanted to break away from the realist view that people commonly have of them and which leads to questions of the type 'are intellectuals bourgeois or petty-bourgeois?' – questions, in other words, about limits and frontiers, questions that are generally settled by juridical acts. Furthermore, there have been situations in which the Marxist theory of classes has been used to find juridical solutions which, sometimes, were executions: depending on whether you were or were not a kulak, you could lose your life or save it. And I think that, if the theoretical problem is asked in these terms, it's because it is still linked to an unconscious intention to classify and catalogue, with all that can ensue. I wanted to get away from the realist definition of class, which sees class as a clearly defined group that exists in the real world as a compact and sharply delimited real entity. This definitional way of thinking gives you the impression that you know whether there are two classes or more than two, and leads you to think you know how many *petits bourgeois* there are. Just recently, a count was made – on allegedly Marxist grounds – of how many *petits bourgeois* there are in France – they gave a figure to the nearest digit, without even rounding the figures up! My work consists in saying that people are located in a social space, that they aren't just anywhere, in other words interchangeable, as those people claim who deny the existence of 'social classes', and that according to the position they occupy in this highly complex space, you can understand the logic of their practices and determine, *inter alia*, how they will classify themselves and others and, should the case arise, think of themselves as members of a 'class'.

Q. Another problem these days concerns the social functions of sociology and the demand for it 'from outside'.

A. You first have to ask whether there really is such a thing as a demand for a scientific discourse in the social sciences. Who wants to know the truth about the social world? Are there people who want the truth, who have an interest in the truth, and, if there are, are they in any position to demand it? In other words, you would have to carry out a sociology of the demand for sociology. Most sociologists, being paid by the state, as civil servants, can get by without asking themselves that question. It's an important fact that, at least in France, sociologists owe their freedom from demand to the fact that they are paid by the state. An important part of orthodox sociological discourse owes its immediate social success to the fact that it answers the dominant demand, which often comes down to a demand for rational instruments for management and domination or to a demand for a 'scientific' legitimation of the spontaneous sociology of those in the dominant position. For example, at the time of our investigation into photography, I had read the available market studies on the question. I remember an ideal-typical study composed of an economic analysis which ended with a simple but false – or, even worse, apparently true – equation, and a second part devoted to a 'psychoanalysis' of photography. On the one hand, a formal knowledge which keeps reality at arm's length and allows you to manipulate it by giving you the means of predicting, in a rough and ready way, the sales line; on the other hand, for that added human touch, psychoanalysis, or, in other cases, metaphysical speculations on eternity and the instant. It's rare that the people who have the means to pay really resent forking out their money when they think they are getting the scientific truth about the social world in return; as for those who have an interest in unveiling the mechanisms of domination, they hardly ever read sociology and, in any case, they can't afford it. Basically, sociology is a social science without a social basis. . . .

Q. One of the effects of the decline of 'positivist' sociology has been that certain sociologists have made an effort to abandon the technical vocabulary that had been built up, and have adopted an 'easy' and 'readable' style – not only to spread their ideas more easily, but also as a way of keeping scientistic illusions at bay. You don't share that point of view. Why not?

A. At the risk of seeming arrogant, I'll refer to Spitzer and what he says about Proust. I think that, literary and stylistic qualities apart, what Spitzer says about Proust's style is something I could say about my own writing. He says, firstly, that what is complex can only be said in a complex way; secondly, that reality is not only complex, but also structured, hierarchically ordered, and that you have to give an idea of this structure: if you want to hold the world in all its complexity and at the same time order and articulate it, show it in perspective, bring what's important into the foreground and so on, you have to use heavily articulated sentences that can be practically reconstructed like Latin sentences; thirdly, he says that Proust does not want to reveal this complex structured reality just as it is, but to present us simultaneously with the point of view from which he sees it, telling us where he locates himself in relation to what he is describing. According to Spitzer, it's Proust's parentheses – which I for my part would compare to the parentheses of Max Weber – that are the place where metadiscourse shows itself as present in discourse. It's the inverted commas or the different forms of indirect style which express the different ways of relating to the things narrated and the people whose remarks you are reporting. How can you mark the distance adopted by the writer from what he or she writes? That is one of the main difficulties of sociological writing. When I say that comic strips are an inferior genre, you might imagine I really think that. So I have to say at one and the same time that that's how it is, but that it isn't *my* opinion. My texts are full of indications meant to stop the reader deforming and simplifying things. Unfortunately, these warnings pass unnoticed or else make what I am saying so complicated that readers who read too quickly see neither the little indications nor the big ones and read more or less the exact opposite of what I wanted to say – witness numerous objections that are made to my work.

In any case, what is certain is that I am not out to make my writing clear and simple and that I consider the strategy of abandoning the rigour of technical vocabulary in favour of an easy and readable style to be dangerous. This is first and foremost because false clarity is often part and parcel of the dominant discourse, the discourse of those who think everything goes without saying, because everything is just fine as it is. Conservative language always falls back on the authority of common sense. It's no coincidence that nineteenth-century bourgeois theatre was called 'the theatre of common sense'. And common sense speaks the clear and simple language of what is plain for all to see. A second reason is that producing an over-simplified and over-simplifying discourse about the social world means inevitably that you are providing weapons that can be used to manipulate this world in dangerous ways. I am convinced that, for both scientific and political reasons, you have to accept that discourse can and must be as complicated as the (more or less complicated) problem it is tackling demands. If people at least come away with the feeling that it *is* complicated, that's already a good lesson to have learnt. Furthermore, I don't believe in the virtues of 'common sense' and 'clarity', those two ideals of the classical literary canon ('what is clearly understood can be clearly expressed', etc.). When it comes to objects of inquiry as overladen with passions, emotions and interests as those of social life, the 'clearest', that is, simplest discourses, are probably those which run the greatest risks of being misunderstood, because they work like projective tests into which each person imports his or her prejudices, unreflective opinions and fantasies. If you accept the fact that, in order to make yourself understood, you have to work at using words in such a way that they say just what you wanted them to say, you can see that the best way of talking clearly consists in talking in a complicated way, in an attempt to transmit simultaneously what you are saying and your relationship to what you are saying, and in avoiding saying, against your will, something more than and different from what you thought you were saying.

Sociology is an esoteric science – initiation into it is very slow and requires a real conversion in your whole vision of the world – but it always seems to be exoteric. Certain people, especially in my generation, which was brought up to hold in contempt – as philosophy encouraged one to do – everything linked with the social sciences, tend to read a sociological analysis in the same way that they would read a political weekly. This opinion is fostered by all those who sell bad journalism under the name of sociology. That is why the most difficult thing is to get the reader to adopt the right attitude, the one he would be immediately constrained to adopt if he were placed in the position of having to uncover, in the interpretation of a statistical table or the description of a certain situation, all the errors that the ordinary attitude – the one he applies to analyses constructed against this very attitude – leads him to commit. A scientific report does without such blunders. Another difficulty in the case of the social sciences is that the researcher has to deal with propositions that are scientifically false but sociologically so powerful – because many people need to think that they are true – that you cannot ignore them if you want to succeed in imposing the truth (I have in mind, for example, all those spontaneous representations of culture, innate intelligence, giftedness, genius, Einstein, and so on, that cultivated people keep in circulation). This sometimes leads you to 'twist the screw the other way' or to adopt a polemical or ironic tone, necessary to wake the reader from his doxic sleep . . .

But that's not all. I have constantly emphasized the fact that the social world is, to adapt the title of Schopenhauer's famous book, 'will and representation'. Representation in the psychological sense but also the theatrical and political senses – that of delegation, of a group of proxies. What we consider to be social reality is to a great extent representation or the product of representation, in all senses of the term. And the sociologist's language plays this game all the time, and with a particular intensity, derived from its scientific authority. In the case of the social world, speaking with authority is as good as doing: if for instance I say with authority that social classes exist, I contribute greatly to making them exist. And even if I rest content with putting forward a theoretical description of the social space and its most adequate divisions (as I did in *Distinction*), I expose myself to bringing into existence in reality, in other words, first and foremost, in people's minds (in the form of categories of perception, principles of vision and division), logical classes that I constructed to explain the distribution of modes of practice. This is all the more the case in that this representation – as everyone knows – acted as a basis for the new socio-professional categories of the National Institute of Economic and Statistical Information and was thus certified and guaranteed by the state . . . All this is not done, you will understand, in order to discourage the realistic and objectivist reading of works of sociology, which are all the more prone to it the more 'realistic' they are, and the closer the way they carve things up, as the Platonic metaphor has it, corresponds to the way reality is articulated. Thus, the sociologist's words contribute to creating the social world. The social world is more and more inhibited by reified sociology. The sociologists of the future (but it's already true of us) will discover more and more in the reality they study the sedimented products of their predecessors.

It's easy to understand why the sociologist is well advised to weigh his words carefully. But that's not all. The social world is the locus of struggles over words which owe their seriousness – and sometimes their violence – to the fact that words to a great extent make things, and that changing words, and, more generally representations (for instance, pictorial representation, like Manet), is already a way of changing things. Politics is, essentially, a matter of words. That's why the struggle to know reality scientifically almost always has to begin with a struggle against words. What very often happens is that in order to transmit knowledge, you have to use the very words that it was necessary to destroy in order to conquer and construct this knowledge: you can see that inverted commas are pretty insignificant when it comes to mark such a major change in epistemological status. In this way I will be able to carry on talking about 'tennis' at the end of a piece of work which has led to all the presuppositions behind a phrase such as 'tennis is becoming more democratic' being exploded – a phrase which relies, among other things, on the illusion that names continue to mean the same thing, and on the conviction that the reality designated by the word twenty years ago is the same as that designated by the same word today.

When dealing with the social world, the ordinary use of ordinary language makes metaphysicians of us. The fact that we are accustomed to political verbalism, and the reification of collective entities that certain philosophers have very often indulged in, means that the logical fallacies and question-begging implied by the most trivial remarks of everyday existence pass unnoticed. 'Public opinion is in favour of an increase in the price of petrol.' People accept a statement like that without wondering whether anything such as 'public opinion' can exist, and if so, how. And yet, philosophy has taught us that there are lots of things that you can talk about without their existing, that you can pronounce phrases which have a meaning ('The King of France is bald') without there being any referent (the King of France doesn't exist). When you pronounce phrases that have as their subject the State, Society, Civil Society, the Workers, the Nation, the People, the French, the Party, the Trade Union, etc., you wish it to be understood that what these words designate exists, just as when you say 'the King of France is bald' you are presupposing that there is a King of France and that he is bald. Each time existential propositions (France exists) are hidden behind predicative statements (France is big), we are exposed to the ontological slippage which leads from the existence of the name to the existence of the thing named, a slippage all the more probable, and dangerous, in that, in reality itself, social agents struggle for what I have called symbolic power, of which this power of constitutive *naming*, which by naming things brings them into being, is one of the most typical demonstrations. I certify that you are a teacher (the teaching diploma), or ill (the doctor's certificate). Or, even more powerfully, I certify that the proletariat exists, or the Occitan nation. The sociologist may be tempted to join in the game, to have the last word in these verbal disputes by saying how things are in reality. If, as I think, his real task lies in describing the logic of struggles over words, you can understand his having problems with the words he has to use in order to talk about these struggles.

Part II

Confrontations

3

From rules to strategies

Q. I would like us to talk about the interest you have shown in your work for questions of kinship and transmission, from the writings in 'Béarn' and the 'Trois études d'ethnologie kabyle' up to *Homo academicus*. You were the first person to tackle the question of the choice of spouse in a French population from a strictly ethnological standpoint,[1] and to emphasize the correlation between the mode of transmission of goods, which happens to be non-egalitarian, and the logic of marriages. Each matrimonial transaction must, you said, be understood as 'the result of a strategy' and may be defined 'as a moment in a series of material and symbolic exchanges . . . depending to a great extent on the position this exchange occupies in the family's *matrimonial history*'.

A. My research into marriage in the Béarn was for me the crossover point, the interface, between ethnology and sociology. Right from the start, I had thought of this work on my own part of the country as a sort of epistemological experimentation: analysing, as an ethnologist, in an environment familiar to me (apart, that is, from social distance), the matrimonial practices that I had studied in a much more distant social environment, namely Kabyle society, was a way of giving me an opportunity to objectify the act of objectification and the objectifying subject; of objectifying the ethnologist not only as a socially situated individual but also as a scientist who professes to analyse and conceptualize the social world, and who for that reason has to withdraw from the game, whether he observes a foreign world in which he has no vested interests, or whether he observes his own world, but while standing back from the game, as

Interview with P. Lamaison, published in *Terrains*, 4 (March 1985).
1 See 'Célibat et condition paysanne', *Études rurales*, 5–6 (April–September 1962), pp. 32–136, and 'Les stratégies matrimoniales dans le systèmè de reproduction', *Annales*, 4–5 (July–October 1972), pp. 1105–27.

far as he can. In short, I wanted less to observe the observer as an individual, which is in itself not particularly interesting, than to observe the effects produced on the observation, on the description of the thing observed, by the situation of the observer – to uncover all the presuppositions inherent in the *theoretical* posture as an external, remote, distant or, quite simply, non-practical, non-committed, non-involved vision. And it struck me that there was an entire, basically false social philosophy which stemmed from the fact that the ethnologist has 'nothing to do' with the people he studies, with their practices and their representations, except to study them: there is an enormous difference between trying to understand the nature of matrimonial relations between two families so as to get your son or daughter married off, investing the same interest in this as people in our own world invest in their choice of the best school for their son or daughter, and trying to understand these relations so as to construct a theoretical model of them. The same goes for trying to understand a ritual.

So the *theoretical* analysis of the theoretical vision as an external vision, one above all without anything practical at stake, was doubtless the source of my breaking away from what others would call the structuralist 'paradigm': it was an acute awareness, which I developed not only by theoretical reflexion, of the gap between the *theoretical* aims of theoretical understanding and the practical and directly concerned aims of practical understanding, that led me to talk of matrimonial *strategies* or of the *social uses* of kinship, rather than of rules of kinship. This change of vocabulary represented a change of point of view: I wanted to try to avoid giving as the source of agents' practice the theory that had to be constructed in order to explain it.

Q. But when Lévi-Strauss talks about rules or models that are reconstructed in order to explain it, he is not really saying anything different from you on this point.

A. In fact, it seems to me that the contradiction is disguised by the ambiguity of the word *rule*, which enables one to spirit away the very problem I tried to raise: it's impossible to tell exactly whether what is understood by rule is a principle of the juridical or quasi-juridical kind, more or less consciously produced and mastered by agents, or a set of objective regularities imposed on all those who join a game. When people talk of a rule of the game, it's one or other of these two meanings that they have in mind. But they may also be thinking of a third meaning, that of the model or principle constructed by the scientist to explain the game. I think that if you blur these distinctions you risk committing one of the most disastrous errors that can be made in the human sciences, that which consists of passing off, in Marx's well-known phrase, 'the things of logic as the logic of things'. To avoid this, you have to include in the theory the real principle behind strategies, namely the practical sense, or, if you prefer, what sports players call a feel for the game, as the practical mastery of the logic or of the immanent necessity of a game – a mastery acquired by experience of the game, and one which works outside conscious control and discourse (in the way that, for instance, techniques of the body do). Notions like that of habitus (or system of dispositions), practical sense, and strategy, are linked to my effort to escape from structuralist objectivism without relapsing into subjectivism. That is why I don't recognize myself in what Lévi-Strauss said recently about research into what he calls 'domestic societies'. This remains true even if I can't feel myself personally concerned, because I contributed to reintroducing into the theoretical discussion in ethnology one of those societies in which acts of exchange, both matrimonial and others, seem to have as 'subject' the house, the *maysou*, the *oustau*; and thus to formulate the theory of marriage as strategy . . .

Q.   Are you referring to the Marc Bloth lecture on 'L'ethnologie et l'histoire', published by the *Annales* ESC,[2] where Lévi-Strauss criticizes what he calls 'spontaneism'?

A.   Yes. When he talks about that critique of structuralism 'that floats around pretty much everywhere and which takes its cue from a modish spontaneism and subjectivism' (all of which is rather unkind), it's clear that Lévi-Strauss is attacking in a rather uncomprehending way – that's the least that can be said – a set of works which in my opinion belong to a different 'theoretical universe' from his. I will pass over the hotchpotch effect which consists of suggesting the existence of a relation between thinking in terms of strategy and what is designated in politics by spontaneism. One's choice of words, especially in polemical exchanges, is not innocent, and the discredit attached, even in politics, to all forms of belief in the spontaneity of the masses is well known. (That being said, incidentally, Lévi-Strauss's political intuition is not completely mistaken, because, via

---

2   No. 6 (November–December 1983), pp. 1217–31.

habitus, practical sense and strategy, what is reintroduced is agent, action, practice, and above all, perhaps, the observer's proximity to agents and practice, the rejection of the distant gaze, none of which are without a relation to theoretical, but also political, dispositions and positions.) The main thing is that Lévi-Strauss, who has always (I am thinking here of his remarks on phenomenology in the preface to Mauss) been locked within the alternative of subjectivism and objectivism, cannot see attempts to transcend this alternative as anything other than a regression to subjectivism. He is, like so many other people, a prisoner of the alternative of individual versus social phenomena, of freedom versus necessity, etc., and so he cannot see in the attempts being made to break away from the structuralist 'paradigm' anything other than so many returns to an individualist subjectivism and thus to a form of irrationalism: according to him, 'spontaneism' substitutes for structure 'a statistical mean resulting from choices made in all liberty or at least unaffected by any external determination', and it reduces the social world to 'an immense chaos of creative acts all arising at the individual level and ensuring the richness of permanent disorder'. (How can one fail to recognize here the real or fantastical image of the 'spontaneism' of May 1968 evinced both by the concept used to designate this theoretical current, and by the allusions to modishness and to critiques 'that float around pretty much everywhere'?) In short, because strategy is for him a synonym of *choice*, a conscious and individual choice, guided by rational calculation or by 'ethical and affective' motivations, and because it is the opposite of constraint and the collective norm, he cannot help but exclude from science a theoretical project which in reality aims at reintroducing the socialized agent (and not the subject) and the more or less 'automatic' strategies of the practical sense (and not the projects or calculations of any conscious mind).

q. But what, in your opinion, is the function of the notion of strategy?

a. The notion of strategy is the instrument I use to break away from the objectivist point of view and from the action without an agent that structuralism presupposes (by relying, for example, on the notion of the unconscious). But one can refuse to see in strategy the product of an unconscious program without making it the product of a conscious, rational calculation. It is the product of the practical sense as the feel for the game, for a particular, historically determined game – a feel which is acquired in childhood, by taking part in social activities, especially, in the case of Kabylia, and doubtless elsewhere, in children's games. The good player, who is so to speak the game incarnate, does at every moment what the game requires. That presupposes a permanent capacity for invention, indispensable if one is to be able to adapt to indefinitely varied and never completely identical situations. This is not ensured by mechanical obedience to the explicit, codified rule (when it exists). For example, I described the double game strategies which consist of playing in conformity with the rules, making sure right is on your side, acting in accordance with your interests while all the time seeming to obey the rules. One's feel for the game is not infallible; it is shared out unequally between players, in a society as in a team. Sometimes it is completely lacking, notably in tragic situations, when people appeal to wise men who, in Kabylia, are often poets too and who know how to take liberties with the official rule, so that the basis of what the rule aimed to guarantee can be saved. But this freedom of invention and improvisation which enables the infinity of moves allowed by the game to be produced (as in chess) has the same limits as the game. The strategies adapted in playing the game of Kabyle marriage, which do not involve land and the threat of sharing it out (because of the joint ownership in the equal sharing out of land between agnates), would not be suitable in playing the game of Béarn marriage, where you have above all to keep hold of your house and your land.

It's clear that the problem should not be discussed in terms of spontaneity and constraint, freedom and necessity, individual and society. The habitus as the feel for the game is the social game embodied and turned into a second nature. Nothing is simultaneously freer and more constrained than the action of the good player. He quite naturally materializes at just the place the ball is about to fall, as if the ball were in command of him – but by that very fact, he is in command of the ball. The habitus, as society written into the body, into the biological individual, enables the infinite number of acts of the game – written into the game as possibilities and objective demands – to be produced; the constraints and demands of the game, although they are not restricted to a code of rules, *impose themselves* on those people – and those people alone – who, because they have a feel for the game, a feel, that is, for the immanent necessity of the game, are prepared to perceive them and carry them out. This can easily be applied to the case of marriage. As I showed in the cases of the Béarn and Kabylia, matrimonial strategies are the product, not of obedience to a rule but of a feel for the game which leads people to 'choose' the best match possible given the game they have at their disposal, that is, the aces or the bad cards (especially girls), and the skill with which they are capable of playing; the explicit rule of the game – for instance, prohibitions or preferences in kinship or laws of succession – defines the value of the playing cards (of boys and girls, elder and younger children). And the regularities that can be observed, thanks to statistics, are the aggregate product of individual actions guided by the same constraints, whether objective (the necessities written into the structure of the game or partly objectified in the rules), or incorporated (the feel for the game, itself unequally distributed, because there are everywhere, in all groups, degrees of excellence).

Q.   But who produces the rules of the game you are talking about, and are they any different from the rules of functioning of societies which, when they are laid down by ethnologists, lead precisely to the working-out of models? What separates the rules of the game from rules of kinship?

A.   The image of a game is doubtless the least inadequate when it comes to talking about social phenomena. Yet it is not without its dangers. Indeed, to talk about a game is to suggest that there is at the beginning someone who invents the game, a 'nomothetes' or legislator who has laid down the rules, and established the social contract. What is more serious is the fact that there exist rules of the game, that is, explicit norms, more often than not written down, etc.; whereas in reality it's much more complicated. You can use the analogy of the game in order to say that a set of people take part in a rule-bound activity, an activity which, without necessarily being the product of obedience to rules, *obeys certain regularities*. The game is the locus of an immanent necessity, which is at the same time an immanent logic. In the game you can't do just anything and get away with it. And the feel for the game, which contributes to this necessity and this logic, is a way of knowing this necessity and this logic. Whoever wants to win this game, appropriate the stakes, catch the ball, in other words the good matrimonial match and the benefits associated with it, for example, must have a feel for the game, that is, a feel for the necessity and the logic of the game. Should one talk of a rule? Yes and no. You can do so on condition that you distinguish clearly between *rule* and *regularity*. The social game is regulated, it is the locus of certain regularities. Things happen *in regular fashion* in it; rich heirs *regularly* marry rich younger daughters. That does not mean that it is a *rule* that rich heirs marry rich younger daughters – even if you may think that marrying an heiress (even a rich one, and *a fortiori* a poor younger daughter) is an error, or even, in the parents' eyes for example, a misdeed. I can say that all my thinking started from this point: how can behaviour be regulated without being the product of obedience to rules? But it is not enough to reject the juridical ideology (what the Anglo-Saxons call the *legalism*) that comes so naturally to anthropologists, always ready to listen to those dispensers of lessons and rules that informants are when they talk to the ethnologist, that is to someone who knows nothing and to whom they have to talk *as if they were talking to a child*. In order to construct a *model* of the game which will not be the mere recording of explicit norms nor a statement of regularities, while synthesizing both norms and regularities, one has to reflect on the different *modes of existence* of the principles of regulation and regularity of different forms of practice: there is, of course, the habitus, that regulated disposition to generate regulated and regular behaviour outside any reference to rules; and, in societies where the work of *codification* is not very advanced, the habitus is the principle of most modes of practice. For instance, ritual practices, as I demonstrated, I believe, in *The Logic of Practice*,[3] are the product of the implementation of *practical taxonomies*, or rather, of classificatory models handled in a practical, pre-reflective state, with all the well-known effects: rites and myths are logical, but only up to a certain point. Their logic is a practical logic (in the way one calls an article of clothing practical), that is, good in practice, necessary and sufficient in practice. Too much logic would often be incompatible with practice, or even contradictory with the practical aims of practice. The same goes for the classifications that we apply to the social or political world. I came to what seems to me to be a correct intuition of the practical logic behind ritual action by envisaging it by analogy with our way of using the opposition between right and left in order to envisage and classify political opinions or politicians (I even tried, some years later, with Luc Boltanski, to grasp how this practical logic works in our ordinary experience by using a technique derived from that used by the inventors of componential analysis to understand native taxonomies in the fields of kinship, botany and zoology: I asked people to classify little pieces of cardboard on which

---

3 P. Bourdieu, *Le sens pratique* (Paris, 1980); trans. as *The Logic of Practice*, tr. R. Nice (Cambridge, 1989).

were written names of political parties and of politicians. I carried out a similar experiment with names of professions.

Q.   There too, you cross the line between ethnology and sociology.

A.   Yes. The distinction between sociology and ethnology prevents the ethnologist from submitting his own experience to the analysis that he applies to his object. This would oblige him to discover that what he describes as mythical thought is, quite frequently, nothing other than the practical logic we apply in three out of four of our actions: even, for instance, in those of our judgements which are considered to be the supreme accomplishment of cultivated culture, the judgements of taste, entirely founded on (historically consti-tuted) couples of adjectives.

But returning to the possible principles of production of regular practices, one has to take into account, along with the habitus, the explicit, express, formulated rules, which can be preserved and transmitted orally (this was the case in Kabylia, as in all societies without writing), or else in writing. These rules can even be constituted as a coherent system, with an intentional and deliberate coherence, at the price of an effort of *codification* that is the responsibility of the professionals of formalization and rationaliz-ation – the jurists.

Q.   In other words, the distinction you were making to start with, between the things of logic and the logic of things, would be what enables one to raise clearly the question of the relation between that regularity of practices based on dispositions and the feel for the game on the one hand, and the explicit rule, the code, on the other?

A.   Absolutely. The regularity that can be grasped statistically, which the feel for the game spontaneously abides by, which you 'recognize' practically by 'playing the game', as they say, does not necessarily spring from the rule of law or of anything 'lawlike' (a custom, saying, proverb, or formula setting out a regularity that is thereby constituted as a 'normative fact': I have in mind, for example, tautologies such as the one which consists of saying of a man that 'he's a man', with the implication that he's a *real* man, *really* a man). However, it sometimes happens that this is the case, especially in official situations. Once this distinction has been clearly made, it is necessary to develop a theory of the labour of explanation and codification, and of the properly symbolic effect produced by codification. There is a link between the juridical formula and the mathematical formula. Law, like formal logic, looks at the form of operations without taking account of the matter to which they are applied. The juridical formula is valid for all values of x. The code is that which means that different agents agree on universal (because formal) formulae (in the double sense of the English word *formal* – official, public – and the French word *formel*, that is, relating to form alone). But I will stop there. I just wanted to show how ambiguous the word 'rule' is and how many meanings it covers (the same error haunts the whole history of linguistics, which, from Saussure to Chomsky, tends to confuse the generative schemes functioning in the practical state with the explicit model – the grammar – constructed in order to explain the statements made).

Q. So, among the constraints which define a social game, there could be more or less strict rules governing marriage and defining bonds of kinship?

A. The most powerful of these constraints, at least in the traditions I have studied directly, are those which result from the custom of succession. It is through them that the necessities of the economy are imposed, and strategies of reproduction – matrimonial strategies being foremost among them – have to take them into account. But customs, even highly codified ones – which is rarely the case in peasant societies – are themselves the object of all sorts of strategies. Thus in each case one has to return to the *reality of practices*, instead of relying, as does Le Roy Ladurie, following Yver, on custom, whether codified (that is, written) or not: being essentially based on the recording of 'moves' or lapses that, being exemplary, are converted into norms, custom gives a very inexact idea of the ordinary routine of ordinary marriages, and it is the object of all sorts of manipulations, notably on the occasion of marriages. If the Béarnais were able to perpetuate their traditions of succession in spite of two centuries of the civil code, it's because they had long ago learnt to play with the rules of the game. That being said, the effect of codification or of simple officialization (to which the effect of what is called preferential marriage is reduced) must not be underestimated: the channels of succession designated by custom are established as 'natural' and they tend to guide matrimonial strategies – though how exactly this happens needs to be explained. This is why one can observe quite a close correspondence between the geography of the modes of transmission of goods and the geography of representations of bonds of kinship.

Q. In fact, you also set yourself apart from the structuralists in the way you view the action of juridical or economic 'constraints'.

A. Absolutely. The coordination of different 'instances' that the structuralists, especially Neo-Marxists, sought in the objectivity of structures, is accomplished in every responsible act, in the proper sense of the word *responsible* – objectively adjusted to the necessity of the game because guided by a feel for the game. The 'good player' takes into account, in each matrimonial choice, the set of pertinent properties, given the structure that has to be reproduced: in Béarn, these properties include gender (i.e. the customary representations of male precedence), the rank of birth (i.e. the precedence of the elder children and, through them, of the land which, as Marx said, inherits the heir who inherits it), the social rank of the house that has to be maintained, etc. The feel for the game, in this case, is, more or less, the sense of honour; but the Béarnais sense of honour, despite the analogies, is not exactly identical with the Kabyle sense of honour, which, being more sensitive to symbolic capital, reputation, fame or 'glory', as they said in the seventeenth century, pays less attention to economic capital, notably to land.

Q. Matrimonial strategies are thus written into the system of strategies of reproduction . . .

A. I must say, for the sake of the anecdote, that it was the concern for stylistic elegance on the part of the editorial staff of *Annales*[4] which meant my article had to be called 'Les stratégies matrimoniales dans le système de reproduction' ['Matrimonial strategies in the system of reproduction'] (which doesn't mean a great deal) and not, as I wanted, 'dans le système des stratégies de reproduction' ['in the system of strategies of reproduction']. This is the main point: matrimonial strategies cannot be dissociated from the set of strategies – I am thinking for instance of strategies of fertility, of educative strategies as strategies of cultural investment or of economic strategies such as investing or saving money, etc. – through which the family aims to reproduce itself biologically and, above all,

---

4 *Annales*: French review of social and economic history, founded in 1929.

socially: aims, that is, to reproduce the properties that enable it to maintain its position, its rank in the social world under consideration.

Q. By talking of the *family* and its strategies, are you not postulating the homogeneity of that group, of its interests, and are you not ignoring the tensions and conflicts inherent for instance in conjugal life?

A. No, quite the opposite. Matrimonial strategies are often the outcome of power relationships within the domestic group and these relationships can be understood only by appealing to the history of this group and in particular to the history of previous marriages. For example, in Kabylia, the woman, when she comes from outside, tends to reinforce her position by trying to find a match in her own lineage and she stands all the more chance of succeeding the more prestigious her lineage is. The struggle between husband and wife can take place by way of an interposed mother-in-law. The husband may also find it in his interest to reinforce the cohesion of the lineage, by an internal marriage. In short, it is via this synchronic power-relationship between members of the family that the history of lineages, and especially of all previous marriages, intervenes on the occasion of each new marriage.

This theoretical model has a very general value and it is indispensable, for instance, if one is to understand the educational strategies of families or, in a completely different field, their strategies for investing or saving money. Monique de Saint-Martin has noted in the great families of the French aristocracy matrimonial strategies altogether similar to those I had observed among the Béarnais peasants. Marriage is not that instantaneous, abstract operation, based on the mere application of rules of descent and marriage, described by the structuralist tradition, but an act which integrates the set of necessities inherent in a position within the social structure, that is, within a particular state of the social game, by the synthetic virtue of the feel for the game shown by the 'negotiators'. The relationships established by families on the occasion of marriages are as difficult and important as the negotiations of our most sophisticated diplomats, and reading Saint-Simon or Proust doubtless provides a better preparation for understanding the subtle diplomacy of Kabyle or Béarnais peasants than does reading *Notes and Queries on Anthropology*. But not all readers of Proust or Saint-Simon are equally prepared to recognize M. de Norpois or the duc de Berry in a rugged, rough-spoken peasant or in a mountain dweller, when the grids we apply to them – those of ethnology – lead us inevitably to treat them as radically other – as barbarians.

Q. Ethnology does not really call peasants or indeed anybody at all 'barbarian' these days, I think. Its developments in France and Europe have, moreover, probably contributed to modifying even more profoundly the way it looks at societies.

A. I know I'm exaggerating. I would none the less maintain that there is something unhealthy about the way ethnology can exist as a separate science, and that we risk, through this division, accepting all that was written into the initial division out of which it came and which is perpetuated, as I think I have shown, in its methods (for example, why should there be this resistance to statistics?) and especially in its modes of thought: for example, the rejection of ethnocentrism which prevents the ethnologist from relating what he observes to his own experiences – as I was doing just now when I related the classificatory operations involved in a ritual act to those that we carry out in our perception of the social world – leads, behind the façade of respect, to the setting up of an unbridgeable distance, as when the idea of a 'primitive mentality' held sway. And this can be just as much the case when one carries out the 'ethnology' of peasants or workers.

Q. To come back to the logic of matrimonial strategies, you mean that the whole history and structure of the game are present, by way of the habitus of the actors and their feel for the game, in each of the marriages that results from the confrontation of their strategies?

A. Exactly. I have shown how, in the case of Kabylia, the most difficult and thus most prestigious marriages mobilize almost everyone in the two groups being brought together and the history of their past transactions, matrimonial or other, so that they can be understood only if one knows the balance sheet of these exchanges at the moment under consideration and also, of course, everything that defines the position of the two groups in the distribution of economic and also symbolic capital. The great negotiators are those who can get the most out of this situation. But this, people will say, is valid only as long as marriage is a family affair.

Q. Yes. One can ask whether the same is true in societies such as ours, in which the 'choice of spouse' is apparently left to the free choice of those involved.

A. In fact, the *laissez-faire* policy of the free market conceals various necessities. I showed this in the case of the Béarn by analysing the passage from a matrimonial regime of the planned type to the free market incarnated in the local dance. The use of the notion of habitus is necessary in this case more than ever: for how otherwise can the homogamy that is observed in spite of everything be explained? There are, of course, all those social techniques which aim at limiting the field of possible matches, by a sort of protectionism: rallies, exclusive balls, society gatherings, etc. But the surest guarantor of homogamy and, thereby, of social reproduction, is the spontaneous affinity (experienced as a feeling of friendly warmth) which brings together the agents endowed with dispositions or tastes that are similar, and thus produced from similar social conditions and conditionings. There is, too, the effect of closure linked to the existence of socially and culturally homogeneous groups, like groups of school friends (secondary school classes, university faculties, etc.), which are responsible, today, for a great number of marriages or love affairs, and which themselves owe much to the effect of affinity of habitus (especially in the operations of cooptation and selection). I showed at some length, in *Distinction*[5] that love too can be described as a form of *amor fati*: to love is always to some extent to love in someone else another way of fulfilling one's own social destiny. I learned this from studying Béarnais marriages.

Q. Lévi-Strauss, defending the structuralist paradigm, says that 'to doubt that structural analysis can be applied to some [of these societies] leads to its being challenged for all societies'. In your opinion, isn't that valid for the paradigm of strategy too?

A. I think it's rather unwise to pretend to propose a universal paradigm and I was careful not to do so starting from the two – actually rather similar – cases that I studied (even if I think it likely that matrimonial strategies are universally written into the system of strategies of social reproduction). In fact, before deciding in favour of monism or pluralism, you would have to verify that the structuralist

---

5   P. Bourdieu, *La distinction. Critique sociale du jugement* (Paris, 1979); trans. as *Distinction. A Social Critique of the Judgement of Taste*, tr. R. Nice (Cambridge, Mass., 1984).

view that was essential in the analysis of societies without writing is not an effect of the relation to the object and of the theory of practice favoured by the ethnologist's external position (marriage with a parallel cousin, which was considered to be the *rule* in the Arabo-Berber countries, was the object of certain structuralist exercises whose weakness I believe I have demonstrated). Some of the work on typically 'cold' societies seems to show that, so long as you go into details, instead of being content with picking out the nomenclatures of kinship terms and abstract genealogies, thus reducing the relations between spouses to mere genealogical distance, you discover that matrimonial exchanges and, more generally, all material or symbolic exchanges, such as the transmission of forenames, are the occasion for complex strategies and that the genealogies themselves, far from determining economic and social relations, are the stake of manipulations whose aim is to encourage or to prevent economic or social relations, to legitimatize or condemn them. I have in mind the work of Bateson who, in *Naven*,[6] opened the way by referring to strategic manipulations whose objects may be names of places or lineages and the relations between them. I could mention too the very recent studies of Alban Bensa, on New Caledonia.[7] Once the ethnologist finds the means of grasping in all their subtlety the social uses of kinship – combining, as Bensa does, the linguistic analysis of toponyms, the economic analysis of the circulation of land, the methodical questioning of the most humdrum political strategies, etc. – he discovers that marriages are complex operations, involving very many parameters that genealogical abstraction, which reduces everything to the kinship relation, excludes without even realizing it. One of the bases of the division between the two 'paradigms' could lie in the fact that you have to spend hours and hours with well-informed and well-disposed informants in order to gather the information necessary to understand a single marriage (or at least to bring to light the parameters that are relevant for constructing a statistically based model of the constraints that organize matrimonial strategies), whereas you need only a single afternoon to establish a genealogy including a hundred marriages or so, and a couple of days to draw up a picture of the terms of address and reference. I tend to think that, in the social sciences, talking in terms of rules is often a way of hiding your ignorance.

6 G. Bateson, *Naven* (Cambridge, 1936).
7 A. Bensa and J. C. Rivierre, *Les chemins de l'alliance: l'organisation sociale et ses représentations en Nouvelle-Calédonie* (Paris, 1982).

Q.   In *The Logic of Practice*, especially with relation to ritual, you suggest that it's the ethnologist who artificially produces a sense of distance and estrangement, because he is incapable of understanding his own relation to practice.

A.   I hadn't read the merciless criticisms addressed by Wittgenstein to Frazer, and which apply to most ethnologists, when I described what seemed to me to be the real logic behind mythical or ritual thinking. Where people saw an algebra, I think one should see a dance or a gymnastic exercise. The intellectualism of ethnologists, which only increases their concern to give a scientific trimming to their work, prevents them from seeing that, in their own everyday practice, whether they are giving a big kick to the pebble that tripped them up, to use Wittgenstein's example, or whether they are classifying professions or politicians, they are obeying a logic very similar to that of the 'primitives' who classify objects according to whether they are wet or dry, hot or cold, up or down, right or left, and so on. Our perception and our practice, especially our perception of the social world, are guided by practical taxonomies, oppositions between up and down, masculine (or virile) and feminine, etc., and the classifications produced by these taxonomies owe their effectiveness to the fact that they are 'practical', that they allow one to introduce just enough logic for the needs of practical behaviour, neither too much – since a certain vagueness is often indispensable, especially in negotiations – nor too little, since life would then become impossible.

Q.   Do you think there are objective differences between societies that mean that some of them, especially the more complex and highly differentiated ones, lend themselves better to strategic play?

A.   Although I am suspicious of big dualist oppositions (hot societies versus cold societies, historical societies versus societies without history), one could say that as societies become more highly differentiated and as those relatively autonomous 'worlds' that I call fields develop in them, the chances that real events (that is, encounters between independent causal series, linked to different spheres of necessity) will happen in them will continue to increase, and so, therefore, will the liberty given to complex strategies of the habitus, integrating necessities of different orders. It's in this way, for instance, that as the economic field establishes itself in its own right by establishing the necessity that sets it apart, that of business, of economic calculation, or of the maximization of material profit ('business is business', 'business is no place for sentiment'), and as the more or less explicit and codified principles that determine the links between relatives cease to apply beyond the limits of the family, only the complex strategies of a habitus shaped by diverse necessities can integrate the different necessities into coherent decisions. The big aristocratic or bourgeois marriages, for instance, are probably the best examples of such an integration of different and relatively irreducible necessities, those respectively of kinship, economics and politics. Perhaps, in societies that are less highly differentiated into autonomous orders, the necessities of kinship, not having to count with any other principle of order that might come into competition, can rule undivided. This would need to be verified.

Q. Do you think, all the same, that kinship studies have a part to play in the interpretation of our societies, but that they should be defined in a different way?

A. They have a major part to play. For instance, I showed in my work with Monique de Saint-Martin on French employers that affinities based on marriage are the basis of certain of the solidarities that unite those incarnations of homo oeconomicus *par excellence*, the captains of industry, and that, in certain economic decisions of the highest importance, such as mergers between companies, the weight of matrimonial links – which themselves lie behind certain affinities in life-style – can prevail over the weight of purely economic reasons or determining factors. And, more generally, it's certain that dominant groups, especially the big families (big in both senses of the term) ensure their perpetuation via strategies – foremost of which are educative strategies – that are not so different, in their principle, from those which Kabyle or Béarn peasants use in order to perpetuate their material capital or symbolic capital.

In short, all my work, for more than twenty years, has aimed at abolishing the separation of sociology from ethnology. This residual, vestigial division prevents both sets of researchers from adequately formulating the most fundamental questions raised by all societies, those of the specific logic of strategies which groups, especially families, use to produce and reproduce themselves, that is, to create and perpetuate their unity, and thus their existence as groups, which is almost always, and in all societies, the condition of the perpetuation of their position in the social space.

Q. So the theory of the strategies of reproduction is inseparable from a genetic theory of groups, which aims at accounting for the logic which determines how groups, or classes, are made and unmade?

A. Absolutely. This was so evident, and so important, for me, that I went as far as to place the chapter devoted to classes, which I had intended as the conclusion of *Distinction*, at the end of the first, theoretical part of *The Logic of Practice*, in which I had tried to show that groups, especially genealogically based units, existed both in the objective reality of established regularities and constraints, and in representations, and also in all the strategies of bargaining, negotiation, bluff, etc., aimed at modifying reality by modifying its representations. I thus hoped to show that the logic that I had discovered in genealogically based groups, families, clans, tribes, etc., was also valid for the most typical groupings of our societies, those that are designated by the name 'classes'. Just as the theoretical units that are drawn up *on paper* by genealogical analysis do not automatically correspond to real, practical units, the theoretical classes drawn up by sociological science to explain modes of practice are, likewise, not always concretely constituted classes. In both cases, we are dealing only with what appear to be groups on paper ... In short, groups – family groups or other sorts – are things you have to keep going at the cost of a permanent effort of maintenance, of which marriages constitute one stage. And the same applies to classes, when they exist, even in a tenuous state (has anyone ever asked what it means, for a group, to exist?): belonging to a group is something you build up, negotiate and bargain over, and play for. And there too, the opposition between voluntarist subjectivism and scientistic and realist objectivism has to be transcended: the social space, in which distances are measured in terms of capital, defines proximities and affinities, distances and incompatibilities, in short, the probabilities of belonging to really unified groups, families, clubs, or concretely constituted classes; but it's in the struggle over classifications, a struggle to impose this or that way of dividing up this space, a struggle to unify or to divide, etc., that real comparisons are made. Class is never something immanent; it is also will and representation, but it has no chance of incarnating itself in things unless it brings closer that which is objectively close and distances what is objectively distant.

4

Codification

When I began working as an ethnologist, I wanted to react against what I called legalism, that is, against the tendency among ethnologists to describe the social world in the language of rules and to behave as if social practices were explained merely by stating the explicit rule in accordance with which they are allegedly produced. So I was very pleased one day to come across a text by Weber which said, in effect: 'Social agents obey the rule when it is more in their interest to obey it than to disobey it.' This good, healthy materialist formula is interesting because it reminds us that the rule is not automatically effective by itself and that it obliges us to ask under what conditions a rule can operate.

Notions that I developed gradually, such as the notion of habitus, came from the desire to recall that beside the express, explicit norm, or the rational calculation, there are other principles that generate practices. This is especially true in societies in which there are very few things codified; so that, to explain what people do, you have to suppose that they obey a certain 'feel for the game', as people say in sport, and that, to understand their practices, you have to reconstruct the capital of informational models that enables them to produce sensible and regular thoughts and practices without any intention of behaving meaningfully and without consciously obeying rules explicitly posed as such. Doubtless you always come across norms and rules, even imperatives and what Gernet called 'pre-legal' formulations: these are proverbs, explicit principles concerning the use of time or the way of bringing in the harvest, codified preferences concerning marriage, and customs. But statistics, which in this case are very useful, show that practices conform only exceptionally to the norm: for example, marriages with one's parallel cousin, which

Paper presented at Neuchâtel in May 1983 and published in *Actes de la recherche en sciences sociales*, 64 (September 1986).

in the Arab and Berber traditions are unanimously recognized as exemplary, are in fact very rare, and most of them are inspired by other reasons, the conformity of practice to the rule bringing an additional symbolic profit, that which consists in being in line, or, as they say, coming into line, paying homage to the rule and to the values of the group.

Having begun with that sort of mistrust of legalism – and of the ethnologists who are often inclined to it, because it's easier to pick up the codified aspects of different practices – I managed to show that, in the case of Kabylia, the most codified, namely customary law, is only the recording of successively produced verdicts, with relation to individual transgressions, based on the principles of the habitus. I do think that one can re-generate all the concrete acts of jurisprudence that are recorded in customary laws on the basis of a small number of simple principles, in other words, on the basis of the fundamental oppositions which organize the entire world-vision, night/day, inside/outside, etc.: a crime committed at night is more serious than a crime committed during the day; a crime committed in the home is more serious than one committed outside, and so on. Once these principles have been understood, you can predict that the one who committed such and such a crime will receive such and such a fine, or, at least, that he will be given a bigger or lesser fine than the person who commits some other crime. In short, even that which is most codified – and the same goes for the agrarian calendar – has as its principle not explicit, objectified and thus themselves codified principles, but practical models. One example is provided by the contradictions one can observe, for instance, in the agrarian calendar, which is, however, specially codified because synchronization is, in all societies, one of the bases of social integration.

The habitus, as the system of dispositions to a certain practice, is an objective basis for regular modes of behaviour, and thus for the regularity of modes of practice, and if practices can be predicted (here, the punishment that follows a certain crime), this is because the effect of the habitus is that agents who are equipped with it will behave in a certain way in certain circumstances. That being said, this tendency to act in a regular manner which, when its principle is explicitly constituted, can act as the basis of a forecast (the specialized equivalent of the practical anticipations of ordinary experience), is not based on an explicit rule or law. This means that the modes of behaviour created by the habitus do not have the fine regularity of the modes of behaviour deduced from a legislative principle: *the habitus goes hand in glove with vagueness and indeterminacy*. As a

generative spontaneity which asserts itself in an improvised confrontation with ever-renewed situations, it obeys a *practical logic*,
that of vagueness, of the more-or-less, which defines one's ordinary
relation to the world.

This degree of indeterminacy, of openness, of uncertainty, means
that one cannot depend on it entirely in critical, dangerous situations. One can formulate the general rule that the more dangerous
the situation is, the more the practice tends to be codified. The
degree of codification varies in proportion with the degree of risk.
This is easy to see in the case of marriage: as soon as you examine
marriages and not marriage as such, you see that there are considerable variations, in particular as regards codification: the more
marriage unites distant and thus prestigious groups, the greater will
be the symbolic profit, but the greater too the risk. It's in this case
that you will find a high degree of formalization of practices; it's here
that there will be the most refined rules of politeness, and the most
highly elaborated rituals. The more a situation is pregnant with
potential violence, the more people will have to *respect the conventions*, the more behaviour freely vested in the improvisations of the
habitus will give way to behaviour expressly determined by a
methodically instituted, even codified *ritual*. You need only think of
the language of diplomacy or the rules of protocol which govern the
order of precedence and the proprieties in official situations. The
same was true in the case of marriages between distant tribes, in
which ritual games, archery for instance, could always degenerate
into war.

To codify means to formalize and to adopt formal behaviour.
There is *a virtue proper to the form*. And cultural mastery is always a
mastery of forms. That is one of the reasons which make ethnology
so very difficult: this cultural mastery cannot be acquired in a single
day . . . All these modes of formalizing which, as can be seen by the
euphemistic way of putting it, are also ways of getting round the
rules of the game, and are thus double games, are a matter for
virtuosi. In order to make sure you are on the right side of the
authorities, you have to have rule, adversaries and game at your
fingertips. If one had to propose a transcultural definition of
excellence, I would say that it's the fact of being able to play the
game up to the limits, even to the point of transgression, while
managing to stay within the rules of the game.

This means that the analysis of the logic of practice is valid far
beyond societies without writing. In most ordinary modes of behaviour, we are guided by practical models, that is, 'principles

imposing order on action' (*principium importans ordinem ad actum*, as the scholastics said), or *informational models*. These are principles of classification, principles of hierarchization, principles of division which are also principles of vision, in a word, everything which enables each one of us to distinguish between things which other people confuse, to operate, that is, a *diacrisis*, a judgement which separates. Perception is basically diacritical; it distinguishes 'figure' from 'background', what is important from what is not, what is central from what is secondary, what is a matter of current concern and what is not. These principles of judgement, of analysis, perception and understanding are almost always implicit, and thus the classifications they work with are coherent, but only up to a certain point. This can be observed, as I have shown, in the case of ritual practices: if you take logical control too far, you see contradictions springing up at every step. And the same goes when you carry out a survey asking people to classify political personalities or political parties, or even professions.

The classificatory models, quasi-bodily dispositions, which operate in the practical state, can in certain cases pass over into the objectified state. What is the effect of objectification? To ask what objectification is means asking about the ethnologist's very work, which, in the fashion of the first legislators, codifies, by the mere fact of recording, things which existed only in the incorporated state, in the form of dispositions, classificatory schemes whose products are indeed coherent, but only partly so. One has to refrain from seeking in the productions of the habitus more logic than they actually contain: the logic of practice lies in being logical to the point at which being logical would cease being practical. In the French army, they used to teach you – and perhaps they still do – how to take a step forward; it's clear that nobody would be able to walk or march if they had to conform to the theory of how to take a step in order to walk. Codification may be antinomic to the application of the code. All codifying activity must thus be accompanied by a theory of the effect of codification, for fear of unconsciously substituting the objectified logic of the code for the codified logic of the practical models and the partial logic of practice that they generate.

The objectification brought about by codification introduces the possibility of a logical control of coherence, of a *formalization*. It makes possible the establishment of an explicit normativity, that of grammar or law. When people claim that language is a code, they don't specify in what sense. Language isn't a code properly speaking: it becomes a code only through grammar, which is an almost juridical codification of a system of informational schemes. Speaking of a code in relation to grammar is to commit the major fallacy, that which consists of putting into the minds of the people you are studying what you have to have in your own mind in order to understand what they are doing. On the pretext that in order to understand a foreign language, you have to have a grammar, people seem to behave as if those who speak the language were obeying a grammar. Codification is a change of nature, a change of ontological status, which occurs when you go from linguistic patterns mastered at the practical level to a code, a grammar, via the labour of codification, which is a juridical activity. This activity has to be analysed in order to find out both what happens in reality when jurists make a code and what happens automatically, without people knowing it, when you carry out the science of practices.

Codification goes hand in glove with discipline and with the normalization of practices. Quine says somewhere that symbolic systems 'enlist' what they code. Codification is an operation of symbolic ordering, or of the maintenance of the symbolic order, which is most often the task of the great state bureaucracies. As can be seen in the case of driving, codification brings the collective benefits of clarification and homogenization. You know what you have to do; you know with a reasonable chance of predictability that at every crossroad in France the people who arrive from the left will have to yield to you. Codification minimizes ambiguity and vagueness, in particular in interactions. It is particularly indispensable and just as efficient in situations in which the risks of collision, conflict and accident, hazard and chance (a word which, as Cournot used to say, designates the encounter between two independent causal series), are particularly important. The encounter between two very distant groups is the encounter between two independent causal series. Between people of the same group, equipped with the same habitus, and thus spontaneously orchestrated, everything goes without saying, even conflicts; they can be understood without people having to spell things out, and so on. But when different systems of dispositions are involved, there appears the possibility of an accident, a collision or a conflict . . . Codification is of capital importance because it ensures a basic minimum level of communication. What is lost is a certain charm . . . Societies in which the degree of codification is slight, in which the essential things are left to a feel for the game and to improvisation, have a tremendous charm about them, and in order to survive in them, above all in order to dominate in them, you have to have a certain genius for social relations, and an absolutely extraordinary feel for the game. You doubtless have to be much more cunning than in our societies.

Certain of the major effects of codification are linked to the objectification that it implies and which are inscribed into the very practice of writing. Havelock, in a work on Plato, analyses the notion of *mimesis*, which can be translated as 'imitation', in the ordinary sense of the word, but which means first and foremost the fact of mimicking. According to Plato, poets are mimes: they don't know what they are saying because they are entirely caught up in what they are saying. They speak in the same way that people dance (and what's more, they dance and mime as they sing their poems), and if it is true that they can invent and improvise (the habitus is a source of invention, but only within certain limits), they do not understand the principles behind their invention. The poet, according to Plato, is the absolute antithesis of the philosopher. He says what is the good and the beautiful, he says, as in archaic societies, whether his people should make war or peace, whether or not they should kill a woman taken in adultery – in short, things that are essential: and he does not know what he is saying. He does not understand the principles behind his own productions. In this condemnation of the poet, in fact, there is an implicit theory of practice. The mime does not know what he is doing because he *is* what he does. He cannot objectify his practice or himself, above all because he does not possess the written word and everything that makes the written word possible: above all, the freedom to go back over your words, the logical control which makes revision possible, the comparing and contrasting of the successive moments of discourse. Logic is always a victory won over chronology, over succession: as long as I remain within a linear time-scale, I can stay content with being logical overall (this is what enables practical logics to be viable). Logic presupposes the confrontation of successive moments, of things which have been said or done at different, separate moments. Like Socrates, who never forgets a thing, and who forces his interlocutors to contradict themselves ('but you said just now that . . .') by contrasting the different moments of their discourse, writing, which synchronizes ('the written word remains'), enables one to grasp at a glance, *uno intuitu*, that is, at one and the same instant, successive moments of the practice that were protected against logic by the gradual unfolding of time.

To objectify is also to bring out into the open, to make visible, public, known to all, published. An *author* in the proper sense of the word is someone who makes public things which everyone felt in a confused sort of way; someone who possesses a special capacity, that of publishing the implicit, the tacit; someone who performs a real task of creation. A certain number of acts become official as soon as they are public, published (such as marriage bans). Publication is the act of officialization *par excellence*. The official is what can and must be made public, displayed, proclaimed, before everyone's eyes, in front of everyone, as opposed to what is unofficial, or even secret and shameful; with official publication ('in the official gazette'), everyone is both invited to be a witness and called upon to check, ratify and sanction, and he or she ratifies or sanctions even by staying silent (it is the anthropological basis for Durkheim's distinction between religion, which is necessarily collective and public, and magic, which condemns itself, subjectively and objectively, by the very fact that it is forced to hide). The effect of officialization can be seen as an effect of ratification: it transforms a practical pattern into a linguistic code of the juridical type. To have a name or a profession which are authenticated and recognized means that you exist officially (commerce, in Indo-European societies, is not a real profession, because it's a profession without a name, unnameable, *negotium*, non-leisure). Publication is an operation which makes things official and thus legal, because it implies divulgation, unveiling in front of everybody, and authenticating, the consensus of everyone regarding the thing which is thus unveiled.

The last feature associated with codification is the effect of *formalization*. To codify means to banish the effect of vagueness and indeterminacy, boundaries which are badly drawn and divisions which are only approximate, by producing clear classes and making clear cuts, establishing firm frontiers, even if this means eliminating people who are neither fish nor fowl. Difficulties in coding, which are the sociologist's daily bread, force one to reflect on those unclassifiable members of our societies (like the students who work in order to pay for their studies, etc.), those creatures who are *indeterminate* from the point of view of the dominant division. And people also discover, conversely, that what can be codified easily is what has already been the object of a juridical or quasi-juridical piece of codification.

Codification makes things simple, clear, communicable; it makes possible a controlled consensus on meaning, a *homologein*: you are sure of giving the same sense to the words. This is the definition of the linguistic code according to Saussure: that which enables the emitter and the receiver to associate the same sound with the same sense and the same sense with the same sound. But, if you transpose the formula in the case of the professions, you immediately see that it isn't quite that simple: do all the members of a society agree in the way they give the same sense to the same names of professions (such as teacher) and in giving the same name (and all that follows – salary, perks, prestige, etc.) to the same professional practices? Certain aspects of social struggle stem from the fact that, precisely, not everything is authenticated and that, when authentication takes place, it does not end discussion, negotiation, or even dispute (even if the agencies that produce juridically guaranteed social classifications, such as the institutes of statistics and the state bureaucracy, give themselves an appearance of scientific neutrality). Indeed, if the highway code (like the linguistic code) imposes its authority without much discussion, it's because, with rare exceptions, it decides between relatively arbitrary possibilities (even if such possibilities – like driving on the right or the left – may cease to be arbitrary once they have been made objective and incorporated into the habitus) and because, too, no great interests are here at stake, on either side (this is a consequence – one that has gone unappreciated – of the 'arbitrary nature of the linguistic sign' that Saussure spoke of). In this case, the collective profits of calculability and predictability linked to codification win out, without any need for discussion, over the interests – nil or, at most, minor – associated with choosing either option on its merits.

That being said, formalization, understood both in the sense of logic or mathematics as well as in the juridical sense, is what enables you to go from a logic which is immersed in the particular case to a logic independent of the individual case. Formalization is what enables you to confer on practices, above all practices of communication and cooperation, that constancy which ensures calculability and predictability over and above individual variations and temporal fluctuations. One might mention here, while giving it a more general extension, the criticism that Leibniz made of a method founded, like that of Descartes, on intuition and thereby exposed to irregularities and accidents. And he proposed replacing Descartes's sense of 'evidence' with the *evidentia ex terminis*, the evidence which comes from the terms, from symbols, a 'blind evidence', as he put it elsewhere, which comes from the automatic functioning of well-constructed logical instruments. As opposed to the person who can count only on his or her intuition, and who always runs the risk of inattention or forgetfulness, the person who possesses a well-constructed formal language can depend on it, and thereby finds himself or herself liberated from the need of having to attend to each particular case.

In the same way, jurists, in order to free themselves from a justice based on the feeling of equity which Weber, probably by virtue of a somewhat ethnocentric simplification, calls *Kadijustiz*, the justice of the cadi, have to establish formal, general laws, based on general, explicit principles, and expressed in such a way as to produce valid answers in all cases and for every person (for every *x*). 'Formal law', says Weber, 'takes into account only the general unequivocal characteristics of the case under consideration.' It is this constitutive abstraction of law which is ignored by the practical prudence of the sense of equity, which goes directly from one individual case to another, from a particular transgression to a particular punishment, without passing via the mediation of the concept or of the general law.

One of the virtues (which is also a vice . . .) of formalization is that, like all rationalization, it allows for an economy of invention, improvisation and creation. A formal law ensures calculability and predictability (at the cost of abstractions and simplifications which mean that the judgement which is most formally in conformity with the formal rules of law may be in formal contradiction with the evaluations of the sense of equity: *summum ius summa injuria*). It ensures above all the perfect interchangeability of agents whose responsibility it is to 'dispense justice' as the saying goes, that is, to apply codified rules in accordance with codified rules. Anybody at all can dispense justice. We don't need a Solomon any more. With customary law, if you have a Solomon, everything's fine. But otherwise, the danger of arbitrariness is very great. It's well known that the Nazis professed a charismatic theory of the 'nomothetes', granting to the Führer, set above the laws, the task of inventing law at each moment. Against this establishing of arbitrariness as a general law, a law, even an iniquitous one, such as the racial laws of the mid-thirties against the Jews (who were already persecuted, stripped of their possessions, etc.), was able to meet with a favourable response on the part of the victims because, when faced with the absolutely arbitrary, a law, even a wicked one, sets a limit to the purely arbitrary and ensures a minimal level of predictability.

But form, formalization and formalism do not act merely through their specific and properly technical effectiveness of clarification and rationalization. There is a properly symbolic effectiveness of form. Symbolic violence, of which the realization *par excellence* is probably law, is a violence exercised, so to speak, in formal terms, and paying due respect to forms. Paying due respect to forms means giving an action or a discourse the form which is recognized as suitable, legitimate, approved, that is, a form of a kind that allows the open production, in public view, of a wish or a practice that, if presented in any other way, would be unacceptable (this is the function of the euphemism). The force of the form, this *vis formae* that the ancients spoke of, is that properly symbolic force which allows force to be fully exercised while disguising its true nature as force and gaining recognition, approval and acceptance by dint of the fact that it can present itself under the appearances of universality – that of reason or morality.

I can now return to the problem I posed at the beginning. Do we have to choose between the legalism of those who believe that the rule is effective and the materialism of Weber, recalling that the rule is effective only when one has an interest in obeying it and, more generally, between a normative definition and a descriptive definition of the rule? In fact, the rule is effective *vi formae*, by the force of form. It is true that if the social conditions of its effectiveness are not met, form can accomplish nothing by itself. None the less, as a rule with ambitions to universality, it adds its own force, that which is written into the effect of rationality or rationalization. The word 'rationalization' should always be taken in the double sense of Weber and of Freud: the *vis formae* is always a force which is both logical and social. It unites the force of the universal, the logical, the formal, of formal logic, and the force of the official. Official publication, the use of formal, official language, in conformity to the forms imposed, which is suitable for official occasions, has by itself an effect of consecration and permission. Certain practices which had been experienced as a drama so long as there were not yet any words to say them and think them – none of those official words, produced by the authorized people, doctors or psychologists, who make it possible to *declare* them, to oneself and to others – undergo a veritable ontological transmutation by virtue of the fact that, being known and recognized publicly, named and authenticated, they are made legitimate, even legalized, and may thus declare and display themselves (this is the case, for instance, with the French notion used to refer to young people who live together without being married, namely 'juvenile cohabitation' which, in its platitude as a bureaucratic euphemism, played a determining role, especially in the countryside, in the task of symbolically accompanying a silent transformation of practices).

So I see two modes of procedure coming into contact these days, each of which has a meaning opposite to the other, and which I performed successively in my research. The effort to break away from legalism and found an adequate theory of practice led to a movement from norms to practical dispositions and from conscious intentions or the explicit levels of a calculating consciousness to the obscure intuitions of the practical sense. But this theory of practice contained the principles of a theoretical questioning of the social conditions of possibility (notably the *scholè*) and the essential effects of that legalism which it had been necessary to combat in order to construct the theory. The legalist illusion imposes itself not only on the researcher. It is also active in reality itself. And an adequate science of practice must take it into account and analyse, as I have tried to do here, the mechanisms at its basis (codification, canonization, etc.). And this comes down – if you take the enterprise to its conclusion – to posing in all its generality the problem of the social conditions of possibility of the very activity of codification and theorization, and of the social effects of this theoretical activity, of which the work of the researcher in the social sciences itself represents a particular form.

5

The interest of the sociologist

Why does the dialogue between economists and sociologists involve so many misunderstandings? Probably because the encounter between two disciplines is the encounter between two different histories, and thus between two different cultures: each one deciphers what the other says in accordance with his or her own code, his or her own culture. . . .

Firstly, the notion of *interest*. I've used this word, rather than others that are more or less equivalent in their meaning of emotional investment, of *illusio*, to show my rejection of the naively idealist tradition which used to haunt the social sciences and its most usual lexicon (motivations, aspirations, etc.). Banal in economics, the word produced an effect of novelty in sociology. That being said, I did not give it the meaning ordinarily granted it by economists. Far from being a sort of anthropological, natural datum, interest, in its historical specification, is an arbitrary institution. There is not an interest, but there are *interests*, variable with time and place, almost infinitely so: there are as many interests as there are fields, as historically constituted areas of activity with their specific institutions and their own laws of functioning. The existence of a specialized and relatively autonomous field is correlative with the existence of specific stakes and interests: via the inseparably economic and psychological investments that they arouse in the agents endowed with a certain habitus, the field and its stakes (themselves produced as such by relations of power and struggle in order to transform the power relations that are constitutive of the field) produce invest-

---

Paper presented to the colloquium on 'The economic model in the social sciences' (Paris, University of Paris – I, 1981) and published in *Économies et sociétés*, 18, no. 10 (October 1984).

ments of time, money and work, etc. (I would note in passing that there are as many forms of work as there are fields and you have to be able to consider the society activities of the aristocrat, or the religious activities of the priest or the rabbi, as specific forms of work oriented towards preserving or increasing specific forms of capital).

In other words, interest is at once a condition of the functioning of a field (a scientific field, the field of *haute couture*, etc.), in so far as it is what 'gets people moving', what makes them get together, compete and struggle with each other, and a product of the way the field functions. In every case, one has to observe the form taken, at a given moment in history, by this set of historical institutions which constitute a given economic field, and the form taken by the economic interest that is dialectically linked to this field. For instance, it would be naive to try and understand the economic behaviour of workers in French industry today without including in the definition of the interest that guides and motivates them not only the state of the juridical institution (property rights, the right to work, collective conventions, etc.), but also the sense of advantages and rights acquired in previous struggles which may, on certain points, anticipate the state of juridical norms, of the right to work for instance, and, on other points, may lag behind expressly codified experience, and thus be what forms the basis of their feelings of indignation and new demands, etc. Interest thus defined is the product of a given category of social conditions: as a historical construction, it cannot be known other than by historical knowledge, *ex post*, empirically, and not deduced *a priori* from a transhistorical nature.

Every field, as a historical product, generates the interest which is the precondition of its functioning. This is true of the economic field itself, which, as a relatively autonomous space obeying its own laws, and endowed with its own specific axiomatics linked to an original history, produces a particular form of interest, which is a particular case of the universe of possible forms of interest. Social magic can constitute more or less anything as interesting, and establish it as an object of struggle. One can extend to the economic domain Mauss's questioning of magic; and, abandoning the quest for the basis of economic power (or capital) in such-and-such an agent or system of agents, such-and-such a mechanism or institution, ask whether the generative principle behind this power isn't the field itself, that is, the system of differences which are constitutive of its structure, and the different dispositions, the different, even antagonistic interests that it generates in agents situated at its different points and concerned to preserve or transform it. This means, among other things, that the inclination to play the economic game, to invest in the economic game which is itself the product of a certain economic game, is at the very basis of the existence of this game. This is something forgotten by every form of economism. Economic production functions only in so far as it first produces a belief in the value of its products (witness the fact that today the proportion of work destined to produce a need for the product is continually growing); and it must also produce a belief in the value of the activity of production itself, that is, for example, the interest for *negotium* rather than for *otium*. This is a problem which arises concretely when the contradictions between the logic of the institution responsible for the production of producers, namely education, and the logic of the economic institution favour the appearance of new attitudes to work, which are sometimes described, with great naivety, as an 'allergy to work', and which are evident in the dying-out of any pride in one's trade, of any sense of professional honour, or any liking for a task well done, etc. What people then retrospectively discover is a number of dispositions that, because they are ceasing to be self-evident, used to be part and parcel of the conditions of the way the economy functioned – conditions that, being tacit, were forgotten in the specialists' equations.

These relatively trivial propositions would lead one, if they were developed, to conclusions which are less so. People would thus see that, through, for example, the juridically guaranteed structure of the distribution of property, thus of power over the field, the structure of the economic field determines everything that occurs in the field, and in particular the formation of prices or wages. The effect of this is that the so-called political struggle to modify the structure of the economic field is at the heart of the object of economic science. Not even the criterion of value, the central bone of contention between economists, can escape being an object of conflict in the very reality of the economic world. So that, in all rigour, economic science should include in its very definition of value the fact that the criterion of value is an object of conflict, rather than claiming that this struggle can be decided by an allegedly objective verdict and trying to find the truth of exchange in some substantial propriety of the goods exchanged. It is no small paradox, indeed, to come across the substantialist mode of thought, with the notion of labour-value, in Marx himself, who denounced, in fetishism, the product *par excellence* of the inclination to impute the property of being a commodity to the physical thing and not to the relations it entertains with the producer and the potential buyers.

I cannot go any further, as I should, within the limits of a brief and half-improvised statement. And I must pass on to the second notion under discussion, that of *strategy*. It's still a term I never use without a certain hesitation. It encourages the fundamental logical error, that which consists in seeing the model that explains reality as constitutive of the reality described, forgetting the 'it all happens as if' which defines the status proper to theoretical discourse. More precisely, it inclines one to a naively finalist conception of practice (that which underlies the ordinary use of notions such as interest, rational calculation, etc.), In fact, my whole effort aims at explaining, via the notion of habitus for instance, how it is that behaviour (economic or other) takes the form of sequences that are objectively guided towards a certain end, without necessarily being the product either of a conscious strategy or of a mechanical determination. Agents to some extent *fall into* the practice that is theirs rather than freely choosing it or being impelled into it by mechanical constraints. If this is how it is, it's because the habitus, a system of predispositions acquired through a relationship to a certain field, becomes effective and operative when it encounters the conditions of its effectiveness, that is, conditions identical or analogous to those of which it is the product. It becomes a generator of practices immediately adjusted to the present and even to the future inscribed within the present (hence the illusion of purpose) when it encounters a space proposing, in the guise of objective opportunities, what it already bears within itself as a *propensity* (to save or invest money, etc.), as a disposition (to calculate, etc.), because it has constituted itself by the incorporation of the structures (scientifically apprehended as probabilities) of a similar universe. In this case, agents merely need to let themselves follow their own social 'nature', that is, what history has made of them, to be as it were 'naturally' adjusted to the historical world they are up against, to do what they have to, to realize the future potentially inscribed in this world where they are like fish in water. The counter-example is Don Quixote, who puts into effect in a transformed economic and social space a habitus which is the product of a previous state of this world. But one need think only of growing old, without forgetting all the cases in which the habitus is discordant because it has been derived from conditions different from those in which it has to function, as is the case with agents that have emerged from pre-capitalist societies when they are thrown into a capitalist economy.

Most actions are objectively economic without being subjectively economic, without being the product of a rational economic calculation. They are the product of an encounter between a habitus and a field, that is, between two more-or-less completely adjusted histories. You need think only of the case of language and situations of bilingualism, in which a well-constituted speaker, since he has acquired his linguistic competence and the practical knowledge of the conditions for optimal use of this competence at the same time, anticipates the occasions in which he can place one or other of his languages with the maximum profit. The same speaker changes his or her expressions, moving from one language to another, without even realizing the fact, by virtue of a practical mastery of the laws of functioning of the field (which functions as a market) in which he or she will place his or her linguistic products. Thus, for as long as habitus and field are in agreement, the habitus 'comes at just the right moment' and, without the need for any calculation, its anticipations forestall the logic of the objective world.

It's at this point one needs to raise the question of the *subject* of calculation. The habitus, which is the generative principle of responses more or less well adapted to the demands of a certain field, is the product of an individual history, but also, through the formative experiences of earliest infancy, of the whole collective history of family and class; through, in particular, experiences in which the slope of the trajectory of a whole lineage is expressed, and which may take the visible and brutal form of a failure, or, on the contrary, may show itself merely as so many imperceptible regressions. This means, in other words, that we are as far away from Walrasian atomism, which gives no place to an economically and socially founded structure of preferences, as from that sort of soft culturalism which, in a sociologist such as Parsons, leads one to postulate the existence of a community of preferences and interests: in fact, every economic agent acts by virtue of a system of preferences proper to him or her, but which is distinguished only by secondary differences from systems of preference common to all agents placed in equivalent economic and social conditions. The different classes of systems of preference correspond to classes of conditions of existence, and thus to economic and social conditionings which impose different structures of perception, appreciation and action. An individual habitus is the product of the intersection of partly independent causal series. You can see that the subject is not the instantaneous *ego* of a sort of singular *cogito*, but the individual trace of an entire collective history. Furthermore, most economic strategies of any importance, such as marriage in pre-capitalist

91

societies or the purchase of real estate in our societies, are the product of a collective deliberation in which one may find reflected the power relationships between the parties concerned (married couples, for instance), and, through them, between the groups that are confronting each other (the lineages of the two marriage partners or the groups defined by the economic, cultural or social capital held by each one of them). In fact, nobody knows any longer who the subject of the final decision is. This is also true when you study business firms which function as fields, so that the place of decision is everywhere and nowhere (this as opposed to the illusion of the 'decision-maker' who is at the basis of numerous case studies on power).

We should ask, finally, whether the illusion of universal economic calculation is not rooted in reality. The most different economies, the economy of religion with its logic of the offering, the economy of honour with the exchange of gifts and counter-gifts, challenges and replies, killings and acts of vengeance, etc., can obey, partly or wholly, the principle of economy and bring into play a form of calculation, of *ratio*, which aims at ensuring the optimization of the cost–profits balance sheet. It's in this way that you discover modes of behaviour that can be understood as investments aimed at the maximization of utility in the most different economic universes (in the extended sense of the word), in prayer or sacrifice, and which obey, sometimes explicitly, the *do ut des* principle, but also in the logic of symbolic exchanges, with all the forms of behaviour that are perceived as wastage so long as they are measured by the principles of economy in the restricted sense. The universality of the principle of economy, that is, of the *ratio* in the sense of calculating the optimum, which means that one can *rationalize* any form of behaviour (one need think only of the prayer wheel), leads one to believe that all economies can be reduced to the logic of *one* economy: via a universalization of the particular case, one reduces all economic logics, and in particular the logic of economies based on the lack of differentiation of economic, political and religious functions, to the altogether singular logic of the economic economy in which economic calculation is explicitly guided by the exclusively economic aims posed, by its very existence, by an economic field constituted as such, on the basis of the maxim expressed by the tautology 'business is business'. In this case, and in this case alone, economic calculation is subordinated to the properly economic aims of the maximization of properly economic profit, and the economy is formally rational, in its aims and in its means. In fact, this perfect rationalization is never realized and it would be easy to show, as I attempted to do in my work on managers, that the logic behind the accumulation of symbolic capital is present even in the most rationalized sectors of the economic field. Not to mention the universe of 'feeling' (one of the privileged areas of which is evidently the family) which evades the axiom 'business is business' or 'business is no place for sentiment'.

One would still need to examine, finally, why the economic economy has not stopped gaining ground compared to economies oriented towards non-economic aims (in the restricted sense of the word) and why, even in our societies, economic capital is the dominant type, as opposed to symbolic capital, social capital and even cultural capital. This would require a lengthy analysis and one would need, for instance, to analyse the bases of the essential instability of symbolic capital which, being based on reputation, opinion and representation ('Honour', the Kabyles say, 'is like a turnip seed'), can be destroyed by suspicion and criticism, and is particularly difficult to transmit and to objectify, not easily convertible, etc. In fact, the particular 'power' of economic capital could spring from the fact that it permits an economy of economic calculation, an economy of economy, that it is, of rational management, of the labour of preservation and transmission – that it is, in other terms, easier to manage rationally (this can be seen in the case of its realization, money), and to calculate and to predict (which means it goes hand in glove with calculation and with mathematical science).

6

Reading, readers, the literate, literature

For several years I studied a particular tradition, the Kabyle tradition, which has this peculiarity: in it, you find ritual practices but very few properly mythical discourses. The fact that I came into contact with relatively unverbalized practices, as opposed to most ethnologists who, at the time I was beginning my work, were interested in corpora of myths, most often collected by other people (so that, despite their methodological care, they often lacked an understanding of the context in which the myths were used), obliged me very early on to think about the problem I would like you in turn to think about and discuss. Can you read a text without wondering what reading is? The precondition for every construction of an object is a tight control over your relationship, which is frequently an unconscious and obscure one, with the object that you are supposed to be constructing (many discourses on the object being, in fact, merely projections of the objective relation from subject to object). It's as an application of this very general principle that I ask: can one read anything at all without wondering what it is that reading means; without asking what are the social conditions of the possibility of reading? There were, at one time, a great number of works in which the word 'reading' cropped up. It was even a sort of password of the intellectual idiolect. And I was inclined to ask myself questions about this unquestioned factor. For example, the mediaeval tradition contrasted the *lector*, who comments on an already-established discourse, with the *auctor* who produces new discourse. This distinction is the equivalent, in the division of intellectual labour, of the

---

Lecture delivered at Grenoble in 1981 and published in *Recherches sur la philosophie et le langage* (Grenoble, Université des sciences sociales, Cahier du Groupe de recherches sur la philosophie et le langage, 1981).

distinction between prophet and priest in the division of religious labour: the prophet is an *auctor* who is the son of his works, who has no legitimacy, no *auctoritas*, other than his person (his charisma) and his practice as an *auctor*, and who is thus the *auctor* of his *auctoritas*; on the other hand, the priest is a *lector*, and holds a legitimacy which is delegated to him by the body of *lectores*, by the Church, and which is based in the final analysis on the *auctoritas* of the original *auctor*, to whom the *lectores* at least pretend to refer.

But this is not enough. Inquiring into the conditions of possibility of reading means inquiring into the social conditions which make possible the situations in which one reads (and it is immediately clear that one of these conditions is the *scholè*, leisure in its educational form, that is, the time of reading, the time of learning how to read) and inquiring also into the social conditions of production of *lectores*. One of the illusions of the *lector* is that which consists in forgetting one's own social conditions of production, and unconsciously universalizing the conditions of possibility of one's own reading. Inquiring into the conditions of this type of practice known as reading means inquiring into how *lectores* are produced, how they are selected, how they are educated, in what schools, etc. One would have to carry out a sociology of the success, in France, of structuralism, of semiology and of all the forms of reading, 'symptomatic' or other. One would need to ask, for instance, whether semiology was not a way of producing an *aggiornamento* of the old tradition of 'explication de textes' and of making it possible, at the same time, to redeploy a certain kind of literary capital. These are a few of the questions one would have to ask. *yes. see Ahmad.*

But, you will say, how can these social conditions of the education of readers – and, more generally, of interpreters – affect the way they read the texts or the documents they use? In his book on language,[1] Bakhtin denounces what he calls philologism, a sort of perversion entailed by the logic of an objectivist kind of thought, and in particular by the Saussurean definition of language: philologism consists of putting oneself in the position of a reader who treats the language as a dead thing, a dead letter, and who constitutes as properties of the language the properties which are properties of the dead, that is, non-spoken language, by projecting into the language as object the relation of the philologist to the dead language, that of

---

1 See *Marxism and the Philosophy of Language* by V. N. Volosinov (sometimes attributed to M. M. Bakhtin), tr. L. Matejka and I. R. Titunik (New York, 1973).

the decipherer faced with a text or an obscure fragment to which he has to find the key, the cipher or the code.

This is, it seems to me, what Bally wanted to point out when he said: the point of view of language, in the Saussurean sense, is the point of view of a listener, that is, the point of view of someone who listens to a language without speaking it. The reader is someone who can do nothing with the language that he or she takes as object, except study it. This is the principle of an altogether general bias, which I have often pointed out and which is part of the so-called 'theoretical' relation to the object: ethnologists tackle kinship relations as a pure object of knowledge and, through leaving out the fact that the theory of kinship relations they are going to produce presupposes in reality their 'theoretical' relation to the kinship relations, they forget that real relatives are not positions in a diagram, a genealogy, but relations that you have to cultivate, to keep up. In the same way, the philologists whose task it is to fix the meaning of words tend to forget that, as the experience of societies without writing goes to show, sayings, proverbs, aphorisms, sometimes proper names – whether of places, of pieces of land one might be able to claim, or of people – are an object of permanent conflict; and I believe that, if a certain verse of Simonides survived through the entire history of Greece, this is precisely because it was so important for the group that, by appropriating it for oneself, one was appropriating for oneself power over the group. The interpreter who imposes his or her interpretation is not only the one who has the last word in a philological quarrel (although this prize is as good as any other); he or she is also, quite frequently, the one who has the last word in a political struggle, who, by appropriating the word, puts *common sense* on his or her side. (One need only think of the slogans – such as democracy, liberty, liberalism – which politicians dispense, and of the energy which they display with the aim of appropriating categoremes which, as principles of structuring, give meaning to the world, in particular the social world, and create a consensus as to the meaning of this world.) Mouloud Mammeri, talking about Berber poetry,[2] used to recall that professional poets, called sages, *imusnawen*, pass their time appropriating sayings which everyone knows by making small displacements of sound and sense. 'Purifying the language of the tribe.' And Jean Bollack[3] has shown that the

---

2 M. Mammeri, 'Dialogue sur la poésie orale en Kabylie' (Interview with P. Bourdieu), *Actes de la recherche en sciences sociales*, 23, 1978, pp. 51–61.
3 See for instance J. Bollack, *Empédocle* (Paris, 1965).

Pre-Socratics, for example Empedocles, carry out a similar work on language, completely renewing the meaning of a saying or a line of Homer by subtly making the meaning of the word *phôs* slip from its most frequent sense of 'light', 'brilliance', to a rarer and often more archaic sense, 'the mortal', 'man'. These are effects that the Kabyle poets produced systematically: by appropriating the common meaning, they ensured a power over the group that, by definition, recognized itself in this common meaning; and this, in certain circumstances, in time of war or in moments of acute crisis, could assure them power of a prophetic type over the group's present and future. In other words, this poetry had nothing in common with pure poetry; the poet was the person who resolved impossible situations, in which the limits of ordinary morality were crossed and in which, for instance, the two camps discovered that according to the principles of this morality, they were both right.

The meaning of this example is self-evident: by forgetting to examine the implicit presuppositions behind the operation which consists in deciphering, in seeking *the* meaning of the words, the 'true' meaning of the words, philologists expose themselves to the risk of projecting into the words they study the philosophy of words which is implied by the very fact of studying words; they also expose themselves to the risk of failing to capture that which constitutes the truth of words, when, in political usage for instance, which knowingly plays on polysemia, their truth is that they have several truths. If the philologist is mistaken when he or she wants to have the last word about the sense of words, this is because different groups may frequently attach their self-interest to one or other possible meanings of those words. The words that are at stake in political or religious struggles, like musical chords, may present themselves in root position, with, as a base, in the foreground, a fundamental meaning, that which the dictionaries give first, then a sense which is understood only as a background meaning, and then a third sense. Struggles over words – those struggles that take place in the eighteenth century over the idea of nature, for instance – will consist in trying to carry out what musicians call inversions of the chord, in trying to overturn the ordinary hierarchy of meanings in order to constitute as a *fundamental* meaning, as the root note of the semantic chord, a meaning that had hitherto been secondary, or, rather, *implied*, thus putting into action a symbolic revolution which may be at the root of political revolutions.

You can see that if the philologist were to reflect on what being a philologist means, he would be obliged to wonder whether the use he makes of language coincides with the use made of it by those who produced it; and whether the gap between linguistic usages and interests does not risk introducing into interpretation an essential bias, one that is far more radical than mere anachronism or any other form of ethnocentric interpretation, since it stems from the activity of interpretation itself. The interpreter, philologist or ethnologist, is situated outside what he interprets; he apprehends action as a spectacle, a *representation*, a reality to be held at a distance and which is held before him as an *object*, because he has at his disposal instruments of objectification – the photograph, schema, diagram, genealogy or, quite simply, writing. Now it is well known that a certain number of works, in particular those of Havelock (*Preface to Plato*),[4] have underlined the notion of *mimesis* and recalled that what Plato denounces in poetry is the fact that the mimetic relation to language that it implies brings into play the whole body: the poet, the bard, calls up poetry in the same way that you call up spirits, and calling up is (as is also the case with the Berber poets) inseparable from a whole bodily gymnastics. One must give Havelock's ideas their greatest general application: apart from the fact that a number of the texts on which hermeneutic scholars work, and not only poetry, were originally created to be danced, mimed, or acted, some of the information they convey in the form of discourse, story, *logos* or *mythos*, had in fact as a referent, at least originally, a *praxis*, a religious practice, and rites – I am here thinking for example of what Hesiod says about Dionysos, Hecate or Prometheus, or of Tiresias' prophecy in the *Odyssey*. And when we behave as readers unaware of the truth of reading, or as logocentric philologists, we always risk forgetting that praxic, practical, mimetic philosophy does not include the symbolic mastery of its own principles. The ethnologists that I call objectivistic, those who, by failing to analyse the ethnologist's relation to his object, project on to their object the relation they have with that object, describe myths or rites as if they were logical practices or mathematical calculations, whereas what they are dealing with are types of dance, often retranslated (in the case of myth) into discourse. Ritual practice is a dance: you turn seven times from left to right; you throw with your right hand over your left shoulder; you go up or down, etc. All the fundamental operations of a ritual are movements of the body, which objectivistic observers describe not as movements but as states (there where I would say go up/come down, the objectivist will say high/low, which changes everything).

---

4   E. Havelock, *Preface to Plato* (Cambridge, Mass. and London, 1982).

One could thus re-engender the entire Kabyle ritual on the basis of a small number of generative schemas, in other words precisely what Plato, as Henri Joly notes,[5] called the *schemata tou sômatos*. The word *schemata* is particularly suitable for what I want to say, since ancient authors (for example Athenaeus, who lived in the first half of the third century) use it to designate the mimetic gestures of the dance they are cataloguing (in the same way as the *phorai*, the significant movements): for example, the hands held out turned to the sky, the suppliant's gesture, or hands held out to the spectator, an apostrophe to the public, the hands held flat out to the ground, a gesture of sadness, etc. The practical schemata of the ritual are indeed *schemata tou sômatos*, schemas which generate fundamental movements such as rising or descending, getting up or lying down, etc. And it is only in the eyes of the observer that ritual can change from dance into algebra, from gymnastics into a symbolic and logical calculus.

By failing to objectify the truth of the objectifying relation to practice, one projects into practices the function of practices as it appears to someone who studies them as something to be deciphered. And ethnologists or philologists are not the first people to make this mistake: when they work on myths, they are dealing with objects that are themselves the product of this logocentric change; for example, in the myth of Prometheus as recounted by Hesiod, one can straightaway recognize rites, but rites which are already reported and reinterpreted by literate people, that is, by readers. So that, for want of knowing what a literate tradition is and what transformation it performs by transcription and permanent reinterpretation, one oscillates between two mistakes: ethnologism, which ignores the fact of scientific reinterpretation, and academic neutralization which, staying on the level of the literate logic of reinterpretation, ignores its ritual foundation. Literate people, indeed, never present rites in their original crude form (the blacksmith slices, cuts, kills, separates what is linked, and he is thus chosen to perform all ritual separations, etc.). They have already emerged from the silence of the ritual praxis which does not aim to be interpreted, and they place themselves within a hermeneutic logic: when Hesiod recounts a rite, his recording finds its *raison d'être* in a universe in which the rite is no longer a sequence of regulated practices that are carried out in order to conform to a social practice or to produce practical effects, but a

---

5 H. Joly, 'Le renversement platonicien: *logos, épistémé, polis* (Paris, Vrin, 1974).

tradition that one intends to transmit and codify by a labour of
rationalization which implies a reinterpretation in the light of new
questions, that is, at the price of a complete change of functions.
From the moment a rite is retold, it changes meaning and you pass
from a mimetic practice, from a bodily logic oriented towards
functions, to a philological relation: the rites become texts which
have to be deciphered, they are pretexts for decipherment. The need
for coherence and logic appears, linked to communication, discussion and comparison. The analogical meaning which resolves
problems one by one, one after another, yields to the effort to keep
together analogies that have already been made. The mythopoet
becomes a mythologist, that is, as Plato was already pointing out, a
philosopher; the speaker becomes a grammarian. The rite is no
longer any use for anything except being interpreted.

Interests and stakes change, or, to put it more simply: people
believe in them in a different way. Does Hesiod believe in the rites
he relates? Does he believe in them in the same way those who really
practised them believed in them? The question is not as empty as it
seems. People have known for a very long time that you go from
ethos to ethics when principles cease to act practically in practice;
you start to make a written record of norms when they are on the
point of dying out. What, we must ask, is implied, from the point of
view of belief, of practice, of practising belief, by the shift from
behaviour patterns implemented in practical terms (in the form:
rising is good; descending is bad, since it means going towards the
west, towards the feminine, etc.) to a table of oppositions, like the
sustoichiai of the Pythagoreans (in which already relatively abstract
oppositions, such as that of limited versus unlimited, appear)? What
else do ethnologists do (re-read Hertz on the right hand and the left
hand) if not draw up tables of oppositions? The philologist studies
the works of philologists who, from the start, were unaware of their
own status as philologists and thus did not realize the essential
distortion they were imposing on the object of their studies, a
distortion at the end of which myth ceases to be a practical solution
to practical problems in order to become an intellectual solution to
intellectual problems. The distortion wrought on practice by the
objectification of practice (for instance, the operation which consists
in distributing properties in tables with two columns, left/right,
feminine/masculine, wet/dry, etc.) is destined to pass unnoticed,
since it is constitutive of the very operation that the ethnologist has
to perform in order to constitute practice as an ethnological object.
The inaugural operation which constitutes practice, a rite for in-

stance, as a spectacle, as a representation capable of being the object of a story, description or account, and secondarily, of an interpretation, produces an essential distortion which has to be theorized if one is to record in the theory the effects both of the act of recording and of the theory.

It is here that the word 'critique' which I often use, takes on its most classic philosophical sense: certain of the operations which social science cannot fail to perform without running the risk of having no object, such as the activity of drawing up a schema, establishing a genealogy, tracing a diagram, setting out a statistical table, etc., produce artefacts, unless one takes them in their turn as an object of study. Philosophy and logic were doubtless born from a reflection on the difficulties created every time that the objectification of the practical sense starts to occur without this process taking as its object the very operation of objectification. I realized this because the logic of the work of theorization of a set of practices and ritual symbols led me to find myself placed in a situation altogether analogous, it seems to me, to that of the great Pre-Socratic prophets. For instance, in the analysis of the logic of rituals, I kept stumbling over oppositions which I didn't really know how to handle, that I couldn't manage to integrate into the series of great fundamental oppositions (dry/wet, spicy/insipid, masculine/feminine, etc.) and which all concerned union and separation, *philia* and *neikos*, as Empedocles said. The ploughshare and the earth have to be united; the harvest and the field have to be separated. I had symbols and operators: separating and reuniting. But Empedocles had already abstracted these operators, and he made them function as logical principles. In other words, when we work on an object such as the work of Empedocles, we must ask ourselves about the theoretical status of the operation which has produced the text. Our reading is that of one of the literate, of a reader, who is reading a reader, a member of the class of literate people. And who thus runs a great risk of taking as evident everything that this literate person took to be evident, unless he or she carries out an epistemological and sociological critique of reading. Re-siting reading and the text read in a history of cultural production and transmission means giving oneself a chance of understanding the reader's relation to his or her object and also of understanding how the relation to the object is part and parcel of that object.

In order to convince you that this double critique is the precondition of an adequate interpretation of the text, I need merely mention a few of the problems that are posed by the structural 'reading' of texts that themselves presuppose 'reading', but which do not ask this question of themselves. For that, I would like to return rapidly to Tiresias' prophecy and show that, however far one goes back in a scholarly tradition, there is nothing that can be treated as a pure document for ethnology, that there is nothing, not even in Homer, which is a rite in its pure, that is, in its practical state. It's well known that the corpus which the ethnologist constitutes, merely by virtue of the fact that it is systematically recorded, totalized and synchronized (thanks, for example, to the synoptic schema), is already, in itself, an artefact: no native masters as such the complete system of relations that the interpreter has to constitute for the purposes of decipherment. But that is even truer of the recording carried out by the story told in a literate culture, not to mention those sociologically monstrous corpora that are constituted by drawing on works from altogether different periods. The temporal gap is not the only thing at stake: indeed, one may have to deal, in one and the same work, with semantic strata from different ages and levels, which the text synchronizes even though they correspond to different generations and different usages of the original material, in this case, of the rite. In this way, Tiresias' prophecy brings into play a set of primary significations, such as the opposition between the salty and the insipid, the dry and the wet, the sterile and the fertile, the oar and the grain-shovel (then the tree), the sailor and the peasant, wandering (or change) and putting down roots (or rest). One can recognize the characteristics of a fertility rite mobilizing agrarian and sexual symbols, such as the oar stuck into the ground, which is part of a rite of death and resurrection reminiscent of the descent to hell and ancestor-worship. The mythico-ritual elements are not to be understood merely by reference to the system that they constitute, that is, if you like, in relation to Greek culture in the ethnological sense of the word; they receive a new meaning by virtue of being inserted into the system of relations that constitutes the work, the story, and also into the scientific culture that is produced and reproduced by professionals. For example, in this particular case, the rite takes its structural value within the work from the fact that it is the obligatory preamble to the union of Ulysses and Penelope. As a story that Ulysses has to tell Penelope before uniting with her, it suggests the relation, introduced by Homer, between the eschatalogical myth and the perpetuation of the lineage or the species: the return to the earth, to the home, and to agriculture, is the end of the indefinite cycle of reincarnations to which the sailor is condemned; it is the aristocratic affirmation (which is also found in Pindar) of the possibility which belongs to a few elect spirits of withdrawing from the world of becoming; it is an access to the permanence of the agrarian king (one may think of the palace of Menelaus, mentioned in the *Odyssey*) who spends a happy old age surrounded by his family, far from the sea; this is the agrarian universe as the seat of happiness, of fertility and prosperity, of the perpetuity of the race, of feasting, a sign of election in the beyond. In short, it is the whole marine adventure of Ulysses, as a symbol of human existence in its eternal new beginning, and of the possibility of emerging from a series of reincarnations, which gives a second, esoteric meaning to each of the primary meanings, for instance the sea, which ceases to be the salty, the dry, the sterile, in order to become the symbol of becoming in its indefinite repetition, and of human existence as an eternal cycle. This analysis, which I owe to various discussions with Jean Bollack – it being understood that, as people say in cases like this, I am responsible for any errors – is important for an understanding of the difference, unknown to the ethnologist's reading, between an oral, non-literate culture, and a literate, scholarly culture, and for our understanding of the logic of passage from one to the other. As soon as one is dealing with an *oeuvre*, that is, a system expressly constructed by a professional – and no longer with a system objectively constituted by the work of successive generations, such as the Hopi or Kabyle language or the mythico-ritual system – one cannot, without carrying out an unjustifiable reduction, treat the cultural characteristics it brings into play as simple elements of ethnographic information. And this is not in the name of a sanctifying prejudice which makes reading into a ritual act of academic humanism (one must re-read, on this point, the Durkheim of *The Evolution of Educational Thought*[6]); it is based on strictly scientific reasons: each of the 'ethnographic' elements takes its meaning from the context of the work in which it is inserted and the set of present or past works to which the work (thus its author, himself or herself in relation with other authors) implicitly or explicitly refers. Literate, scholarly culture is defined by reference; it consists of the permanent game of references referring mutually to each other; it is nothing other than this universe of references which are at one and the same time differences and reverences, contradictions and congratulations. Ulysses will remind anyone who feels at home in this universe, like

---

6 É. Durkheim, *The Evolution of Educational Thought: Lectures on the Formation and Development of Secondary Education in France*, tr. P. Collins (London, 1977).

the original literate person or interpreter, of Dionysos, the seafarer, who sails across the wine-dark sea, and is also a fertility god: such a person will recall that Ulysses goes down into Hades just as Dionysos does. As far as planting the oar in the ground is concerned, the interpreter will not fail to refer to the struggle between Athena and Poseidon. But it is probable – and here the problem of the modality proper to belief crops up – that Homer does not have to cultural themes the ludic, Hellenistic relation which defines the cultural game in its most academic phases. In fact, one cannot understand the secondary, eschatalogical meaning without first awakening, as Homer did, the primary and properly ritual significance which one can present as self-evident because author and audience are fully at home with it. The return to the earth is immediately admitted, by one of those non-thetic theses that are constitutive of ritual practice, to be the equivalent of a return to the world of the ancestors, to the central pillar which symbolizes the perpetuity of the lineage, which plunges underground, into the world of the ancestors (one need only think of the descent into hell), etc. One could carry out the same demonstration with Hesiod and his account of the Prometheus myth, which includes the quasi-ethnographic mention of a marriage rite and the philosophical reinterpretation of that rite. Reinterpretation is not entirely free; it presupposes on the part of the hermeneutic narrator (Homer, Hesiod or the Kabyle poet) an immediate familiarity with the first-degree structure, a sort of structural intuition of this structure, which characterizes a living relation to a living culture.

But this practical sense, this practical mastery of the sense invested in ritual practice, is worn away with time or, more exactly, dies out in agents who, although they participate in the same cultural tradition, are situated, as *lectores*, in an altogether different relation to these practices. And this is true *without their being aware of the fact*. That is why anachronism is written into the traditional attitude towards culture; the traditionally literate person experiences his or her culture as living, and sees himself or herself as contemporary with all his or her predecessors. Culture and language change because they survive in a changing world: the meaning of a line of verse, of a maxim or an entire work changes by virtue of the sole fact that the universe of maxims, lines of verse or works simultaneously proposed to those who apprehend them changes: this universe can be called the space of 'co-possibles'. Anachronism detemporalizes the work, tears it out of time (just as academic reading will do) at the same time that it temporalizes it by 'reactivating it' ceaselessly, by permanent reinterpretation, both faithful and unfaithful. This process reaches its culmination when the literate reinterpretation of the *lector* is applied to the works of a literate tradition and the logic of reinterpretation is the same as the logic of the thing interpreted.

This raises the question of the social and epistemological traditions of the passage from the analogical reinterpretation of the myth, in which one mythologizes on mythology, to the paradigmatic usage of the myth, as in Plato, or from the practical use of analogy to a questioning of analogy as such, as in Aristotle.

7

A reply to some objections

I

Most of the questions and objections which have been put to me reveal a high degree of misapprehension, which can go as far as total incomprehension. Some of the reasons for this are to be found on the consumption side, others on the side of production. I shall begin with the latter.

I have said often enough that any cultural producer is situated in a certain space of production and that, whether he wants it or not, his productions always owe something to his position in this space. I have relentlessly tried to protect myself, through a constant effort of self-analysis, from this effect of the field. But one can be negatively 'influenced', influenced *a contrario*, if I may say, and bear the marks of what one fights against. Thus certain features of my work can no doubt be explained by the desire to 'twist the stick in the other direction', to react in a somewhat provocative manner against the professional ideology of intellectuals. This is the case for instance with the use I make of the notion of interest, which can call forth the accusation of economism against a work which, from the very beginning (I can refer here to my anthropological studies), was conceived in opposition to economism. The notion of interest – I always speak of *specific* interest – was conceived as an instrument of rupture intended to bring the materialist mode of questioning to bear on realms from which it was absent and into the sphere of cultural production in particular. It is the means of a deliberate (and provisional) reductionism which is used to put down the claims of the prophets of the universal, to question the ideology of the *frei-schwebende Intelligenz*. On this score, I feel very close to Max Weber

This is the revised transcription of a presentation made to the session on 'Soziologische Theorien uber "Klassen und Kultur"' at the Meetings of the German Sociological Association, Düsseldorf, Germany, 12–14 February 1987. Translated from French by Loïc J. D. Wacquant.

who utilized the economic model to extend materialist critique into the realm of religion and to uncover the specific interests of the great protagonists of the religious game, priests, prophets, sorcerers, in the competition which opposes them to one another. This rupture is more necessary and more difficult in the sphere of culture than in any other. Because we are all both judge and judged. Culture is our specific capital and, even in the most radical probing, we tend to forget the true foundation of our specific power, of the particular form of domination we exercise. This is why it seemed to me essential to recall that the thinkers of the universal have an interest in universality (which, incidentally, implies no condemnation whatsoever).

But there are grounds for misunderstanding that stand on the side of consumption: my critics rely most often on *only one* book, *Distinction*,[1] which they read in a 'theoretical' or theoreticist vein (an inclination reinforced by the fact that a number of concrete analyses are less 'telling' to a foreign reader) and ignore the empirical work published by myself or by others in *Actes de la recherche en sciences sociales* (not to mention the ethnographic works which are at the origin of most of my concepts); they criticize outside of their context of use *open* concepts designed to guide empirical work; they criticize not my analyses, but an already simplified, if not maimed, representation of my analyses. This is because they invariably apply to them the very modes of thought, and especially distinctions, alternatives and oppositions, which my analyses are aimed at destroying and overcoming. I think here of all the antinomies that the notion of habitus aims at eliminating: finalism/mechanism, explanations by reasons/explanation by causes, conscious/unconscious, rational and strategic calculation/mechanical submission to mechanical constraints, etc. In so doing, one can choose either to reduce my analyses to one of the positions they seek to transcend, or, as with Elster, to act as if I simultaneously or *successively* retained both of these contradictory positions.[2] These are so many ways of ignoring what seems to me to be the anthropological foundation of a theory of action, or of practice, and which is condensed in the notion of habitus: the relation which obtains between habitus and the field to

---

1 P. Bourdieu, *La distinction. Critique sociale du jugement* (Paris, 1979); trans. as *Distinction. A Social Critique of the Judgement of Taste*, tr. R. Nice (Cambridge, Mass., 1984).
2 J. Elster, *Sour Grapes: Studies in the Subversions of Rationality* (Cambridge, 1983).

which it is objectively adjusted (because it was constituted with regard to the specific necessity which inhabits it) is a sort of ontological complicity, a subconscious and pre-reflexive fit. This complicity manifests itself in what we call the sense of the game or 'feel' for the game (or *sens pratique*, practical sense), an intentionality without intention which functions as the principle of strategies devoid of strategic design, without rational computation and without the conscious positing of ends.[3] (By way of aside, habitus is one principle of production of practices among others and although it is undoubtedly more frequently in play than any other – 'We are empirical', said Leibniz, 'in three-quarters of our actions' – one cannot rule out that it may be superseded under certain circumstances – certainly in situations of crisis which disrupt the immediate adjustment of habitus to field – by other principles, such as rational and conscious computation. This being granted, even if its theoretical possibility is universally allocated, the propensity or the ability to have recourse to a rational principle of production of practices has its own social and economic conditions of possibility: the paradox, indeed, is that those who want to admit no principle of production of practices, and of economic practices specifically, other than rational consciousness, fail to take into account the economic preconditions for the development and the implementation of economic rationality.)

Hence we have a first break with the utilitarian theory with which the concept of interest is commonly associated. An action in conformity with the interests of the agent who performs it is not necessarily guided by the conscious and deliberate search for the satisfaction of this interest posited as an end. In a number of social universes, one of the privileges of the dominant, who move in their world as fish in water, resides in the fact that they need not engage in rational computation in order to reach the goals that best suit their interests. All they have to do is to follow their dispositions which, being adjusted to their positions, 'naturally' generate practices adjusted to the situation. This is the paradox of 'natural distinction' which Elster cannot understand, locked as he is in a hypersubjectivist vision excluding any principle of action other than consciousness, conscious intention. Agents whose dispositions are the product of conditionings associated with positively distinguished positions (which differ from other positions in that they possess a set of

---

3 P. Bourdieu, *Le sens pratique* (Paris, 1980); trans. as *The Logic of Practice*, tr. R. Nice (Cambridge, 1989).

distinctive properties acknowledged as socially desirable), have only to give way to their dispositions in order to produce practices that are 'naturally' distinguished; they can do so without having to take distinction as a goal, without pursuing it as such (as do the upstarts evoked by Veblen) consciously, methodically, as part of a rational schema or plan, of a strategy designed to maximize the symbolic profit of distinction. They are distinguished in the only manner that is socially recognized, that is, 'naturally', on the basis of a principle which tends to appear innate, instinctive, as a 'natural gift' which rational principles, such as intelligence or calculating reason, can only ape, and which defines true excellence (in opposition to the awkwardness of the strained, laboured ease of the upstart). One sees in passing that the theory of habitus is the theoretical foundation of the critique of the ideology of gift – an ideology so powerful in the intellectual universe – which I developed in my first works[4] (a 'gift' is nothing other than the feel for the game socially constituted by early immersion in the game, that class racism turns into a nature, a natural property unequally allocated by nature and thereby legitimated).

But interest as I conceive of it differs from the natural and universal interest of utilitarian theories in yet another manner. I said earlier that the strategies of habitus as sense of the game could be understood as the manifestation of a form of well-understood interest which does not need to ground itself in a conscious and calculated understanding of interest. (Let me mention in passing that there are degrees in this feel for the game, excellence consisting in the perfect mastery which allows one to anticipate so perfectly the necessity of the game that the latter is no longer experienced as such: actions which are said to be *reasonable* differ from rational actions, with which everything apparently identifies them, in that they provide the primary profits – success – and secondary profits – approval of the group – that come with submission to realities, that is, to objective chances, without having to pursue them as such, without having to constitute them as a conscious project. One should recall here the Husserlian distinction between protension, the positing of a future immediately inscribed in the present, as an objective potentiality and endowed with the doxic modality of the present, and project, the positing of a future grasped as such, that is, as

---

4 P. Bourdieu and J. C. Passeron, *Les héritiers, les étudiants et la culture* (Paris, 1964); trans. as *The Inheritors: French Students and their Relation to Culture*, tr. R. Nice (Chicago, 1979).

contingent, liable to come to pass or not.)

If this is so, it is because the sense of the game is the internalized form of the necessity of the game. It is necessity made into virtue (or disposition), or *amor fati*. This means that there will be as many senses of the game, as many practical understandings of interest as there are games. Hence there are as many interests as there are games. The *specific* interest which defines a game is identical with investment in the game, with the *illusio* as tacit recognition of the stakes of the game. Each field produces and calls forth a specific form of interest (this fundamental investment, which constitutes the admission fee tacitly demanded by every game, that is, the recognition of the value of the game and its stakes, is shared by all participants who are thereby tied by an agreement – not a contract – on the grounds for disagreement). And this specific interest, implied by involvement in the game, further specifies itself according to the position occupied in the game. (In fact, this agreement on the grounds for disagreement is found again at the cognitive level: common sense, as objectively recorded in the *topics*, commonplaces, as paired oppositions which structure the vision of the world, is the product of the embodiment of social structure; by internalizing his or her position in social space, each agent internalizes both his or her definite position – high, intermediate or low – and the structure within which this position is defined, the opposition high/low.)

To highlight the difference between the interest socially constituted in and by the necessity of a field and the interest presupposed by economics, there is no instance better than the interest called forth by the artistic field. Inasmuch as this field, particularly in its most autonomous sectors, defines itself by eschewing or inverting the rules and regularities that constitute the economic field, one can say that the interest promoted by this field is an interest in disinterestedness (in the ordinary sense of the term), that is to say, an interest which proves irreducible to economic interest in its ordinary sense.[5] This economically disinterested interest remains none the less an interest, and one which can enter into conflict or competition with others, as well as determine actions as strictly interested, nay egoistic, as those of which the economic field is the site. Thus the interest institutionalized in the rules and regularities of functioning of the scientific field and which, in the most advanced stages of this field, can be described as an interest in the universal, can lead to the

5 P. Bourdieu, 'The Field of Cultural Production or: the Economic World Reversed', *Poetics*, 12, no. 4–5 (November 1983), pp. 311–56.

most brutally interested and egoistic confrontations (which can go so far as the forgery of scientific results, as is more and more frequently the case today).[6]

Thus we have different fields where different forms of interest are constituted and expressed. This does not imply that the different fields do not have *invariant properties*. Among these invariant properties is the very fact that they are the site of a struggle of interests, between agents or institutions unequally endowed in specific capital (as specific resources or specific weapons for the conquest or domination over the field), or the fact that these struggles presuppose a consensus on what is at stake in the struggle, etc. The charge of economism which is often brought against me consists of treating the homology between the economic field (or the political field) and the fields of cultural production (scientific field, artistic field, literary field, philosophical field, etc.) as an identity, pure and simple, and by the same token to cause the specificity of the form which the different invariant properties (and first of all interest) take in each field to disappear. The reduction of all fields to the economic field (or the political field) goes hand in hand with the reduction of all interests to the interest characteristic of the economic field. And this twin reduction brings the accusation of reductionist economism or of economistic reductionism to a theory whose major purpose is undoubtedly to avoid economistic reduction.

II

A second main set of questions or objections relate to the autonomy of the symbolic. Here again, I believe that I must clear up various misunderstandings.

I contend that a power or capital becomes symbolic, and exerts a specific effect of domination, which I call symbolic power or symbolic violence, when it is known and recognized (*connu et reconnu*), that is, when it is the object of an act of knowledge and recognition. But what must we understand by 'knowledge'? One of the roots of misunderstanding lies, once more, in the fact that people apply to my analyses distinctions or modes of thought against which the latter have been constructed. When I write 'knowledge', people read *connaissance connaissante*, scholarly knowledge, conscious

---

6 P. Bourdieu, 'The Peculiar History of Scientific Reason', *Sociological Forum*, Winter 1990 (in press).

knowledge, explicit, if not reflexive, representation; in a word, the specific mode of thought of the scientist is projected into the mind of agents. Here is a paradigmatic form of what I call the *scholastic fallacy*: this fallacy, encouraged by the situation of *scholè*, leisure and school, induces them to think that agents involved in action, in practice, in life, think, know and see as someone who has the leisure to think thinks, knows and sees, as the scientist whose mode of thought presupposes leisure both in its genesis and its functioning, or at least distance and freedom from the urgency of practice, the practical bracketing of the necessities of practice. It must be asserted *at the same time* that a capital (or power) becomes symbolic capital, that is, capital endowed with a specifically symbolic efficacy, only when it is *misrecognized* in its arbitrary truth as capital and *recognized* as legitimate and, on the other hand, that this act of (false) knowledge and recognition is an act of *practical* knowledge which in no way implies that the object known and recognized be posited as object. It is the scientist who raises the question of legitimacy; he or she forgets that this question does not arise as such for the dominated and that the answer that the dominated give to it in practice appears as an answer only to those who raise the question; he forgets, as a consequence, that the practical recognition of legitimacy which is inscribed in certain actions or certain abstentions is not an act of free consent accomplished as the outcome of an explicit cognitive operation. It is inscribed, rather, in the immediate relationship between a habitus and a situation and finds no expression more indisputable than the silence of shyness, abstention or resignation, by which the dominated manifest practically, without even considering the possibility of doing otherwise, their practical acceptance (in the mode of *illusio*) of the possibilities and the impossibilities inscribed in the field. (Think for instance of the expression 'This is not for us' by which the most deprived exclude themselves from possibilities from which they would be excluded anyway.)

All of this holds true at a more general level. It is the immediate relation between a habitus structured in accordance with the objective structures of a field, and thus predisposed to apply to it principles of vision and division that are adjusted, adapted to its objective divisions (for example, couples of adjectives such as studious and bright which have currency in the university field), which establishes the specifically symbolic effect of a property, and thus the transmutation of a power into a symbolic power. (This means that this effect is not automatic, but exerts itself only when a social space or a power is perceived, known, according to the cognitive structures it imposes by its very existence – for example, the opposition between male and female, and all the homologous oppositions between high and low, wet and dry, east and west, etc., in societies where the sexual division of labour provides the fundamental principle of differentiation.) For a habitus structured according to the very structures of the social world in which it functions, each property (a pattern of speech, a way of dressing, a bodily hexis, an educational title, a dwelling-place, etc.) is perceived in its relation to other properties, therefore in its positional, distinctive value, and it is through this distinctive distance, this difference, this distinction, which is perceived only by the seasoned observer, that the homologous position of the bearer of this property in the space of social positions shows itself. All of this is exactly encapsulated in the expression 'that looks' (*'ça fait . . .'*: 'that looks petty-bourgeois', 'that looks yuppie', 'that looks intellectual', etc.) which serves to locate a position in social space through a stance taken in symbolic space.

It is because the analyses reported in *Distinction* are read in a realist and substantialist way (as opposed to a relational one) – thus assigning directly this or that property or practice to a 'class', playing soccer or drinking *pastis* to workers, playing golf or drinking champagne to the traditional *grande bourgeoisie* – that I am taken to task for overlooking the specific logic and autonomy of the symbolic order, thereby reduced to a mere *reflection* of the social order. (In other words, once again, the charge of reductionism thrown at me is based on a reductionist reading of my analyses.) In reality, the space of symbolic stances and the space of social positions are two independent, but homologous, spaces. (It bears recalling here that the aim of the whole theory of fields of cultural production is to account for the autonomy of these social universes – the artistic field, literary field, juridical field, scientific field – where cultural products are produced and reproduced according to specific logics, and whose differential appropriation, through struggles of competition and a whole set of processes that are entirely ignored by conventional studies of 'consumption', is the focus of *Distinction*.) What allows saying that a particular practice or property 'looks' (*fait*) this or that (petty-bourgeois or upstart) is the sense of the game acquired through prolonged immersion in the game, a sense of positioning (*placement*), which Goffman calls the 'sense of one's place', the sense of the position occupied in social space, which always involves a *sense of the place of others* and, more precisely, a practical mastery of the two independent and homologous spaces and of their correspondence. This is to say that the meaning of a practice is necessarily distinctive, differential, and that the relationship between golf and the old bourgeoisie is established only through the mediation of the relation between the space of stances adopted and the space of positions within which the *value* (in the Saussurean sense) of the practice of golf is defined.

This is the reason why the statics of the system, that is, the correspondence between the two spaces at a given point in time, is the mainspring of the dynamics of the system: any action aimed at modifying this correspondence – for instance, the 'pretentiousness' which spurs the new bourgeoisie to appropriate to themselves an 'attribute' of the old bourgeoisie – determines a transformation of the whole system of relations between the two spaces. (One could study this process in the case of the recent evolution of tennis.) The motor-cause of this ongoing transformation is the dialectic of pretension and distinction, which I have described at length in *Distinction* and which properly defines symbolic space. The various agents involved in this struggle, of which snobbery is one aspect, arm themselves with the products that are continuously offered to them by the various fields of cultural production (by the field of high culture no less than by the field of high fashion), which themselves obey a specific form of the logic of pretension and distinction in order to preserve or transform the state of the correspondence between social positions and distinctive properties or, to put it more simply, to maintain or bridge the state of *distinctive distances*.

There is a risk that the language that I have just used, and the mention of snobbery, will suggest that the principle of this dynamic is the explicit search for distinction. In fact, as an in-depth analysis of any one instance would show, this is not at all the case. Take the example of those tennis players who entered the competition organized for the official ranking (*classement*) during the 1970s and now retire to a less competition-oriented practice of tennis or turn to other sports, such as golf. They are not driven by an explicit concern to distinguish themselves from the new players who have progressively invaded the clubs, bringing with them a different 'tennis culture' (new styles, patterns of play, of training, etc.); they move to another sport, or to another manner of practising the same sport (as in other realms one moves to new authors, new composers, new painters and new film directors), more often than not in an imperceptible manner, from the experience of new aspects of this practice which their habitus makes unpleasant or unbearable. For instance,

114

repeated losses against younger players who play a game which seems to them less elegant, more aggressive, less in keeping with norms of fair play, or merely from experiencing overcrowding, congestion on the courts, as elsewhere on ski slopes and lifts, and the intolerance of waits, or the displeasure arising from associating with people whose style of life – and play – is scarcely congenial, or the feeling of lassitude and weariness arising from the routinization of a practice or an experience: listening to a piece of music which is becoming well-known, Vivaldi or Schubert, too often heard in concert, on the radio and even in supermarkets. One should examine in each case the social dimension of the process of imperceptible adulteration through which initial infatuation gives way to dislike, by focusing particularly on all the judgements in such forms as 'it has become impossible . . .', 'nowadays one can no longer . . .' (do such and such thing, read such and such newspaper, patronize such and such theatre, etc.), in which is expressed more than a mere factual impossibility: a true intolerance of the intolerable.

The vocabulary of strategy – which is indispensable to retain the active, constructive side of the most ordinary choices of the symbolic struggles of daily life – must not deceive us. The most efficacious strategies of distinction are those which find their principle in the practical, pre-reflexive, quasi-instinctual choices of habitus. The 'naturalness' of the dominant life-style (which makes it inimitable) is without a doubt the most secure foundation of self-valuation: in it, the monopoly of the scarcest, and at the same time most universal, cultural goods conferred by possession of economic and cultural capital finds a justification. Nature and the natural have always been the best instruments of sociodicies.

EXPLANATORY NOTES

On the notion of symbolic power: I have offered a 'theoretical' (that is, scholastic) genealogy of this concept in a lecture delivered at the University of Chicago in 1973 and subsequently published in *Annales.*[7]

---

7 'Sur le pouvoir symbolique', *Annales*, 3 (May–June 1977), pp. 405–11; trans. as 'Symbolic Power', in *Identity and Structure: Issues in the Sociology of Education*, ed. D. Gleason (Driffield, 1977), pp. 112–19, and *Critique of Anthropology*, 4, no. 13–14 (Summer 1979), pp. 77–85.

– On the 'durability' of habitus and the charge of 'determinism' which goes with it. First, habitus realizes itself, becomes active only *in the relation* to a field, and the same habitus can lead to very different practices and stances depending on the state of the field. An illustration of this is given by French bishops of aristocratic birth who express the same aristocratic inclinations to keep their distance from common practices in different ways in different situations:[8] in the 1930s by embracing the most traditional form of the role of the seigneurial prelate; in the seventies, that is, since the Episcopate has become dominated by oblates who come from the middle classes and are inclined to reject the traditional role, by assuming the role of leftist bishop (*prêtre gauchiste*), championing the cause of immigrant workers and spurning all the attributes and attributions of the old role. It can be inferred from this example that one should be careful not to describe as an effect of the conversion of habitus what is nothing more than the effect of a change in the relation between habitus and field. Secondly, habitus, as the product of social conditionings, and thus of a history (unlike *character*), is endlessly transformed, either in a direction that reinforces it, when embodied structures of expectation encounter structures of objective chances in harmony with these expectations, or in a direction that transforms it and, for instance, raises or lowers the level of expectations and aspirations (which can in turn lead to social crises proper). It has often been noted that the children who are labelled 'unstable' by academic specialists as well as by the evaluations of psychologists or physicians (who often do little more than give the former a sort of 'scientific' seal of approval), bear inscribed in their habitus the instability of the living conditions of their family, that of the sub-proletariat doomed to insecurity in their conditions of employment, housing, and thereby of existence. Habitus can, in certain instances, be built, if one may say so, upon contradiction, upon tension, even upon instability – and I believe that there is a sociogenesis of psychoses and neuroses. Thirdly, not only can habitus be practically transformed (always within definite boundaries) by the effect of a social trajectory leading to conditions of living different from initial ones, it can also be *controlled* through awakening of consciousness and socioanalysis.

---

8 P. Bourdieu and M. de Saint Martin, 'La sainte famille. L'épiscopat français dans le champ du pouvoir', *Actes de la recherche en sciences sociales*, 44–45 (November 1982), pp. 2–53.

A reply to some objections

– On the problem of classes. The intention of *Distinction*, on which most of my critics rely, was not to propound a theory of social classes (which, if I remember correctly, was announced in it, but in a footnote), but rather to put forth an explanatory model, that is, a system of factors capable of explaining in the most economical manner possible a set of practices apparently quite dissimilar and traditionally treated by different subfields of sociology (whence the fact that it is perhaps, of all my books, the one which seems most 'deterministic' and 'objectivist'). The purpose was thus to uncover principles of differentiation capable of accounting in the fullest possible way for the largest possible number of observed differences; or, in other words, to construct the multidimensional space enabling us to reproduce the distribution of these differences (by making use of the fundamental property of space according to Strawson, namely, the reciprocal externality of objects). In the end, the *major*, primary principles of differentiation (other principles are at work, such as ethnic origins or place of residence, but they are less powerful) which had to be applied in order theoretically to reproduce, to re-generate the space of differences or, to be more precise, the space of differential positions (defined both intrinsically, as capturing a definite type of material conditions of living, and thus of conditionings, etc., and relationally, as defined by their distinctive distance to other positions), turned out to be global volume of capital held (all the different species of capital, economic, cultural and social, being lumped together), the structure of this capital (as defined by the relative weight of the different species) and, lastly, evolution over time of these two parameters, which measures both intra- and inter-generational social trajectory. Having thus constructed this space, it became possible to cut up 'regions' (all the more homogeneous as they become smaller) or, if one wishes, 'classes' in the logical sense of the term. These 'classes on paper' necessarily include the effect of occupation: as testified in the fact that they are often designated by names of occupations or clusters of occupations, 'classes' were delimited by taking into account occupational criteria and affinities in working conditions within a space itself constructed according to criteria which are not randomly distributed across different occupational categories.

These 'classes on paper', these 'theoretical classes', constructed for explanatory purposes, are not 'realities', groups which would exist as such in reality. Inasmuch as they correspond to classes of material conditions of living, and thus to classes of similar conditionings, they bring together agents who have in common dispositional

117

properties (habitus), hence a certain propensity to come together in reality, to constitute themselves into real groups (as revealed in the fact that homogamy becomes greater as the size of the classes gets smaller), and thus more homogeneous from the standpoint of the criteria used in constructing the space.[9] All I want to say, in opposition to the realist interpretation of the construction of classes shared by theories of stratification and Marxist theory, is that 'classes' can become real groups, actually mobilized or organized, only at the cost of a political work: classes in Marx's sense of the term are to-be-made (as the title of E. P. Thompson's book *The Making of the English Working Class* appropriately reminds us).[10] Now the theoretical construction of social space, and the theoretical cutting-up, within the limits of this theoretical space, of theoretical classes, defines the limits (or the probabilities) of any attempt to turn theoretical classes into real classes. Groups must be made, groups are to be constructed, but one cannot construct anything anyhow. The political work of *group-making* (whose specific logic must be analysed) is all the more likely to be successful when the social collective it endeavours to constitute as group is less scattered in theoretical space. The effect of theory, which a well-constructed theory exerts by making real divisions visible, is all the more powerful when this theory is better grounded in reality.

– The problem of change. I do not see where my readers could have found the model of circular reproduction which they attribute to me (structure → habitus → structure). Indeed, I could show how the opposition between statics and dynamics, structure and history, reproduction and transformation, etc., is totally fictitious, in so far as it is the structure (the tensions, the oppositions, the relations of power which constitute the structure of a specific field or of the social field as a totality at a given point in time) which constitutes the principle of the strategies aimed at preserving or transforming the structure.[11] But rather than launching into a lengthy and tedious

---

9   I shall not rehearse here the full demonstration developed in my Frankfurt lecture, *Sozialerraum und 'Klassen', Leçon sur la leçon* (Frankfurt, 1985); first part trans. as 'Social Space and the Genesis of Groups', *Theory and Society*, 14 (November 1985), pp. 723–44.

10   See P. Bourdieu, 'What Makes a Social Class?', *Berkeley Journal of Sociology*, 32 (1987), pp. 1–17, for an elaboration.

11   P. Bourdieu, *Homo academicus* (Paris, 1984; trans. as *Homo academicus*, tr. P. Collier, Cambridge, 1988) demonstrates this point in the case of the French academic field around 1968.

argument, let me use a brief example to bring out the inadequacy of the ordinary mode of thought. The section of *Distinction* entitled 'Clan, Mobility and Mobile Classes' contains a model of one of the most distinctive principles of social change in modern societies, to wit, the contradictions of the school-mediated mode of reproduction. In effect, the contradictions built into the mechanisms which tend to secure the reproduction of the social structure by eliminating children differentially according to the volume of their inherited cultural capital are at the basis of the individual and collective strategies (such as student movements) through which the victims of elimination (or at least the most socially privileged of them) aim at transforming the structures which the mechanisms of elimination, and thereby of reproduction of structures, tend to preserve.

– On the question of politics and of the political means for breaking out of the limits of the system of reproduction – and especially on the role of trade unions, parties, on the role of the state – I can only refer to other works.[12] I fear that these objections, like many others, stem from the fact that *Distinction* is read as one of these theoretical books which claim to say everything on everything and in the right order, whereas it is a synthetic account of a set of empirical investigations geared to a well-defined objective, which I have recapitulated above. It is neither possible nor desirable, under these circumstances, to assert or repeat everything over again in each publication. In a word, to ask of it a general theory of the social world, of social classes, of politics, of the effects of the welfare state on practices, etc., is to grant much too much to this book. I would fully concur with this reading which, after all, does me great honour (at least in its intent) by treating my work as a 'Grand Theory' if it did not lead one to overlook or to misconstrue what seems to me to constitute its specific contribution: a theory of action, or of practice, in rupture with ordinary alternatives; a construction of social space which solves, by dissolving it, the long-standing issue of social 'classes'; a theory of symbolic domination which recognizes the specificity of symbolic logic at the same time that it grounds it in the objective structures of the distribution of the different species of capital (or powers).

---

12 In particular to *Homo academicus*, and 'La représentation politique. Éléments pour une théorie du champ politique', *Actes de la recherche en sciences sociales*, 36–37 (February–March 1981), pp. 3–24.

Part III

New Directions

constructivism
socialgenesis
of

habitus

fields/groups

8

Social space and symbolic power

I would like, within the limits of a lecture, to try and present the theoretical principles which underlie the research whose results are presented in *Distinction*,[1] and draw out certain of the theoretical implications which are most likely to elude the reader, especially here in the United States, by virtue of the differences between our two cultural traditions. If I had to characterize my work in a couple of words, that is, as is often done these days, to apply a label to it, I would talk of *constructivist structuralism* or of *structuralist constructivism*, taking the word structuralist in a sense very different from that given to it by the Saussurean or Lévi-Straussian tradition. By structuralism or structuralist, I mean that there exist, in the social world itself, and not merely in symbolic systems, language, myth, etc., objective structures which are independent of the consciousness and desires of agents and are capable of guiding or constraining their practices or their representations. By constructivism, I mean that there is a social genesis on the one hand of the patterns of perception, thought and action which are constitutive of what I call the habitus, and on the other hand of social structures, and in particular of what I call fields and groups, especially of what are usually called social classes.

(I think this setting straight of the record is particularly necessary here: indeed, the hazards of translation are such that, for instance,

---

Text of the lecture delivered at the University of San Diego in March 1986.

1 P. Bourdieu, *La distinction. Critique sociale du jugement* (Paris, 1979); trans. as *Distinction. A Social Critique of the Judgement of Taste*, tr. R. Nice (Cambridge, Mass., 1984).

123

Reproduction[2] is known, which will lead certain commentators – and some of them have not hesitated to do so – to classify me among the structuralists, while works that come from a much earlier period are not known (they are so old that they even antedate the appearance of the typically 'constructivist' works on the same subjects): these works would mean, no doubt, my being perceived as a 'constructivist': thus, in a book called *Rapport pédagogique et communication*,[3] we showed how a social relation of understanding is constructed in and by misunderstanding, or in spite of misunderstanding; how teachers and students agree, by a sort of tacit transaction, tacitly guided by the need to minimize costs and risks, to accept a minimal definition of the situation of communication. Likewise, in another study, called 'The Categories of Professorial Judgement',[4] we try to analyse the genesis and functioning of the categories of perception and appreciation through which teachers construct the images of their pupils, of their performance and value, and produce, by practices of cooption guided by the same categories, their own group, that of their colleagues and, thereby, the body of teachers. Now that this brief parenthesis is out of the way, I can return to my main theme.)

Speaking in very general terms, social science, in anthropology as in sociology or in history, oscillates between two apparently incompatible points of view, two apparently irreconcilable perspectives: objectivism and subjectivism, or, if you prefer, physicalism and psychologism (which can take on diverse colourings, phenomenological, semiological, etc.). On the one hand, it can 'treat social phenomena as things', in accordance with the old Durkheimian maxim, and thus leave out everything that they owe to the fact that they are objects of cognition – or of miscognition – in social existence. On the other hand, it can reduce the social world to the representations that agents make of it, the task of social science then consisting in producing an 'account of the accounts' produced by social subjects.

It is rare that these two positions are expressed and above all realized in scientific practice in such a radical and contrasting way.

---

2 P. Bourdieu and J. C. Passeron, *La reproduction. Éléments pour une théorie du système d'enseignement* (Paris, 1970); trans. as *Reproduction in Education, Society and Culture*, tr. R. Nice (Beverley Hills, Calif., 1977).
3 P. Bourdieu, J. C. Passeron and M. de Saint Martin (eds), *Rapport pédagogique et communication* (Paris and The Hague, 1965).
4 Published in English as the 'Postscript' in *Homo academicus*, tr. P. Collier (Cambridge, 1988), pp. 194–225.

You know that Durkheim is doubtless, together with Marx, the person who has expressed the objectivist position most consistently: 'We find fruitful the idea that social life must be explained not by the conception of those who participate in it, but by the deep causes which lie outside consciousness.' But, as a good Kantian, he was not unaware of the fact that this reality cannot be grasped without bringing logical instruments into operation. That being said, objectivist physicalism is often associated with the positivist inclination to imagine classifications as 'operative' ways of cutting things up or as a mechanical recording of 'objective' breaks and discontinuities (for example in distributions). It is doubtless in Schütz and the ethnomethodologists that one could find the purest expressions of the subjectivist vision. Thus Schütz takes exactly the opposite standpoint to that of Durkheim: 'The observational field of the social scientist, social reality, has a specific sense and structure of pertinence for the human beings who live and act and think in it. By a series of commonsense constructions, they have preselected and preinterpreted this world that they apprehend as the reality of their daily life. These are the objects of thought that determine their behaviour by motivating it. The objects of thought constructed by the social scientist so as to grasp this social reality must be based on the objects of thought constructed by the commonsense thinking of people who live their daily lives in their social world. Thus, the constructions of the social sciences are, so to speak, second-degree constructions, that is, constructions of the constructions made by actors on the social stage.'[5] The opposition is total: in one case, scientific knowledge can be obtained only by breaking away from the primary representations – called 'pre-notions' in Durkheim and 'ideology' in Marx: this break leads to the positing of unconscious causes. In the other case scientific knowledge is continuous with common-sense knowledge, because it is only a 'construction of constructions'.

If I have rather laboured this opposition, one of the most unfortunate of those 'paired concepts' which, as Richard Bendix and Benett Berger have shown, flourish in the social sciences, this is because the most constant and, in my eyes, most important intention of my work has been to transcend it. At the risk of appearing very obscure, I could sum up in one phrase the whole analysis I am setting out for you today: on the one hand, the objective structures which the sociologist constructs in the objectivist moment, by setting aside

5 A. Schütz, *Collected Papers*, vol. I, *The Problem of Social Reality* (The Hague, n.d.), p. 59.

the subjective representations of the agents, are the basis of subjective representations and they constitute the structural constraints which influence interactions; but, on the other hand, these representations also have to be remembered if one wants to account above all for the daily individual and collective struggles which aim at transforming or preserving these structures. This means that the two moments, objectivist and subjectivist, stand in a dialectical relation and that, even if for instance the subjectivist moment seems very close, when it is taken separately, to interactionist or ethnomethodological analyses, it is separated from them by a radical difference: the points of view are apprehended as such and related to the positions in the structure of the corresponding agents.

In order fully to transcend the artificial opposition that tends to be established between structures and representations, one also has to break away from the mode of thought that Cassirer calls substantialist, and which leads people to recognize no realities except those that are available to direct intuition in ordinary experience, individuals and groups. The major contribution of what one has to call the structuralist revolution consisted in applying to the social world a relational way of thinking, which is that of modern physics and mathematics, and which identifies the real not with substances but with relations. The 'social reality' which Durkheim talked of is a set of invisible relations, those very same relations that constitute a space of positions exterior to each other and defined by their proximity to, neighbourhood with or distance from each other, and also by their relative position – above or below, or even in between, in the middle. Sociology, in its objectivist moment, is a social topology, an *analysis situs*, as this new branch of mathematics was called at the time of Leibniz, an analysis of relative positions and objective relations between these positions.

This relational way of thinking is the point of departure of the construction presented in *Distinction*. But it's a fair bet that the space, that is, the relations, will go unnoticed by the reader, despite the use of diagrams (and of correspondence analysis which is a very sophisticated form of factorial analysis): on the one hand, because the substantialist way of thinking is easier, more 'natural'; secondly, because, as often happens, the means one is obliged to employ to construct social space and in order to manifest it risk concealing the results they enable one to obtain. The groups that one has to construct in order to objectify the positions they occupy conceal those positions and the chapter in *Distinction* on fractions of the dominant class is read as a description of the different life-styles of those fractions, instead of being read as an analysis of the way they have to be seen as positions in the space of power positions – what I call the field of power. (In parenthesis, I would note that changes in vocabulary are, as you can see, both the condition and the result of breaking away from the ordinary representation associated with the idea of *ruling class*.)

One can, at this point of the discussion, compare the social space to a geographical space within which regions are divided up. But this space is constructed in such a way that the agents, groups or institutions that find themselves situated in it have more properties in common the closer they are to each other in this space; and fewer common properties, the further they are away from each other. Spatial distances – on paper – coincide with social distances. The same is not true in real space: it is true that one can observe almost everywhere a tendency to segregation in space; people close to each other in the social space tend to be close together – by choice or necessity – in the geographical space; however, people who are very distant from each other in the social space can encounter one another, enter into interaction, at least briefly and intermittently, in physical space. The interactions, which are accepted at their face value by people of an empiricist disposition – one can observe them, film them, record them, in short they are tangible – conceal the structures that are realized in them. It's one of those cases in which the visible, that which is immediately given, conceals the invisible which determines it. One thus forgets that the truth of the inter- action is never entirely to be found in interaction as it is available to observation. One example will suffice to show the difference be- tween structure and interaction, and, at the same time, between the structuralist vision, which I would defend as a necessary moment of research, and the so-called interactionist vision in all its forms (in particular ethnomethodology). I have in mind what I call strategies of condescension, by which agents occupying a higher position in one of the hierarchies of objective space symbolically deny the social distance which does not thereby cease to exist, thus ensuring they gain the profits of recognition accorded to a purely symbolic negation of distance ('he's unaffected', 'he's not stand-offish', etc.) which implies the recognition of a distance (the sentences I have quoted always have an implicit rider: 'he's unaffected, for a duke', 'he's not stand-offish, for a university professor', etc.). In short, one can use the objective distances so as to have the advantages of proximity and the advantages of distance, that is, the distance and the recognition of the distance that is ensured by the symbolic negation of distance.

How can one thus concretely grasp these objective relations which are irreducible to the interactions in which they are manifested? These objective relations are relations between the positions occupied in the distributions of resources which are or may become active, effective, like the trumps in a game of cards, in competition for the appropriation of the rare goods of which this social universe is the locus. These fundamental social powers are, according to my empirical researches, economic capital, in its different forms, and cultural capital, and also symbolic capital, a form which is assumed by different kinds of capital when they are perceived and recognized as legitimate. Thus agents are distributed in the overall social space, in the first dimension in accordance with the overall volume of the capital that they possess in different kinds and, in the second dimension, in accordance with the structure of their capital, that is, in accordance with the relative weight of the different kinds of capital, economic and cultural, in the total volume of their capital. The misunderstanding in the reading of the analyses that I set out, especially in *Distinction*, thus results from the fact that classes on paper risk being apprehended as real groups. This realist reading is objectively encouraged by the fact that the social space is so constructed that agents who occupy similar or close positions are placed in similar conditions and submitted to similar conditionings, and have every chance of having similar dispositions and interests, and thus of producing practices that are themselves similar. The dispositions acquired in the position occupied imply an adjustment to this position, which Goffman called the 'sense of one's place'. It's this sense of one's place which, in interactions, leads people who are in French called 'les gens modestes', that is, 'ordinary people', to keep to their 'ordinary' place and the others to 'keep their distance' or 'respect their rank', and 'not get familiar'. These strategies, it should be noted in passing, may be perfectly unconscious and may take the form of what is called timidity or arrogance. In fact, social distances are written into bodies, or, more exactly, into the relationship to the body, to language and to time (so many structural aspects of practice that are ignored by the subjectivist vision).

If you add to this the fact that this sense of one's place, and the affinities of the habitus experienced as sympathy or antipathy, are at the basis of all forms of cooperation, friendships, love affairs, marriages, associations, etc., thus of all the relationships that are

128

long-lasting and sometimes sanctioned by law, you see that every-thing leads one to think that classes on paper are real groups – all the more real in that the space is better constructed and the units into which this space is subdivided are smaller. If you want to found a political movement or even an association, you will have a better chance of bringing together people who are in the same sector of space (for example in the north-west of the diagram, where the intellectuals are) than if you want to bring together people situated in the regions at the four corners of the diagram.

But, just as subjectivism inclines people to reduce structures to interactions, objectivism tends to deduce actions and interactions from the structure. So the main error, the theoreticist error that you find in Marx, seems to consist in treating classes on paper as real classes, in concluding from the objective homogeneity of conditions, of conditionings, and thus of dispositions, which all come from the identity of position in the social space, that the people involved exist as a unified group, as a class. The notion of social space allows one to go beyond the alternative of nominalism and realism when it comes to social classes: the political enterprise meant to produce social classes as 'corporate bodies', permanent groups, endowed with permanent organs of representation, acronyms, etc., has all the more chance of succeeding since the agents that it wishes to bring together, unify, and constitute as a group, are closer in the social space (and thus belong to the same class on paper). Classes in Marx's sense have to be produced by a political enterprise which has all the more chance of succeeding in that it is sustained by a theory that is well founded in reality, and thus capable of exercising a *theory effect* – *theorein*, in Greek, means to see – capable, in other words, of imposing a vision of divisions.

With the theory effect, we have left pure physicalism, but without abandoning the experience acquired in the objectivist phase: groups – social classes, for instance – have to be *made*. They are not given in 'social reality'. We have to take literally the title of the famous book by E. P. Thompson, *The Making of the English Working Class*:[6] the working class in the form in which it may appear to us today, via the words meant to designate it, 'working class', 'proletariat', 'workers', 'workers' movement', etc., via the organizations which are meant to express it, the acronyms, the offices, secretariats and flags, etc., is a well-founded historical artefact (in the sense in which Durkheim said of religion that it is a well-founded illusion). But that does not mean

---

6   E. P. Thompson, *The Making of the English Working Class* (London, 1963).

that one can construct just anything at all, in any old way, either in theory or in practice.

We have thus moved from social physics to social phenomenology. The 'social reality' objectivists talk about is also an object of perception. And social science must take as its object both this reality and the perception of this reality, the perspectives, the points of view which, by virtue of their position in objective social space, agents have on this reality. The spontaneous visions of the social world, the 'folk theories' which ethnomethodologists talk about, or what I call spontaneous sociology, but also scientific theories, and sociology, are all part of social reality, and, like the Marxist theory for instance, can acquire an altogether real constructive power.

The objectivist break with pre-notions, ideologies, spontaneous sociology, and 'folk theories', is an inevitable and necessary moment of the scientific procedure – you cannot do without it (as do interactionism, ethnomethodology and all the forms of social psychology which rest content with a phenomenal vision of the social world) without exposing yourself to grave mistakes. But you have to carry out a second and more difficult break away from objectivism, by reintroducing, in a second stage, what had to be excluded in order to construct social reality.

Sociology has to include a sociology of the perception of the social world, that is, a sociology of the construction of the world-views which themselves contribute to the construction of this world. But, given the fact that we have constructed social space, we know that these points of view, as the word itself suggests, are views taken from a certain point, that is, from a given position within social space. And we know too that there will be different or even antagonistic points of view, since points of view depend on the point from which they are taken, since the vision that every agent has of space depends on his or her position in that space.

By doing this, we repudiate the universal subject, the transcendental ego of phenomenology that the ethnomethodologists take over as their own. No doubt agents do have an active apprehension of the world. No doubt they do construct their vision of the world. But this construction is carried out under structural constraints. And one may even explain in sociological terms what appears as a universal property of human experience, that is, the fact that the familiar world tends to be 'taken for granted', perceived as natural. If the social world tends to be perceived as evident and to be grasped, to use Husserl's terms, with a doxic modality, this is because the dispositions of agents, their habitus, that is, the mental structures through which they apprehend the social world, are essentially the product of an internalization of the structures of the social world. As perceptual dispositions tend to be adjusted to position, agents, even the most disadvantaged, tend to perceive the world as natural and to find it much more acceptable than one might imagine, especially when one looks at the situation of the dominated through the social eyes of the dominant.

So the search for the invariant forms of the perception or the construction of social reality masks different things: firstly, the fact that this construction is not carried out in a social vacuum, but that it is subjected to structural constraints; secondly, that the structuring structures, the cognitive structures, are themselves socially structured, because they have social origins; thirdly, the construction of social reality is not only an individual enterprise, but may also become a collective enterprise. But the so-called microsociological vision leaves out a good number of other things: as often happens when you look too closely, you can't see the wood for the trees; and, above all, since you haven't constructed the space, you have no chance of seeing the point from which you can see what you see.

So the representations of agents vary with their position (and the interest associated with it) and with their habitus, as a system of models of perception and appreciation, as cognitive and evaluative structures which are achieved through the lasting experience of a social position. The habitus is at once a system of models for the production of practices and a system of models for the perception and appreciation of practices. And in both cases, its operations express the social position in which it was constructed. As a result, the habitus produces practices and representations which are available for classification, which are objectively differentiated; but they are immediately perceived as such only in the case of agents who possess the code, the classificatory models necessary to understand their social meaning. Thus, the habitus implies a 'sense of one's place' but also a 'sense of the other's place'. For example, we say of an item of clothing, a piece of furniture or a book: 'that's petty-bourgeois' or 'that's intellectual'. What are the social conditions of possibility of such a judgement? Firstly, it presupposes that taste (or the habitus) as a system of classificatory models is objectively referred, via the social conditionings which produced it, to a social condition: agents classify themselves, expose themselves to classification, by choosing, in conformity with their tastes, different attributes, clothes, types of food, drinks, sports, friends, which go well together and which they also find agreeable or, more exactly, which they find suitable for their position. More exactly: they classify themselves by choosing, in the space of available goods and services, goods which occupy a position in this space homologous to the position they occupy in social space. This means that nothing classifies somebody more than the way he or she classifies.

Secondly, a classificatory judgement such as 'that's petty-bourgeois' presupposes that, as socialized agents, we are capable of seeing the relation between practices or representations and positions in the social space (as when we guess a person's social position from his or her accent). Thus, via the habitus, we have a world of common sense, a social world which seems self-evident.

I have so far adopted the position of the perceiving subjects and I have mentioned the principal factor in variations of perception, namely, position in the social space. But what about variations whose principle is more on the level of the object, of this space itself? It is true that the correspondence established, via habitus, disposition and taste, between positions and practices, preferences demonstrated, opinions expressed, etc., means that the social world is not presented as a pure chaos, totally devoid of necessity and capable of being constructed in any old way. But this world does not present itself as totally structured either, or as capable of imposing on every perceiving subject the principles of its own construction. The social world may be described and constructed in different ways in accordance with different principles of vision and division – for example, economic divisions and ethnic divisions. If it is true that, in the societies that are most advanced from the economic point of view, economic and cultural factors have the greatest power of differentiation, the fact remains that the strength of economic and social differences is never such that one cannot organize agents by means of other principles of division – ethnic, religious or national, for instance.

Despite this potential plurality of possible structurings – what Weber called the *Vielseitigkeit* of the given – it is none the less true that the social world presents itself as a highly structured reality. This is because of a simple mechanism, which I want rapidly to sketch out. The social space as I have described it above presents itself in the form of agents provided with different properties that are systematically linked to each other: those people who drink champagne are opposed to those who drink whisky, but they are also opposed, in a different way, to those who drink red wine; but those who drink champagne are more likely than those who drink whisky, and far more likely than those who drink red wine, to have antique furniture, play golf, ride horses or go to see light comedies at the theatre. These properties, when they are perceived by agents endowed with the pertinent categories of perception (capable of seeing that playing golf makes you 'look' like a traditional member of the upper-middle class), function, in the very reality of social life, as signs: the differences function as distinctive signs, and as signs of distinction, either positive or negative, and this happens outside any intention of distinction, any desire for *conspicuous consumption* (this is to say, in passing, that my analyses have nothing in common with those of Veblen: this is all the more true in that distinction, from the point of view of indigenous criteria, excludes any desire for distinction). In other words, via the distribution of properties, the social world presents itself, objectively, as a symbolic system which is organized in accordance with the logic of difference, of a differential variation. The social space tends to function as a symbolic space, a space of life-styles and status groups, characterized by different life-styles.

Thus perception of the social world is the product of a double structuring, on the objective level, it is socially structured because the properties attributed to agents or institutions present themselves in combinations which have very unequal probabilities: just as feathered animals are more likely to have wings than are furry animals, so the possessors of a sophisticated mastery of language are more likely to be seen in a museum than those who don't have this mastery. On the subjective level, perception of the social world is structured because the models of perception and evaluation, especially those which are written into language, express the state of relations of symbolic power: I am thinking for example of the couples of adjectives: heavy/light, brilliant/dull, etc., which structure taste in the most diverse domains. These two mechanisms together act to produce a common world, a world of common sense or, at least, a minimum consensus about the social world.

But the objects of the social world, as I have suggested, can be perceived and expressed in different ways, since they always include a degree of indeterminacy and vagueness, and, thereby, a certain degree of semantic elasticity: indeed, even combinations of the most constant properties are always based on statistical connections between interchangeable characteristics; and, furthermore, they are submitted to variations in time so that their meaning, in so far as they depend on the future, is itself held in suspense and relatively indeterminate. This objective element of uncertainty – which is often reinforced by the effect of categorization, since the same word can

133

This uncertainty

cover different practices – provides a basis for the plurality of world-views, which itself is linked to the plurality of points of view; and, at the same time, it provides a base for symbolic struggles for the power to produce and to impose a vision of the legitimate world. (It is in the middle positions of the social space, especially in the United States, that the indeterminacy and objective uncertainty of relations between practices and positions is at a maximum; and also, as a consequence, the intensity of symbolic strategies. It is easy to understand that it is this universe which provides the privileged terrain of interactionists and in particular of Goffman.)

Symbolic struggles over the perception of the social world may take two different forms. On the objective level, one may take action in the form of acts of representation, individual or collective, meant to show up and to show off certain realities: I am thinking for example of demonstrations whose objective is to demonstrate a group, its number, its strength, its cohesion, to make it exist visibly; and on the individual level, of all the strategies of self-presentation, so well analysed by Goffman, designed to manipulate one's self-image and especially – something omitted by Goffman – the image of one's position in social space. On the subjective level, one may act by trying to change the categories of perception and evaluation of the social world, the cognitive and evaluative structures. The categories of perception, the systems of classification, that is, essentially, the words, the names which construct social reality as much as they express it, are the crucial stakes of political struggle, which is a struggle to impose the legitimate principle of vision and division – is, that is, a struggle for the legitimate exercise of the theory effect. I have shown, in the case of Kabylia, that groups, households, clans or tribes, and the names that designate them, are the instruments and objects of innumerable strategies, and that agents are ceaselessly occupied in the negotiation of their own identity: for example, they may manipulate genealogy, as we manipulate, and for other ends, the texts of the 'founding fathers' of our discipline. In the same way, on the level of the daily class struggle that social agents carry out in an isolated and dispersed state, they are insults, like magical attempts at categorization – gossip, rumours, calumnies, insinuations, etc. On the collective and more properly political level, they include all the strategies which aim at imposing a new construction of social reality by rejecting the old political lexicon, or else aim at maintaining the orthodox view by keeping those words, which are often euphemisms (just now I referred to the expression 'ordinary people'), designed to describe the social world. The most typical of these strategies of construction are those which aim at reconstructing retrospectively a past adjusted to the needs of the present – as when General Flemming, on landing in France in 1917, says: 'La Fayette, here we come!' – or else aim at constructing the future, by a creative prediction destined to limit the ever-open sense of the present.

These symbolic struggles, both the individual struggles of daily life and the collective, organized struggles of political life, have a specific logic, which grants them a real autonomy from the structures in which they are rooted. By virtue of the fact that symbolic capital is nothing more than economic or cultural capital which is acknowledged and recognized, when it is acknowledged in accordance with the categories of perception that it imposes, the symbolic power relations tend to reproduce and to reinforce the power relations which constitute the structure of the social space. More concretely, the legitimatization of the social order is not the product, as certain people believe, of a deliberately biased action of propaganda or symbolic imposition; it results from the fact that agents apply to the objective structures of the social world structures of perception and appreciation that have emerged from these objective structures and tend therefore to see the world as self-evident.

Objective power relations tend to reproduce themselves in symbolic power relations. In the symbolic struggle for the production of common sense or, more precisely, for a monopoly over legitimate naming, agents put into action the symbolic capital that they have acquired in previous struggles and which can be juridically guaranteed. In this way, titles of nobility, like educational qualifications, represent real titles of symbolic property which give one a right to the profits of recognition. Here too, one has to move away from marginalist subjectivism: the symbolic order is not constituted, like a market price, by the mere mechanical addition of the individual orders. On the one hand, in the determination of the objective classification and the hierarchy of values granted to individuals and groups, not all judgements have the same weight, and those people who have a large symbolic capital, the *nobiles*, that is, etymologically, those who are acknowledged and recognized, are in a position to impose the scale of values most favourable to their products – notably because, in our societies, they hold a *de facto* monopoly over institutions which, like the education system, officially establish and guarantee rank. On the other hand, symbolic capital may be officially sanctioned and guaranteed, and juridically established by the effect of an official nomination. Official nomination, in other words the act by which one grants someone a title, a socially recognized qualification, is one of the most typical demonstrations of that monopoly of legitimate symbolic violence which belongs to the state or to its representatives. A diploma such as a school diploma is a piece of universally recognized and guaranteed symbolic capital, valid on all markets. As an official definition of an official identity, it releases its holder from the symbolic struggle of all against all by imposing the universally approved perspective.

The state, which produces the official classification, is in one sense the supreme tribunal to which Kafka refers in *The Trial*, when Block says of the advocate who claims to be one of the 'great Advocates': 'any man can call himself "great", of course, if he pleases, but in this matter the Court tradition must decide.'[7] Science doesn't have to choose between relativism and absolutism: the truth of the social world is at stake in the struggles between agents who are unequally equipped to reach an absolute, that is, self-verifying vision. The legalization of symbolic capital confers on a perspective an absolute, universal value, thus releasing it from a relativity which is by definition inherent in every point of view, as a view seen from a particular point of the social space.

There is an official point of view, which is the point of view of officials and which is expressed in official discourse. This discourse, as Aaron Cicourel has shown, accomplishes three functions: firstly, it performs a diagnostic, that is, an act of cognition which enforces recognition and which, quite often, tends to affirm what a person or a thing is and what it is universally, for every possible person, and thus objectively. It is, as Kafka clearly saw, an almost divine discourse, which assigns to everyone an identity. In the second place, the administrative discourse, via directives, orders, prescriptions, etc., says what people have to do, given what they are. Thirdly, it says what people really have done, as in authorized accounts such as police reports. In each case, it imposes a point of view, that of the institution, especially via questionnaires, official forms, etc. This point of view is set up as a legitimate point of view, that is, as a point of view which everyone has to recognize at least within the limits of a given society. The representative of the state is the repository of common sense: official nominations and school certificates tend to have a universal value on all markets. The most typical effect of the 'raison d'État' is the effect of codification which is at work in operations as simple as the granting of a diploma: an expert, doctor, jurist, etc., is someone who is appointed to produce a

---

7 F. Kafka, *The Trial*, tr. E. and W. Muir (Harmondsworth, 1953), p. 197.

point of view which is recognized as transcending individual points of view, in the form of sickness notes, certificates of competence or incompetence, a point of view which confers universally recognized rights on the holder of the certificate. The state thus appears as the central bank which guarantees all certificates. One may say of the state, in the terms Leibniz used of God, that it is the 'geometral locus of all perspectives'. This is why one may generalize Weber's famous formula and see in the state the holder of the monopoly of legitimate symbolic violence. Or, more precisely, the state is a referee, albeit a very powerful one, in struggles over this monopoly.

But, in the struggle for the production and imposition of a legitimate vision of the social world, the holders of bureaucratic authority never obtain an absolute monopoly, even when they add the authority of science, as do state economists, to their bureaucratic authority. In fact, there are always, in a society, conflicts between symbolic powers which aim to impose their vision of legitimate divisions, that is, to construct groups. Symbolic power, in this sense, is a power of 'worldmaking'. 'Worldmaking' consists, according to Nelson Goodman, 'in separating and reuniting, often in the same operation', in carrying out a decomposition or analysis, and a composition or synthesis, often by the use of labels. Social classifications, as is the case in archaic societies, which often work via dualist operations, masculine/feminine, high/low, strong/weak, etc., organize the perception of the social world and, in certain conditions, can really organize the world itself.

So we can now turn to examine on what conditions a symbolic power can become a power of constitution, taking the term, with Dewey, both in the philosophical sense and in the political sense of the term: that is, a power of keeping or transforming the objective principles of union or separation, marriage and divorce, association and dissociation which are at work in the social world, a power of conserving or transforming present classifications when it comes to gender, nation, region, age and social status, a power mediated by the words that are used to designate or to describe individuals, groups or institutions.

To change the world, one has to change the ways of making the world, that is, the vision of the world and the practical operations by which groups are produced and reproduced. Symbolic power, whose most exemplary form is seen in the power to produce groups (already-established groups, which have to be recognized, or groups which are still to be established, such as the Marxian proletariat), is based on two conditions. Firstly, like every form of performative

137

discourse, symbolic power has to be based on the possession of symbolic capital. The power of imposing on other minds a vision, old or new, of social divisions depends on the social authority acquired in previous struggles. Symbolic capital is a credit, it is the power granted to those who have obtained sufficient recognition to be in a position to impose recognition: in this way, the power of constitution, a power of making a new group, by mobilization, or of making it exist by procuration, by speaking on its behalf, as an authorized spokesperson, can be obtained only at the end of a long process of institutionalization, at the end of which a representative is chosen, who receives from the group the power to form the group.

Secondly, symbolic effectiveness depends on the degree to which the vision proposed is based on reality. Evidently, the construction of groups cannot be a construction *ex nihilo*. It has all the more chance of succeeding the more it is founded in reality: that is, as I have said, in the objective affinities between people who have to be brought together. The theory effect is all the more powerful the more adequate the theory is. Symbolic power is a power of creating things with words. It is only if it is true, that is, adequate to things, that a description can create things. In this sense, symbolic power is a power of consecration or revelation, a power to conceal or reveal things which are already there. Does this mean that it does nothing? In fact, as a constellation which, according to Nelson Goodman, begins to exist only when it is selected and designated as such, a group, class, 'gender', region, or nation, begins to exist as such, for those who are part of it and for others too, only when it is distinguished, according to one principle or another, from other groups, that is, via cognition and recognition.

It is thus, I hope, easier to understand what is at stake in the struggle over the existence or non-existence of classes. The struggle of classifications is a fundamental division of class struggle. The power of imposing a vision of divisions, that is, the power of making visible and explicit social divisions that are implicit, is the political power *par excellence*: it is the power to make groups, to manipulate the objective structure of society. As with constellations, the performative power of designation, of nomination, brings into existence in an instituted, constituted form (that is, as a 'corporate body', a *corporatio*, as the mediaeval canonists studied by Kantorowicz said), what existed up until then only as a *collectio personarum plurium*, a collection of multiple persons, a purely additive series of merely juxtaposed individuals.

Here, if we bear in mind the main problem that I have tried to resolve today, that of knowing how one can create things, that is, groups, with words, we are confronted with one last question, the question of the *mysterium* of the *ministerium*, as the canonists liked to put it: how does the spokesman become invested with the full power of acting and speaking in the name of the group which he produces by the magic of the slogan, the watchword or the command, and by his mere existence as an incarnation of the group? As the king of archaic societies, *rex*, who, according to Benveniste, has the job of *regere fines* and of *regere sacra*, of tracing out and stating the frontiers between groups and, thereby, of bringing them into existence as such, the leader of a trades union or a political party, the civil servant or the expert invested with state authority, are so many personifications of a social fiction to which they give existence, in and through their very being, and from which they receive in return their power. The spokesman is the substitute of the group which exists only through this delegation and which acts and speaks through him. He is the group personified. As the canonists say: *status*, the position, is *magistratus*, the magistrate who occupies it; or, as Louis XIV said: 'L'État, c'est moi'; or again, in Robespierre's words, 'Je suis le peuple.' The class (or the people, or the nation, or any other social reality ungraspable in any other way) exists if there exist people who can say that they are the class, by the mere fact of speaking publicly, officially, in its place, and of being recognized as justified in so doing by people who thereby recognize themselves as members of the class, people or nation, or of any other social reality which a realist construction of the world can invent and impose.

I hope that I have convinced you, within the limits of my linguistic capacities, that the complexity lies in the social reality and not in the somewhat decadent desire to say complicated things. 'The simple', Bachelard used to say, 'is never anything more than the simplified.' And he demonstrated that science has never progressed except by questioning simple ideas. A similar questioning needs to be applied, it seems to me, in the social sciences, by virtue of the fact that, for all the reasons that I have said, we tend to satisfy ourselves too easily with the obvious pictures we derive from our common-sense experience or our familiarity with a scientific tradition.

9

The intellectual field:
a world apart

Q. Let's take a particular domain of the social space that you have discussed in an article in German: the literary field. 'It is remarkable', you write, 'that all those who have busied themselves scientifically with literary or artistic works . . . have always neglected to take into account the social space in which are situated those who produce the works and their value.' An analysis which grasps this social space solely as a 'milieu', 'context' or 'social background' seems to you insufficient. So what is a 'literary field', what are its principles of construction?

A. The notion of field of cultural production (which is specified as artistic field, literary field, scientific field, etc.) allows one to break away from vague references to the social world (via words such as 'context', 'milieu', 'social base', 'social background') with which the social history of art and literature usually contents itself. The field of cultural production is this altogether particular social world referred to in the traditional notion of a republic of letters. But we must not remain on the level of what is merely a convenient image. And if one can observe all kinds of structural and functional homologies between the social field as a whole, or the political field, and the literary field, which, like them, has its dominated and its dominators, its conservatives and its avant-garde, its subversive struggles and its mechanisms of reproduction, the fact remains that each of these phenomena assumes within it an altogether specific form. The homology may be described as a resemblance in difference. Talking of a homology between the political field and the literary field is to

Interview with Karl-Otto Maue, for the *Norddeutscher Rundfunk*, recorded in Hamburg in December 1985.

affirm the existence of structurally equivalent – which does not mean identical – characteristics in different groupings. This is a complex relation which those who have the habit of thinking in terms of all or nothing will hasten to demolish. From a certain point of view, the literary field (or the scientific field) is a field like all the others (this remark is directed against all forms of hagiography or, quite simply, against the tendency to think that social universes in which these exceptional realities, art, literature or science are produced cannot but be totally different, different from every point of view): it involves power – the power to publish or to refuse publication, for instance; it involves capital – the capital of the established author which can be partly transferred into the account of a young and still unknown author by a highly positive review or a preface; one can observe here, as in other fields, power relations, strategies, interests, etc. But there is not a single one of the characteristics designated by these concepts which does not assume in the literary field a specific and altogether irreducible function. For example, if it is true that the literary field is, like every field, the locus of power relationships (and of struggles aiming to transform or maintain them), the fact remains that the power relations which are imposed on all the agents entering the field – and which weigh with a particular brutality on the new entrants – assume a special form: they are, indeed, based on a very particular form of capital, which is both the instrument and the object of competitive struggles within the field, that is, symbolic capital as a capital of recognition or consecration, institutionalized or not, that the different agents or institutions have been able to accumulate in the course of previous struggles, at the cost of specific activities and specific strategies. One would still need to specify the nature of this recognition which can be measured neither by commercial success – it would be, rather, its opposite – nor by mere social recognition – belonging to academies, winning prizes, etc. – nor even by mere fame, which, if acquired for the wrong reasons, may discredit you. But what I have said will be enough to show you that I'm talking about something very particular. In short, with the notion of field, one gives oneself the means of grasping particularity in generality, and generality in particularity. One may demand of the most highly specialized monograph (on the French literary field at the time of Flaubert, on the revolution brought about by Manet within the artistic field, on struggles within the literary field at the end of the nineteenth century, studies which I am carrying out at present) that it provide general propositions on the functioning of the fields, and from a general theory of the functioning of the fields one can draw very powerful hypotheses on the functioning of a particular state of a particular field (for example, the field of producers of individual houses, which I am studying). But mental habits are so strong – and especially among those who deny their existence – that the notion of literary (or artistic) field is doomed to two reductions, each the opposite of the other: one can see in it a reaffirmation of the irreducibility of the world of art or literature, thus instituted as a universe apart, above the strategies, interests and struggles of everyday life; or, on the other hand, one can reduce it to the very thing against which it is constructed, by reducing these strategies, these interests or these struggles to those which take place in the political field or in ordinary existence. To give you at least one example of these uncomprehending criticisms which destroy a complex notion by reducing it, often in all good faith, to the level of ordinary or scientific common sense in opposition to which it was erected – and such criticisms have every likelihood of receiving the approval of all those who are reassured by a return to the obvious – I would like to refer rapidly to an article by Peter Bürger, who writes: 'Bourdieu, as opposed to [Adorno], defends a functionalist approach' [the labelling, which is the 'scholarly' equivalent of the insult, is also a common strategy, and all the more powerful the more the label is, as here, both more of a stigma and more imprecise, thus irrefutable – P. B.]. 'He analyzes the actions of subjects in what he calls the "cultural field" by taking into account exclusively the chance of winning power and prestige and considers objects merely as strategic means which the producers employ in the struggle for power.'[1] Peter Bürger accuses me of reductionism, a theory which he has himself taken the precaution of first reducing: he behaves as if I reduced the functioning of the literary field to that of the political field (by adding 'exclusively' and 'merely'). In reality, what I say is that, like the political field, or any other field, the literary field is the site of struggles (and who could deny it? Not Peter Bürger, in any case, given the strategy he has just employed against me . . .); but that these struggles have specific stakes, and that the power and prestige which they pursue are of an altogether particular type (if you have been following me, you have probably noticed that I've had to use, despite its lack of elegance, the adjective 'specific' some twenty times!). In short, Peter Bürger reproaches me with leaving out the specificity of artistic struggles and of the interests that are engaged in them, the very thing, that is, that he began by excluding,

---

1 P. Bürger, 'On Literary History', *Poetics*, August 1985, pp. 199–207.

by a strange blind spot on his part, from the notion of field which aimed precisely at explaining this specificity. This sort of selective blindness, of which my writings are often the victim, seems to me to bear witness to the resistances aroused by a scientific analysis of the social world.

To return to your question – but I think this critical preamble wasn't without its use – I would say that the literary field is a force-field as well as a field of struggles which aim at transforming or maintaining the established relation of forces: each of the agents commits the force (the capital) that he has acquired through previous struggles to strategies that depend for their general direction on his position in the power struggle, that is, on his specific capital. Concretely, these are, for example, the permanent struggles that oppose the ever-emergent avant-gardes to the recognized avant-garde (and which must not be confused with the struggle which sets the avant-garde in general against 'bourgeois artists', as they said in the nineteenth century). Poetry is thus the locus, in France since the mid-nineteenth century, of a permanent revolution (the cycles of renewal of the dominant school are very short): the new entrants, who are also the youngest, question what was in the preceding revolution set up against the previous orthodoxy (you have, for instance, the revolt of the Parnassians against romantic 'lyricism'). This incessant revolt against the establishment is expressed, on the level of works of literature, by a process of purification. Poetry is more and more completely reduced to its 'essence', that is, to its quintessence, in the alchemical sense, the more it is stripped in successive revolutions of everything which, although it is an accessory, seemed to define 'the poetic' as such: lyricism, rhyme, metre, so-called poetic metaphor, etc.

As far as the question of limits is concerned, we must be wary of the positivist vision which, for the needs of statistics, for example, determines limits by a so-called operational decision which arbitrarily settles in the name of science a question which is not settled in reality, that of knowing who is an intellectual and who isn't, who are the 'real' intellectuals, those who really realize the essence of the intellectual. In fact, one of the major issues at stake in the struggles that occur in the literary or artistic field is the definition of the limits of the field, that is, of legitimate participation in the struggles. Saying of this or that tendency in writing that 'it just isn't poetry' or 'literature' means refusing it a legitimate existence, excluding it from the game, excommunicating it. This symbolic exclusion is merely the reverse of the effort to impose a definition of legitimate practice, to constitute, for instance, as an eternal and universal essence a historical definition of an art or a genre corresponding to the specific interests of those who hold a certain specific capital. When it succeeds, this strategy which, like the competence it mobilizes, is inseparably artistic and political (in the specific sense), is of a nature to ensure that these people have power over the capital held by all the other producers, in so far as, through the imposition of a definition of legitimate practice, it is the rule of the game which will most favour the trumps that they hold which tends to be imposed on everybody (and especially, at least in the long run, on the consumers); it is their accomplishments which become the measure of all accomplishments. You see, in passing, that the aesthetic concepts that a certain aesthetic theory forces itself to ground in reason, deductively, on the Aristotelian model, and whose inconsistency, incoherence, or mere vagueness people have noted before me (here I could mention Wittgenstein), are, paradoxically, necessary only if one sets them back in the purely sociological logic of the field in which they are generated and have functioned as symbolic strategies in struggles for symbolic domination, that is, for control over a particular use of a particular category of signs and, thereby, over the way the natural and social world is envisaged.

This dominant definition imposes itself on everyone, and in particular on the new entrants, as a more or less absolute right of entry. And it is easy to understand that struggles over the definition of genres, of poetry at the turn of the century, of the novel since the Second World War and later with the defenders of the 'nouveau roman', are something altogether different from futile wars of words: the overthrowing of the dominant definition is the specific form taken by revolutions in these universes. And it is easier to understand how confrontations which will become the object of academic analyses or debates, like all the quarrels between the Ancients and the Moderns and all revolutions, romantic or other, are experienced by the protagonists as questions of life or death.

Q. The field of power, in so far as it exercises its domination within the totality of fields, exercises an influence over the literary field. However, you grant to this field a 'relative autonomy' whose historical process of formation you analyse. What, today, is the concrete situation with regard to the autonomy of this literary field?

A. The fields of cultural production occupy a dominated position in the field of power: that is a major fact ignored by ordinary theories of art and literature. Or, to retranslate this into a more common (but inadequate) language, I could say that artists and writers, and more generally intellectuals, are a dominated fraction of the dominant class. They are dominant, in so far as they hold the power and privileges conferred by the possession of cultural capital and even, at least as far as certain of them are concerned, the possession of a volume of cultural capital great enough to exercise power over cultural capital; but writers and artists are dominated in their relations with those who hold political and economic power. To avoid any misunderstanding, I have to emphasize that this domination is not exercised any longer, as it used to be, through personal relations (like that between a painter and the person who has commissioned a painting or between writer and patron), but takes the form of a structural domination exercised through very general mechanisms, such as those of the market. This contradictory position of dominant-dominated, of dominated among the dominant or, to make use of the homology with the political field, of the left wing of the right wing, explains the ambiguity of the positions they adopt, an ambiguity which is linked to this precariously balanced position. Despite their revolt against those they call the 'bourgeois', they remain loyal to the bourgeois order, as can be seen in all periods of crisis in which their specific capital and their position in the social order are really threatened (one need think only of the positions adopted by writers, even the most 'progressive', like Zola, when faced with the Commune).

The autonomy of the fields of cultural production, a structural factor which determines the form of struggles internal to that field, varies considerably depending on different periods within the same society, and depending on different societies. And the relative strength, within the field, of the two poles, and the relative importance of the roles allotted to the artist or the intellectual, thereby also vary. With, on the one hand, at one extreme, the function of expert, or technician, offering his or her symbolic services to the dominant (cultural production also has its technicians, like the conveyor-belt producers of bourgeois theatre or the hack producers of pulp literature), and, on the other hand, at the other extreme, the role, won and defended against the dominant, of the free, critical thinker, the intellectual who uses his or her specific capital, won by virtue of autonomy and guaranteed by the very autonomy of the field, to intervene in the field of politics, following the model of Zola or Sartre.

Q. Intellectuals in West Germany define themselves, at least since the '68 movement, as being pretty much on the left; they think of themselves as being in opposition to the dominant class. This is demonstrated by the relatively large impact of the 'critical theory' of the Frankfurt School or of philosophers such as Ernst Bloch. You, however, assign to intellectuals, in relation to your analysis of symbolic struggles, a place within the dominant class. The theatre of these symbolic struggles, as you say, is 'the dominant class itself'; it is thus a question of 'fractional struggles' within a class of which intellectuals form a part. How do you come to this analysis? Shouldn't we raise the question of the possibilities for the literary field or for certain of its sectors of acting on the field of power? Isn't this precisely the claim of a committed, active and realist literature?

A. Cultural producers hold a specific power, the properly symbolic power of showing things and making people believe in them, of revealing, in an explicit, objectified way the more or less confused, vague, unformulated, even unformulable experiences of the natural world and the social world, and of thereby bringing them into existence. They may put this power at the service of the dominant. They may also, in the logic of their struggle within the field of power, put their power at the service of the dominated in the social field taken as a whole: it is well known that 'artists', from Hugo to Mallarmé, from Courbet to Pissarro, have often identified their struggles of dominated-dominant against the 'bourgeois' with the struggles of the dominated as such. But, and this is true also of the so-called 'organic intellectuals' of revolutionary movements, alliances founded on the homology of position (dominant-dominated = dominated) are always more uncertain, more fragile, than solidarities based on an identity of position and, thereby, of condition and habitus.

The fact remains that the specific interests of cultural producers, in so far as they are linked to fields that, by the very logic of their functioning, encourage, favour or impose the transcending of personal interest in the ordinary sense, can lead them to political or intellectual actions that can be called universal.

Q. What change does your theory involve for the science of literature, the interpretation of the literary work, or for the traditional space of the science of literature? You reject both internal hermeneutics and intertextuality, both an essentialist analysis and the 'philosophy of biography', to take up the critical terms you use to describe Sartre's work on Flaubert. When you grasp 'the work of art as an expression of the field in its totality', what sort of consequences does that have?

A. The theory of the field does lead both to a rejection of the direct relating of individual biography to the work of literature (or the relating of the 'social class' of origin to the work) and also to a rejection of the internal analysis of an individual work or even of intertextual analysis. This is because what we have to do is all these things at the same time. I postulate the existence of a pretty rigorous correspondence, a homology, between the space of works considered in their differences, their variations (in the manner of intertextuality), and the space of producers and institutions of production, reviews, publishing houses, etc. We have to note the different positions in the field of production as they may be defined by taking into account the genre being practised, rank in this genre, which can be decided by such factors as places of publication (publisher, review, gallery, etc.) and the signs of recognition or, quite simply, the length of time that has elapsed since they entered the game, but also by more external indicators, such as social and geographical origin, which can be retranslated into positions occupied within a field. To all these different positions correspond the positions adopted in the space of modes of expression, of literary or artistic forms (alexandrine or other metres, rhyme or free verse, sonnet or ballad, etc.), of themes and, of course, of all sorts of more subtle signs that traditional literary analysis detected long ago. In other words, to read a work adequately, in the singularity of its textuality, one has to read it consciously or unconsciously in its intertextuality, that is, across the system of variants by which it is situated within the space of contemporary works; but this diacritical reading is inseparable from a structural apprehension of the relevant author who is defined, in his dispositions and the aesthetic positions he adopts, by the objective relations which define and determine his position in the space of production and which determine or guide the relations of competition that he entertains with other authors and the set of strategies, formal strategies especially, which make of him a 'real' artist or a 'real' writer – in opposition to the 'naive' artist or writer, such as 'le douanier' Rousseau or Brisset, who do not know, properly speaking, what they are doing. This doesn't mean that non-naive artists, whose paradigm, in my eyes, is Duchamp, are totally aware of everything that they are doing, which would amount to making of them cynics or impostors. It is necessary and sufficient for them to be 'with it', for them to be up to date with what has happened and is happening in the field, for them to have a 'historical feel' for the field, for its past and also its future, for its future developments, for all that still remains to be done. All of this is a form of the feel for the game, which excludes cynicism, which even demands that you get caught up in the game, taken up by the game to the point of being able to anticipate its future. But this doesn't at all imply a theory of the game as game (which would be enough to transform the *illusio* as an investment in the game or interest in the game, into an illusion pure and simple) nor even a theory of the game, of the laws according to which it functions and the rational strategies that are necessary to win in it. Non-naivety does not exclude a form of innocence . . . In short, the essentially diacritical nature of the production which occurs within a field means that one can and must read the whole field, both the field in which people adopt certain positions in order to make a stand and the field of positions as such, in every work produced in these conditions. This implies that all the oppositions habitually made between external and internal, hermeneutics and sociology, text and context, are totally fictitious; they are meant to justify sectarian refusals, unconscious prejudices (and in particular the aristocratism of the *lector* who doesn't want to get his hands dirty by studying the sociology of the producers) or, quite simply, the desire for the least expenditure of effort. This is because the method of analysis that I am proposing cannot really be put into operation other than at the cost of an enormous amount of work. It demands that you do everything done by the adepts of each of the methods known (internal reading, biographical analysis, etc.), in general on the level of one single author, and that everything that you also do has to be done in order to really construct the field of works and the field of producers and the system of relations established between these two sets of relations.

Q. What place, in your opinion, is occupied by the subject who produces literature or art? Does the old representation of the writer as a 'creator of the symbolic', as the person who 'names' or who 'sees' in the sense Cassandra sees, that old but still intact and active representation, still seem to you to be important? What use can a writer draw from your theory?

A. The author really is a creator, but in an entirely different sense from that understood by literary or artistic hagiography. Manet, for

148

instance, brings about a real symbolic revolution, in the same way as do certain great religious or political prophets. He profoundly transforms our world-view, that is, the categories of perception and evaluation of the world, the principles of construction of the social world, the definition of what is important and what isn't, of what deserves to be represented and what doesn't. For example, he inaugurates and imposes the representation of the contemporary world, men wearing top hats and carrying umbrellas, the urban landscape, in its ordinary triviality. This is a rejection of all the hierarchies, both intellectual and social, which identify the most noble (worthy as such of being represented) with the most ancient – ancient costume, the plaster casts of painting studios, the obligatory subjects of the Greek or biblical tradition, etc. In this sense, the symbolic revolution, which overturns mental structures and deeply upsets people's minds – which explains the violence of the reactions of bourgeois critics and public – may be called the revolution *par excellence*. The critics, who perceive and denounce the avant-garde painter as a political revolutionary, aren't altogether wrong, even if the symbolic revolution is doomed, most of the time, to remain confined to the symbolic domain. The power of naming, in particular of naming the unnameable, that which is still unnoticed or repressed, is a considerable power. Words, said Sartre, can wreak havoc. This is the case, for instance, when they bring into public and thus official and open existence, when they show or half-show, things which existed only in an implicit, confused, or even repressed state. To represent, to bring to light, is no small task. And one can, in this sense, speak of creation.

149

10

The uses of the 'people'

To throw some light on discussions about the 'people' and the 'popular', one need only bear in mind that the 'people' or the 'popular' ('popular art', 'popular religion', 'popular medicine', etc.) is first of all one of the things at stake in the struggle between intellectuals. The fact of being or feeling authorized to speak about the 'people' or of speaking *for* (in both senses of the word) the 'people' may constitute, in itself, a force in the struggles within different fields, political, religious, artistic, etc. – a force that is all the greater the weaker the relative autonomy of the field under consideration. It is at a maximum in the political field, where one can play on all the ambiguities of the word 'people' ('the populace' or the 'working classes', proletariat or nation, *Volk*), and at a minimum in the literary or artistic field which has gained a high degree of autonomy in which 'popular' success leads to a form of devaluation, even of disqualification, of the producer (Zola's efforts to rehabilitate the 'popular' and overthrow the dominant image in the field are well known). The religious field is situated between the two, but is not entirely immune from the contradiction between internal demands which lead one to seek out that which is rare, distinguished and separate – for instance, a purified and spiritualized religion – and external demands, often described as 'commercial', which impel one to offer the profane clientele which is culturally the poorest a ritualist religion with strong magical connotations (that of the great 'popular' pilgrimages – Lourdes, Lisieux, etc., for example).

A second proposition: the stances adopted towards the 'people' or the 'popular' depend in their form and content on specific interests linked first and foremost to belonging to a cultural field of production and, secondly, to the position occupied within this field. Over and above everything which sets them against one another,

Paper given at the Lausanne colloquium on the sociology and history of art, 4–5 February 1982.

150

specialists agree at least in laying claim to a monopoly of legitimate competence which defines them as such and in reminding people of the frontier which separates professionals from the profane. The professional tends to 'hate the common layman' who negates his professional status by doing without his services: he is quick to denounce all forms of 'spontaneism' (political, religious, philosophical, artistic) that will dispossess him of the monopoly of the legitimate production of goods or services. Those in possession of the legitimate competence are ready to mobilize against everything that might favour popular self-help (magic, 'popular medicine', self-medication, etc.). In this way, the clerics are always inclined to condemn a magical or ritualist superstition and to subject to 'purification' the religious practices which, from the point of view of the religious virtuosi, do not demonstrate the 'disinterest' or, as people say elsewhere, the 'distance' associated with the idea that they form of what an acceptable practice is.

If the negative form of the 'popular', that is, the 'vulgar', is thus defined above all as the set of cultural goods or services which present obstacles to the imposition of the legitimacy by which the professionals aim at producing the market (as much as conquering it) through creating a need for their own products, the positive 'popular' (for instance, 'naive' painting or 'folk' music) is the product of a re-evaluation that certain clerics, most often dominated in the field of specialists (and originally coming from the dominated regions of the social space), perform out of a desire for rehabilitation which is inseparable from the desire for their own ennoblement. For instance, in the thirties, the 'populist school' of Louis Lemonnier, André Thérive or Eugène Dabit (all from a very low social class and educationally deprived) defined itself against the aristocratic and worldly psychological novel (and also against naturalism, which they rebuked for its excesses), just as the 'proletarian school' of Henri Poulaille was to define itself against populism, which it criticized for its petty-bourgeois spirit. Most of the types of discourse which have been or are produced in support of the 'people' come from producers occupying dominated positions in the field of production. And, as Rémy Ponton has demonstrated with regard to regionalist novelists, the more-or-less idealized 'people' is often a refuge against failure or exclusion. One can even observe that the relationship which the producers who come from the 'people' entertain with it tend to vary, even during their lifetime, depending on the fluctuations of their symbolic capital within the field (one could show this in the exemplary case of Léon Cladel).

151

The different representations of the people thus appear as so many transformed expressions (by virtue of the censorships and norms of formalization proper to each field) of a fundamental relation to the people that depends on the position occupied in the field of specialists – and, more broadly, in the social field – as well as the trajectory that has led to that position. Writers who have come from the dominated regions of the social space may, with a smaller chance of success the greater the autonomy of the field under consideration, play on their supposed proximity to the people, in the manner of a Michelet, who tries to convert the stigma into an emblem, by proudly advertising his origins, and who uses 'his' 'people' and his 'feeling for the people' to win a position in the intellectual field. As a recognized intellectual (different, for example, from populists or most regionalist novelists, forced to return to their region and their 'own country' because of failure), he is in a position to advertise with some pride his poor origins, knowing that he can only draw a surplus of merit and scarcity value from them (which obliges him to apologize to his aunts who don't like seeing their family devalued in this way . . .). That being said, his exaltation of the people expresses less 'the people' than the experience of a double break, both with the 'people' (he feels it very early on, as Viallaneix shows), and with the intellectual world.

But it is clearly in the political field that the use of 'people' and the 'popular' is most directly profitable, and the history of struggles within progressive parties or workers' unions bears witness to the symbolic effectiveness of workerism: this strategy permits those who can lay claim to a form of proximity with the dominated to set themselves up as holders of a sort of pre-emptive right over the 'people' and, thereby, of an exclusive mission, at the same time as setting up as a universal norm modes of thought and expression that have been imposed on them by conditions of acquisition that are pretty unfavourable to intellectual refinement; but it is also what allows them to accept or to lay claim to everything that separates them from their competitors at the same time as concealing – first and foremost from themselves – the break with the 'people' that is implied by gaining access to the role of spokesperson.

In this case as in all the others, the relation to one's origins is experienced in too visceral and dramatic a manner for one to be able to describe this strategy as the result of a cynical calculation. In fact, the principle of different ways of situating oneself in relation to the 'people', whether we are talking about populist workerism or the *völkisch* mood of the 'conservative revolutionary' and all forms of the 'popular right', still resides in the logic of the struggle within the field of the specialists, that is, in this case, in that very particular form of anti-intellectualism which is often inspired within first-generation intellectuals by a horror of the artistic life-style (Proudhon, Pareto and many others denounce the 'pornocracy') and a horror of the intellectual game, idealized from a distance, which may go as far as the vengeful hatred expressed by all the Zhdanovite Hussonnets,[1] when this hatred is fed by resentment at the failure of one's intellectual endeavours or by the failure to be integrated into the dominant intellectual group (here one can cite the case of Céline).

It is easy to understand that the prior analysis of the objective relation to the object is particularly imperative for the researcher if he or she wishes to escape from the alternative of class ethnocentrism versus a populism which is its inverted form. Inspired by the need to rehabilitate, populism, which may also take the form of a certain relativism, tends, as one of its effects, to disguise the effects of domination: by striving to show that the 'people' has nothing to envy the 'bourgeois' when it comes to culture and distinction, it forgets that its cosmetic or aesthetic innovations are disqualified in advance as excessive, misplaced or out-of-place, in a game in which the dominant determine at every moment the rule of the game (heads, I win; tails, you lose) by their very existence, measuring innovation by the rule of discretion and simplicity by the norm of refinement.

You will object that one can escape from this hall of mirrors by carrying out direct surveys. And by asking the 'people' to judge, so to speak, the struggles that intellectuals take part in 'about' the people. But is everything commonly designated as 'the people' really 'popular' and is everything which comes out of the mouth of the 'true' 'people' the real truth of the 'people'? At the risk of giving the do-gooders of the 'people's cause' an occasion for affirming their noble feelings by condemning this iconoclastic attack on populist imagery, I would say that nothing is less sure. This can be seen when peasants, in whom the 'conservative revolutionary tradition' has always wanted to see the incarnation of the authentic, come out, in all good faith, with the hackneyed stereotypes of primary school essays or of the ruralist, palaeo- or neo-ecological vulgate which has been transmitted to them and inculcated in them by the work of

---

1 Hussonnet is a character in Flaubert's *L'Éducation sentimentale* who, after a radical youth, becomes one of the officials responsible for the censorship of the theatre.

several generations of cultural intermediaries, schoolteachers, priests, educators, JACs,[2] etc., and that, if you trace their genealogy, go back to that very special category of authors that haunt primary school manuals, regionalist novelists and minor poets, often led towards the celebration of the 'people' and of 'popular' virtues by their incapacity (often imputable to 'popular' or petty-bourgeois origins) to triumph in the major genres. And the same is true of working-class discourse, even if, via the union member or the party school, it owes more to Marx or to Zola than to Jean Aicard, Ernest Perrochon, Jean Richepin or François Coppée. To understand this discourse, which populist recordings (consecrated by the triumph of tape-recorder literature and the vogue for life stories) constitute as the most important subject-matter, one must grasp anew the whole system of relations of which it is the product, the whole set of social conditions of production of the producers of discourse (in particular, primary school) and of the discourse itself, thus the whole field of production of the discourse on the 'people', especially the dominated regions of the literary field and the political field. And you thus find yourself back where you started, in any case far from the 'people' as the populist imagination conceives of it.

In short, 'popular culture' resembles Lewis Carroll's 'snark', in that the very categories with which one pursues it in order to conceptualize it, and the questions one asks of it, are inadequate. Rather than speaking in general about 'popular culture', I will take the example of what is called 'popular language'. Those who rebel against the effects of domination that are exercised through the use of the legitimate language often arrive at a sort of inversion of the relation of symbolic force and think they are doing the right thing by consecrating as such the dominated language, for instance in its most autonomous form, namely slang. This reversal from *for* to *against*, which can also be observed, when it comes to culture, when people talk about 'popular culture', is still an effect of domination. It is indeed paradoxical to define the dominated language by relation to the dominant language which itself can be defined only by relation to the dominated language. Indeed, there is no other definition of the legitimate language other than that it is a refusal of the dominated language, with which it institutes a relation which is that of culture to nature: it is no chance that people talk about 'crude' language, 'langue verte' (literally 'green language') or 'underworld slang'.

---

2 Jeunesse agricole catholique: a social movement (literally: Catholic Agricultural Youth).

154

What is called 'popular language' are modes of speaking which, from the point of view of the dominant language, appear as natural, savage, barbarous, vulgar. And those who, out of a need for rehabilitation, talk about popular language or culture are victims of the logic which leads stigmatized groups to claim the stigma as a sign of their identity.

As a distinguished form – even in the eyes of certain of the dominant – of the 'vulgar' language, slang is the product of a quest for a distinction that is none the less dominated, and condemned by that fact to produce paradoxical effects, which cannot be understood when one tries to enclose them within the alternative of resistance or submission which determines ordinary thinking about 'popular language'. When the dominated quest for distinction leads the dominated to affirm what distinguishes them, that is, that in the name of which they are dominated and constituted as vulgar, do we have to talk of resistance? In other words, if, in order to resist, I have no other resource than to lay claim to that in the name of which I am dominated, is this resistance? Second question: when, on the other hand, the dominated work at destroying what marks them out as 'vulgar' and at appropriating that in relation to which they appear as vulgar (for instance, in France, the Parisian accent), is this submission? I think this is an insoluble contradiction: this contradiction, which is inscribed into the very logic of symbolic domination, is something those who talk about 'popular culture' won't admit. Resistance may be alienating and submission may be liberating. Such is the paradox of the dominated, and there is no way out of it. In fact, a proper treatment would be even more complicated, but I think this is enough to confuse somewhat the simple categories, especially the opposition between resistance and submission, with which these questions are usually thought. Resistance occurs on terrains altogether different from that of culture in the strict sense of the word – where it is never the possession of the most destitute, witness all the forms of 'counter-culture' that, as I could show, always presuppose a certain cultural capital. And it takes the most unexpected forms, to the point of remaining more or less invisible to the cultivated eye.

11

Programme for a sociology of sport

A number of the obstacles to a scientific sociology of sport stem from the fact that the sociologists of sport are, so to speak, doubly dominated, both in the universe of sociologists and in the universe of sport. As it would take too long to develop this somewhat brutally phrased argument, I will proceed, in the manner of the prophets, by a parable. Yesterday evening, in a discussion with one of my American sociologist friends, Aaron Cicourel, I learned that the great black athletes who, in the United States, are often sponsored by great universities, such as Stanford, live in a sort of gilded ghetto, for the reason that people on the right don't find it easy to talk to blacks and people on the left don't find it easy to talk to sportspeople. If you think about it, by developing this paradigm, one could perhaps find here the basis of the particular difficulties encountered by the sociology of sport: it is disdained by sociologists, and despised by sportspeople. The logic of the social division of labour tends to reproduce itself in the division of scientific labour. One thus has, on the one side, people who know sport very well in the practical sense but can't talk about it and, on the other, people who don't know sport at all well on the practical level and who could talk about it but disdain to do so, or do so badly. . . .

In order that a sociology of sport can be constituted, one must first of all note that it is impossible to analyse a particular sport independently of the set of sporting practices; one has to imagine the space of sporting practices as a system from which every element derives its distinctive value. In other words, in order to understand a

Paper presented to the study group 'Physical life and games', CEMEA, in November 1980 and opening lecture to the Eighth Symposium of the ICSS, 'Sport, social classes and sub-culture', Paris, July 1983.

sport, whichever one it may be, one has to recognize the position it occupies in the space of sports. This space may be constructed on the base of indicators such as, on the one hand, the distribution of players according to their position in social space, the distribution of the different federations according to their number of members, their wealth, the social characteristics of their leaders, etc., or, on the other, the type of relation to the body that it favours or requires, whether it implies direct contact, hand-to-hand, such as wrestling or rugby, or whether on the contrary it excludes all contact, like golf, or authorizes it only by the interposing of a ball, like tennis, or the intermediary of instruments, like fencing. This space of sports has first of all to be related to the social space that is expressed in it. This is in order to avoid the errors that are linked to the direct relating of a sport and a group as suggested by ordinary intuition. Indeed, one can immediately sense the privileged relation that is today established between wrestling and members of the working classes or aikido and the new petty bourgeoisie. Indeed, these are things that can be understood too hastily. The sociologist's work consists in establishing the socially pertinent properties that mean that a sport has an affinity with the interests, tastes and preferences of a determinate social category. Thus, as Jean-Paul Clément clearly shows, in the case of wrestling, for instance, the importance of close combat, emphasized by the nudity of the combatants, leads to a rough and direct bodily contact, whereas in aikido the contact is ephemeral and distanced, and fighting on the ground is non-existent. If the sense of the opposition between wrestling and aikido can be understood so easily, this is because the opposition between 'down to earth', 'virile', 'hand-to-hand', 'direct', etc., and 'aerial', 'light', 'distanced', 'gracious', transcends the terrain of sport and the antagonism between two practices of combat. In short, the determining element of the system of preferences is here the relation to the body, to the way the body is put into action, which is associated with a social position and an innate experience of the physical and social world. This relation to the body is part and parcel of one's whole relation to the world: the most distinctive practices are those which ensure the most distanced relation to the adversary; they are also the most aestheticized, in so far as violence is more euphemized in them, and form and formalities win out over force and function. Social distance can be easily retranslated into the logic of sport: golf everywhere establishes distance from non-players, through the reserved and harmoniously arranged space in which this sporting activity takes place, and distance from adversaries by the very logic

157

of confrontation which excludes all direct contact, even by the intermediary of a ball.

But this isn't enough and may even lead to a realist and substantialist vision both of each of the sports and of the set of corresponding players and of the relation between the two: we must beware of establishing a direct relation, as I have just done, between a sport and a social position, between wrestling or football and workers, or between judo and the lower middle classes – if only because it would be easy to verify that workers are far from being the most numerous football players. In fact, the correspondence, which is a real homology, is established between the space of sporting practices, or, more precisely, the space of the different finely analysed modalities of the practice of different sports, and the space of social positions. It is in the relation between these two spaces that the pertinent properties of every sporting practice are defined. And the very changes in practices can be understood only on the basis of this logic, in so far as one of the factors which determine them is the desire to maintain in practice the gaps which exist between different positions. The history of sporting practices must be a structural history, taking into account the systematic transformations entailed for instance by the appearance of a new sport (Californian sports) or the spread of an existing sport, such as tennis. In parenthesis: one of the difficulties of the analysis of sporting practices resides in the fact that the nominal unity (tennis, skiing, football) registered by statistics (including the best and most recent of them) masks a dispersal, greater or less depending on the sports, of the ways of playing them, and this dispersal increases when the increase in number of players (which may be the effect of a mere intensification of the practice of categories that already play) is accompanied by a social diversification of those who play. This is the case with tennis, whose nominal unity conceals the fact that, under the same name, there coexist ways of playing that are as different as, in order, off-piste skiing, cross-country skiing and ordinary skiing: the tennis played in small municipal clubs, in jeans and Adidas shoes on hard courts, doesn't have a great deal in common with tennis in whites and pleated skirts which was the rule some twenty years ago and which is kept up in select clubs (a whole universe of differences could be found in the style of players, their relation to competition, training, etc.).

In short, the priority of priorities is the construction of the structure of the space of sporting practices whose effects will be recorded by monographs devoted to particular sports. If I don't know that the perturbations of Uranus are determined by Neptune, I will think I am grasping what happens in Uranus whereas in reality I will be grasping the effects of Neptune. The object of history is the history of these transformations of structure which can be understood only on the basis of a knowledge of what the structure at a certain moment was (which means that the opposition between structure and change, between static and dynamic, is altogether fictitious and one can understand change only on the basis of a knowledge of structure). That's my first point.

My second point is that this space of sports is not a universe closed in on itself. It is inserted into a universe of practices and consumptions themselves structured and constituted as a system. We are altogether justified in treating sporting practices as a relatively autonomous space, but you shouldn't forget that this space is the locus of forces which do not apply only to it. I merely mean that you can't study the 'consumption' of sport, if you will grant me the use of the term, independently of the consumption of food or of the consumption of leisure in general. Sporting practices which are apt to be recorded by statistical inquiry may be described as the result of the relation between a supply and a demand or, more precisely, between the space of products in supply at a given moment and the space of dispositions (associated with the position occupied in the social space and capable of being expressed in the form of other consumptions in relation to another space of supply).

When you bear in mind the structural logic within which each of the practices is defined, what must concrete scientific practice consist in? Does the researcher's work consist merely in drawing this space, relying for instance on the structure of the distribution of wrestlers, boxers, rugby players, etc., by gender, age, or profession? In fact, this structural framework may, for a certain time, remain as a rough outline, and can be measured by the general statistics which are available, bearing in mind the limits of these statistics and the codes according to which they are constructed.

That is a very general methodological principle: rather than remaining content with knowing really well a small sector of reality which it is more or less impossible – the question has never been formulated – to properly situate in the space from which it was detached, or to say what its functioning may owe to that position, one must – at the risk of frustrating positivist expectations that everything, be it said in passing, seems to justify ('it is better to make a modest and precise contribution than to build up big superficial constructions') – one must, then, in the manner of academic architects who used to present a charcoal sketch of the building as a whole within which one could find the individual part worked out in detail, endeavour to construct a summary description of the whole of the space considered.

We at least know that this provisional framework, however imperfect it may be, has to be filled out, and that even the empirical work it orientates will contribute to doing so. The fact remains that these works are radically different, even in their intention, from what they would have been in the absence of this frame which is the precondition of an adequate construction of the objects of a particular piece of empirical research. This theoretical model (here, the idea of the space of sports; elsewhere, the notion of the field of power), even if it remains for the most part empty, even if what it provides us with are above all warnings and programmatic guidelines, means that I will choose my subjects in a different way and that I will be able to maximize what I get out of monographs: if, for example, being able to study only three sports, I bear in mind the space of sports, and hypotheses concerning the axes around which this space is constructed, I will be able to choose to maximize the return on my scientific investments by choosing three points that are far from each other in space. Or else I will be able, as for instance Jean-Paul Clément did, to choose a sub-space within this space, the sub-space of combat sports, and study, on this level, the effect of structure by taking wrestling, judo and aikido as three points in the same sub-space of forces. I will be able, without running the risk of getting lost in details, to examine them in close-up (something which strikes me as the very precondition of scientific work), to film the fights, measure chronometrically how much time people spend on the ground in wrestling, judo and aikido; in short, I will be able to measure everything that can be measured, but on the basis of a construction that determines the choice of objects and of pertinent characteristics. Since my time is limited, I am aware of the somewhat abrupt, peremptory and perhaps apparently contradictory side of what I have just been saying. None the less, I believe that I have given enough details of what can be a method whose aim is to set up a dialectic between the general and the particular, which alone may enable one to reconcile the general and synoptic view demanded by the construction of the overall structure with the close-up, finely-detailed view. The antagonism between the large, macrosociological view and the microscopic view afforded by microsociology, or between the construction of objective structures and the description of the subjective representations entertained by the agents, and of their practical constructions, disappears, as do all the oppositions which take the form of an 'epistemological couple' (between theory and empirical work, etc.), as soon as one has succeeded – which, it strikes me, is the art *part excellence* of the researcher – in investing a large-scale theoretical problematic within an empirical object, both well-constructed with reference to the overall space in which it is situated, and capable of being mastered by the means available, that is, if necessary, by an isolated researcher, reduced to his or her individual labour force.

But I must correct the appearance of objectivist realism that my mention of a 'structural framework', conceived as pre-existing empirical analysis, may give. I am always saying that structures are nothing other than the objectified product of historical struggles in the form in which this product can be grasped at a given moment. And the universe of sporting practices that statistical surveys photograph at a certain moment is merely the result of a relation between a supply, produced by the entire preceding history, that is, a set of 'models' of practices (rules, equipment, specialized institutions, etc.), and a demand that is inscribed within dispositions. The supply itself, in the form in which it presents itself, at a given moment, in the form of a set of sports capable of being practised (or watched) is already the product of a long series of relations between models of practice and dispositions to practice. For example, the programme of bodily practices designated by the word rugby is not the same – even though, in its formal, technical definition, it has remained identical, apart from a few rule changes – in the 1930s, in 1950 and in 1980. It is marked, in its objective nature and in the ways in which it is represented, by the appropriations to which it has been subjected and by specific factors (for instance 'violence') which it has assumed in the concrete 'realization' that agents endowed with socially constituted dispositions of a particular form have made of it (for instance, in the thirties, students of the PUC and the SBUC or at Oxford and Cambridge and, in the eighties, Welsh miners and farmers, small shopkeepers or lower-middle-class people from Romans, Toulon or Béziers). This effect of social appropriation means that, at every moment, each of the 'realities' offered under the name of a sport is marked, in its objective nature, by a set of properties that are not inscribed within the purely technical definition, or may even be excluded from it, and which guide practices and choices (*inter alia* by giving an objective basis to judgements of the type 'that's petty-bourgeois', or 'intellectual', etc.).

Thus, the differential distribution of sporting practices results from the relating of two homologous spaces, a space of possible practices, the supply, and a space of dispositions to practice, the demand: on the supply side, you have a space of sports understood as programmes of sporting practices, which are characterized, firstly, by their intrinsic, technical properties (that is, especially, the possibilities and above all the impossibilities for the expression of different bodily dispositions which they provide) and, secondly, by their relational, structural properties, as they are defined with regard to the set of other programmes of sporting practices that are simultaneously offered, but which do not find their full realization at a given moment except by receiving the properties of appropriation conferred on them, both in reality and in representation, by their dominant association, via their modal participants, with a position in the social space; on the other hand, on the demand side, a space of dispositions to play a sport which, as an element of the system of dispositions (of the habitus) are relationally, structurally characterized as well as the positions to which they correspond, and which are defined in the particularity of their specification at a given moment by the present state of supply (which contributes to producing need by presenting it with the effective possibility of its realization) and also by the realization of the supply in its previous state. That is, I believe, a very general model which determines the most different practices of consumption. Thus we have seen Vivaldi receive, over a period of twenty years, completely opposite social meanings, and pass from being a musicological 'rediscovery' to being background music for supermarkets.

Even if it is certain that a sport, a musical work or a philosophical text define, by virtue of their intrinsic properties, the limits of the social usages which can be made of them, they lead to a diversity of uses and are marked at every moment by the dominant use made of them. A philosophical author, Spinoza or Kant for instance, in terms of the truths which are grasped by our perception, can never be reduced to the intrinsic truth of his work and, in terms of its social truths, that work includes the major readings which are made of it, by the Kantians and Spinozists of the time, they themselves being defined by their objective or subjective relation to the Kantians and Spinozists of the preceding period and to their readings, but also to the promoters or defenders of other philosophies. It is to this indivisible complex constituted by the Kant appropriated by Kantians who project on to Kant, and not only by the way they read him, their own social properties, that Heidegger is reacting when he contrasts a metaphysical and quasi-existentialist Kant (with, for instance, the theme of finitude) to the cosmopolitan, universalist, rationalist, progressive Kant of the neo-Kantians.

You must be asking yourselves what I am trying to get at. In fact, just as the social meaning of a work of philosophy may thus be reversed (and most works, Descartes, Kant, or even Marx, do not cease to change meaning, each generation of commentators over-throwing the reading of the preceding generation), in the same way, a sporting practice which, in its technical, 'intrinsic' definition, always presents a great elasticity, thus offering a great availability for usages that are altogether different and even opposed, may also change meaning. More exactly, the dominant meaning, that is, the social meaning attached to it by its dominant social users (numerically or socially speaking) may change: indeed, it is frequent that at one and the same time – and this is true of a philosophical work too – a sport may be given two very different meanings, and the objectified programme of sporting practice designated by a term such as track running or swimming, or even tennis, rugby, wrestling or judo, will be an object of conflict – by virtue of its objective polysemia, its partial indeterminacy, which makes it available for different uses – between people who disagree over its true use, its proper use, the right way of practising the practice proposed by the objectified programme of practice under consideration (or, in the case of a philosophical or musical work, by the objectified programme of reading or performance). A sport, at a given moment, is rather like a musical work: it is both the musical score (the rules of the game, etc.), and also the various competing interpretations (and a whole set of sedimented interpretations from the past); and each new interpreter is confronted by this, more unconsciously than consciously, when he proposes 'his' interpretation. We would need to analyse in accordance with this logic the 'returns' (to Kant, to period instruments, to French boxing, etc.).

I said that the dominant meaning may change: in fact, especially because it is defined in opposition to this dominant meaning, a new type of sporting practice can be constructed with elements of the dominant programme of sporting practice which had been left in a virtual, implicit or repressed state (for instance, all the violence which was excluded from a sport by the demand for 'fair play'). The principle of these reversals, which the logic of distinction alone cannot explain, resides, no doubt, in the reaction of new entrants, and the socially constituted dispositions they import into the field, to the socially marked complex constituted by a sport, or by a work of philosophy, as an objectified programme of practice but one which is socially realized, incarnated in socially marked agents, thus marked by the social characteristics of those agents, by the effect of appropriation. While for the synchronic vision, one or other of these programmes – that designated by the name of a sport (wrestling, horse-riding, tennis) or the proper name of a philosopher or composer or the name of a genre, opera, operetta, light comedy, or even a style, realism, symbolism, etc. – seems directly linked to the dispositions incorporated by the occupants of a certain social position (this is, for instance, the link between wrestling or rugby and the dominated), a diachronic vision may lead to a different representation, as if the same object being supplied could be appropriated by agents endowed with very diverse dispositions, in short, as if absolutely anyone could appropriate any programme and as if any programme could be appropriated by absolutely anyone. (This healthy 'relativism' has at least the virtue of warning us away from the tendency – a recurrent one in art history – to establish a direct link between social positions and aesthetic positions, between 're-alism', for instance, and the dominated, forgetting that the same dispositions will be able, with reference to different spaces of supply, to express themselves in different positions.)

In fact, semantic elasticity is never infinite (one need only think of golf and wrestling) and above all, at any moment, choices are not distributed at random between the different possibilities on offer, even if, when the space of possibilities is very restricted (for instance, young Marx versus old Marx), the relation between dispositions and positions adopted is very obscure because of the fact that the dispositions which, in more open, less codified universes, can directly project their structure of demands, must in this case be limited to negative choices or second-bests. One can say, I believe, that the dispositions associated with different positions in the social space, and in particular the structurally opposed dispositions linked to opposed positions in this space, always find a means of expressing themselves, but, sometimes in the unrecognizable form of specific oppositions which are tiny and imperceptible if you do not have adequate categories of perception which organize a given field at a given moment. It is not forbidden to think that the same dispositions which led Heidegger towards a 'revolutionary conservative' form of thought could, in reference to another space of philosophical supply, have led him to the young Marx; or even that the same person (but he wouldn't have been the same person) who today finds in aikido a way of escaping from judo, in all its objectively cramped, competitive, petty-bourgeois aspects – I am here talking about judo in its socially appropriated form, of course – could have sought the same things, thirty years ago, in judo itself.

I would like to have gone on to mention, even superficially, the whole programme of research involved in the idea that there progressively develops a field of professional production of sports goods and services (among which, for instance, are the sports shows), within which there develop specific interests, linked to competition, as well as specific power relations, etc. I will content myself with mentioning one consequence among others of the constitution of this relatively autonomous field, namely the continual widening of the gap between professionals and amateurs, which goes together with the development of a sports show totally separate from ordinary sport. It is remarkable that one can observe a similar process in other domains, notably that of dance. In the two cases, the progressive constitution of a relatively autonomous field reserved for professionals is accompanied by a dispossession of the profane, who are little by little reduced to the role of spectators: in opposition to village dancing, often associated with ritual functions, courtly dance, which becomes a spectacle, presupposes specific forms of knowledge (one has to know the beat and the steps), and thus requires dancing masters inclined to emphasize technical virtuosity and to perform a work of exegesis and codification; from the nineteenth century onward there appear professional dancers, who appear in the salons in front of people who themselves can dance and can appreciate dancing with a connoisseur's eye; then, finally, you have a total break between star dancers and spectators who do not practise dance and who are reduced to passive understanding. From then on, the evolution of professional practice depends more and more on the internal logic of the field of professionals, non-professionals being relegated to the rank of a public that is less and less capable of that understanding which comes through practice. As far as sport is concerned, we are often, in the best cases, still in the stage of the nineteenth-century dance, with professionals who appear in front of amateurs who still dance or used to dance; but the spread of sports shows encouraged by television creates more and more spectators who lack all practical competence and pay attention only to the extrinsic aspects of practice, such as the result, the victory. And this entails certain effects, via the intermediary of the reward (financial or other) given by the public, in the very way the field of professionals functions (such as the quest for victory at any price and with it, *inter alia*, the rise of violence).

I will end here because the time given me has practically run out. I will sketch out my last point in a few brief seconds. I started off by referring to effects within the scientific field of the division of labour between theorists and practitioners. I think that sport is, with dance, one of the terrains in which is posed with the maximum acuteness the problem of the relations between theory and practice, and also between language and the body. Certain physical-education teachers have tried to analyse what it is, for example, for a trainer or a music teacher to command a body. How can you make someone understand, that is, make someone's body understand, how he can correct the way he moves? The problems raised by the teaching of a bodily practice seem to me to involve a set of theoretical questions of the greatest importance, in so far as the social sciences endeavour to theorize the behaviour that occurs, in the greatest degree, outside the field of conscious awareness, that is learnt by a silent and practical communication, from body to body one might say. And sporting pedagogy is perhaps the terrain *par excellence* in which the problem can be raised that is raised ordinarily on the terrain of politics: the problem of coming to conscious awareness. There is a way of understanding which is altogether particular, and often forgotten in theories of intelligence: that which consists of understanding with one's body. There are heaps of things that we understand only with our bodies, outside conscious awareness, without being able to put our understanding into words. The silence of sportspeople which I was talking about at the beginning stems partly from the fact that, when you are not a professional analyst, there are certain things you can't say, and sporting practices are practices in which understanding is bodily. Very often, all you can do is say: 'Look, do what I'm doing.' It has often been noticed that books written by very great dancers transmitted practically nothing of what constituted the 'genius' of their authors. And Edwin Denby, thinking of Théophile Gautier or Mallarmé, used to say that the most pertinent remarks on dance come less from dancers or even critics than from enlightened amateurs. This is easy to understand if you know that dance is the only one of the scientific arts whose transmission – from dancers to public, but also from master to disciple – is entirely oral and visual or, at least, mimetic. This is because of the absence of any objectification in an adequate form of writing (the absence of any equivalent to the musical score, which allows one to distinguish clearly between score and performance, leads to the identifying of the work with the performance, the dance with the dancer). One could, from this point of view, try to study what have been the effects, in dance as in sport, of the introduction of the video recorder. One of the questions raised is certainly that of knowing whether one has to go through the medium of language in order to make the body understand certain things, whether, when you talk to the body in words, it is the words which are theoretically, scientifically, correct which are best able to make the body understand, or whether, sometimes, words which have nothing to do with an adequate description of what one wants to communicate are not better understood by the body. Thinking about this understanding of the body, one could perhaps contribute to a theory of belief. You may think that I am jumping to conclusions in seven-league boots. But I think there is a link between the body and what in French we call 'esprit de corps' ('corporate loyalty', or 'team spirit'). If most organizations – the Church, the army, political parties, industrial concerns, etc. – give such a big place to bodily disciplines, this is to a great extent because obedience is belief and belief is what the body grants even when the mind says no (one could, on the basis of this logic, reflect on the notion of discipline). It is perhaps by thinking about what is most specific about sport, that is, the regulated manipulation of the body, about the fact that sport, like all disciplines in all total or totalitarian institutions, convents, prisons, asylums, political parties, etc., is a way of obtaining from the body an adhesion that the mind might refuse, that one could reach a better understanding of the usage made by most authoritarian regimes of sport. Bodily discipline is the instrument *par excellence* of every kind of 'domestication': it is well known how the pedagogy of the Jesuits made use of dancing. One would have to analyse the dialectical relation which unites bodily postures and the corresponding feelings: adopting certain positions or certain postures is, as has been known since Pascal, a way of inducing or reinforcing the feelings they express. The gesture, according to the paradox of the actor or the dancer, reinforces the feeling which reinforces the gesture. Thus is explained the place that all totalitarian regimes give to collective bodily practices which, by symbolizing the social, contribute to somatizing it and which, by the bodily and collective *mimesis* of social orchestration, aim at reinforcing this orchestration. *The Soldier's Tale* reminds us of the old popular tradition: making someone dance means possessing them. 'Spiritual exercises' are bodily exercises and numerous modern forms of training are a form of secular ascesis.

12

Opinion polls: a 'science' without a scientist

To begin with, a paradox: it is remarkable that the same people who view with suspicion the social sciences, and, above all, sociology, greet with open arms opinion polls which are an often rudimentary form of sociology (for reasons which stem less from the quality of the people entrusted with conceiving them, carrying them out and analysing them, than with the constraints of the contract and the pressures of time).

Polling corresponds to the common idea of science: it gives to the questions which 'everyone asks themselves' (everyone or, at least, that small section of the populace that can finance opinion polls, newspaper or weekly review editors, politicians and businessmen) rapid, simple and quantitative answers, in appearance easy to understand and to comment on. However, in these affairs even more than elsewhere, simple truths cannot do justice to complex problems, and the real problems of editorial writers and political commentators are often false problems that scientific analysis must destroy in order to construct its object. The commercial research institutions do not have the means, or even, to begin with, the time, to carry out this questioning of first questions, and even if they did, they doubtless have no interest in so doing, given the present state of the market and the information available to those who commission polls. That is why they most often content themselves with translating into aptly phrased questions the problems the client may ask.

But, you will say, doesn't a practice which formulates questions in the terms in which the customer himself poses them, have the perfect form of that 'neutral' science called for by positivist 'common sense'? (In parenthesis I would like to add a note of qualification: it happens

Text published in *Pouvoirs*, 33 (1985).

that the first questions, when they are inspired by practical forms of knowledge and practical preoccupations, such as those introduced by market surveys, provide us, on condition that they are reinterpreted in virtue of a theoretical problematic, with information of the highest value, often superior to that given us by the more pretentious questionings of semi-scientists.) The 'science without a scientist' of the positivist ideal realizes, in the relations between dominant and dominated within a field of power, the equivalent of what is, in another context, the dream of a 'bourgeoisie without a proletariat'. The success of all the metaphors which lead one to conceive of surveys as a pure mechanical recording, a 'barometer', 'photograph' or 'X-ray', and the contracts that political leaders of every complexion, ignoring the state-financed research institutes, continue to place with private research enterprises testify to this deep-seated expectation of a made-to-measure science, a science without those hypotheses that are easily seen as presuppositions or even prejudices, and those theories which, as everyone knows, do not have a good press.

What is at stake, as can be seen, is the existence of a science of the social world capable of affirming its autonomy against all forms of power: the history of the visual arts shows that artists have had to struggle for centuries to free themselves from creating to order, and to impose their own intentions, those that were defined by competition within the artists' world, and above all by manner, execution and form, in short, by everything that properly depended on the artist, and only secondly by the choice of the object itself. And the same goes for scientists who investigate the physical and biological world. The conquest of autonomy is clearly much more difficult, and thus slower, in the case of the sciences of the social world, which have to liberate each of their problems from the pressures of the contract and from the seductions of demand: these are never so insidious as when they operate, as is the case today, in the opinion poll business, via the impersonal mechanisms of a social functioning which leaves them with no time to correct themselves, recapitulate what has been learnt, strengthen their techniques and methods, or redefine problems, by suspending people's instinctive reaction, which is to accept them as they are, because they find an immediate complicity in vague and confused questions about everyday practice.

And then, why should those who, in order to make sure their business runs smoothly, have to sell products that are rapidly parcelled and skilfully fitted to the taste of those who placed the order, be more royalist than the real king, the consumer? And how could they do it? They have their well-tested samples, their experienced teams of surveyors, their tried and trusted programmes of analysis. They are left, in each case, with the mere task of finding out what the customer wants to know, that is, what he wants to see being sought, or even better, found. Supposing that they can find what they think the truth to be, would they be interested in telling it to the politician interested in getting re-elected, to the industrial manager whose business is in trouble, the newspaper editor more avid for sensation than information, if they were at all interested in keeping their clientele? And this happens as soon as they have to reckon with the competition of the new merchants of illusion who today are all the rage with commercial directors and those in charge of public relations: reviving the ancestral art of the fortune-tellers, palmists and other clairvoyants, those sellers of scientifically unlabelled designer products who translate into a vaguely psychological language, and one always very close to ordinary intuition ('high livers', 'pioneers', 'go-getters' or 'adventurers' . . .), very mysteriously established 'life-styles', and are past masters in the art of giving their customers accommodating answers tricked out with all the magic of a methodology and terminology that sound highly scientific. How and why should they work at posing and imposing problems that would only disappoint or shock, when they need only let themselves follow the inclinations of spontaneous sociology – which the scientific community constantly comes up against in its very midst – to satisfy their customers by producing answers to problems that are posed only by those who ask the pollsters to pose them, and which, very frequently, did not pose themselves to those polled before they were imposed on them? It is clear that they have no interest in telling their customers that their questions are without interest or, worse, without object. And they would need to have a great deal of virtue or faith in science to refuse to conduct a survey into 'the image of Arab countries', knowing that a less scrupulous competitor will happily take over the task, even when they presume that this survey will merely register – without any great accuracy – people's dispositions towards immigrants. In this case, the survey will measure at least one thing, but not what people think they are measuring; in other cases, it will measure nothing but the effect exercised by the measuring instrument: this is the case every time the pollster imposes on those polled a problematic which isn't theirs – which will not prevent them from answering it all the same, out of submission, indifference or pretension, thus eliminating the only interesting problem, the question of the economic and cultural determinants of the capacity for broaching the problem as such, a capacity which, in the realm of politics, defines one of the fundamental dimensions of specific competence.

One would need to draw up a list (not with any naively polemical intention, but in order to work at frustrating and annulling them) of the, from the scientific point of view, altogether disastrous effects that market constraints have on the practice of conducting opinion polls. I will merely mention, in order to try and exorcise it, the memory of that minister of education who, at the beginning of the eighties, asked three different polling firms to analyse the attitudes of teachers from three orders of education (primary, secondary, higher), thus obtaining three perfectly incommensurable surveys, both in the procedures of sampling and in the questions asked, and thus eliminating everything which only a comparative approach could have established with regard to each of the populations under consideration. And, so that the full horror of the thing can be measured, I will add that this survey cost more or less ten times the annual budget of a state-maintained university laboratory which, if it had only been consulted, would have been able to avoid these mistakes and invest in the development of the questionnaire and the programme of analysis a capital of theoretical and empirical experi-ence which private bureaux of research clearly cannot mobilize, given the diversity of the domains to which they are applied, and the conditions of urgency in which they work, which can only have the effect of rendering practically impossible any pooling of resources.

The effects that the market's 'invisible hand' have both on the analysis and on the recording of data (it is well known, for example, that it is easier to get clients to finance questions which are in their opinion of direct interest to them than questions meant to provide information indispensable for the explanation of the answers) go together with an absence of the reserve of personnel freed from the urgencies of immediate demand and equipped with a common capital of theoretical and technical resources which could ensure the pooling of experience (if only for the methodical archiving of previous surveys) so as to favour a descriptive usage of polling, which is, indeed, what the commissioners unconsciously want. This does not prevent the most intrepid of those whom I call, with Plato, the 'doxosophists', from proposing explanations which go far beyond the limits incorporated in the system of explanatory factors, always few in number and often poorly measured, that they have at their disposal. Everyone can see them, at electoral evenings, improvising off-the-cuff explanations and interpretations to which only the

171

all-too-evident bad faith of politicians can give a sense of depth and objectivity. I will merely give as an example the explanations that have been put forward for the decline of the French Communist Party and which gave practically no place to structural changes as important as the generalizing of access to secondary education and the structural downclassing of educational qualifications which, it is clear, have exercised definite effects on people's dispositions towards politics.

I had planned to end at this point my analysis of the scientific limits inherent in the functioning of institutes of commercial research, when I read the text by Alain Lancelot which closes, crowns and concludes the 1984 SOFRES anthology: in this 'reply' to a sort of vague and general amalgam of objections addressed to polls, I think I can detect the intention of replying to me, but I do not recognize my own objections, which have to do with questions of science – hence, no doubt, the misunderstanding – and not, as is commonly believed, with questions of politics (even though false science has real political effects). So I will take one last example, which I had resolved to omit, because it reveals, in a somewhat too brutal and cruel way, the social limits of understanding of the doxosophists. It is known that 'don't-knows' are the trauma, cross and misery of polling institutes which endeavour by all means at their disposal to reduce them, minimize them, even to conceal them. Thus doomed to remain unnoticed by the pollster, who represses them, makes them merely part of the machinery of the poll and the advice that has to be given to pollsters, these wretched 'don't-knows' crop up again in the writings of the 'politologist' in the shape of the problem of 'abstention', that flaw of democracy, or of 'apathy', a relapse into indifference and indifferentiation (the stagnant pool of 'floating voters'). It is easy to understand how the politological pollster who sees in every criticism of polling, identified with universal suffrage (and indeed, the analogy isn't a false one), a symbolic attack on democracy, cannot suspect the decisive problem posed for science, politics and any political science worthy of the name by the existence of 'don't-know' responses which vary with gender (women 'abstain' more frequently), with position in the social space (people abstain more the more they are economically and culturally deprived) and also with the nature of the questions asked (factors inclining you to 'abstention' are all the more active the more the questions asked are more openly 'political', that is, closer in letter and spirit to the problems which ordinary doxosophists, pollsters, politologists, journalists and politicians ask themselves). To bring to light these simple truths which, however, are hidden beneath the evident facts of the daily routine of the reader of dailies ('The abstention rate reached 30 per cent'), it was necessary to give a positive value to this unfortunate feature of the poll and of democracy, this lack, this gap, this void (think of those calculations of percentages labelled ' "don't-knows" excluded') and, by one of those re-evaluations which define the way science moves to distance itself from mere common sense, discover that in every opinion poll, the most important information resides in the number of 'don't-knows', which is a measure of the probability of producing a reply characteristic of a certain category: to such a degree that the distribution of answers, of yes and no, of for and against, which defines a certain category, men or women, rich or poor, young or old, workers or bosses, has no meaning except a second, secondary and derived one, in the form of a *conditional probability* which is valid only by reference to the primary, original probability of producing a reply. This probability attached to a statistical unit defines the competence, in the quasi-juridical sense of the term, socially granted to the agents concerned. Science does not have the task of celebrating or deploring the fact of the unequal distribution of political competence as it is socially defined at any given moment; science must analyse the economic and social conditions which determine it and the effects it produces, in a political life based on the ignorance (active or passive) of this inequality.

I don't want to place undue emphasis on my own ideas, but to make myself understood: the discovery, in the true sense of the term, of something so evident that, as they say, it was 'staring us in the face' was itself no more than a point of departure. It was not enough to discover that the propensity to abstain or express an opinion instead of delegating it, tacitly, to representatives, Church, political party or trade union, or, better, to plenipotentiaries endowed with the *plena potentia agendi*, with full powers of speaking and acting in place and on behalf of those who have supposedly granted them a mandate to do so, is not distributed at random; the particular propensity of those who were most economically and culturally deprived to abstain from replying to the most properly political questions still had to be related to the tendency to concentrate power in the hands of leaders, a tendency which characterizes parties founded on the suffrage of those most economically and culturally deprived, above all, the Communist parties. In other words, the liberty enjoyed by the leaders of these organizations, the liberties they may take with regard to those who have given them a mandate (witness, especially, their extraordinary about-turns), repose fundamentally on the almost unconditional self-surrender which is implied in the feeling of incompetence, even of political indignity – the very thing that was revealed by 'don't-knows'. And it is easy to see that, far from being based on the prejudice that democracy cannot be recognized on any other condition than that it is popular (as Alain Lancelot insinuates), this discovery of a relation that the ordinary politologist cannot see (among other reasons, because his right hand, which 'analyses' polls, does not know what his left hand, which 'analyses' 'political life', is doing) leads to the principle of the tendential law which dooms the organizations meant to defend the interests of the dominated to a monopolistic concentration of the power of protest and mobilization, and which found the fullest conditions of its flourishing in the 'popular democracies'. I should, to avoid creating any misunderstanding, add that this discovery, which is after all pretty commonplace, allows us to take up some of the classical analyses which Neo-Machiavellians, notably Mosca and Michels, devoted to the functioning of political or trade union hierarchies, without accepting their essentialist philosophy of history which ascribes to the *nature* of the 'masses' the propensity to let themselves be dispossessed to the benefit of agitators: we must also keep in mind the fact that the effectiveness of the historical laws which they naturalize would be suspended, or at least weakened, if the economic and cultural conditions of their operation were to be suspended or weakened.

I hope I have convinced you, by this example, that the 'critique of polls', if there is a critique, isn't situated on the (political) terrain on which those who make it their duty to defend it situate it, thinking thereby that they can, through a tried and trusted strategy, evade a properly scientific critique. And I hope I have shown that if scientific critique, in this case more than ever, has to take the form of a sociological analysis of the institution, this is because the limits of scientific practice are, as is always the case, albeit to different degrees, essentially inscribed in the constraints that influence the institution and, through it, the brains of those who participate in it. It is, in any case, a good method and a good tactic because, unlike the strategies of 'politicization' which use slyly *ad hominem* arguments, it frees people from the responsibilities incumbent on them far less than they would like to think.

Part IV

Conclusion

13

A lecture on the lecture

One ought to be able to deliver a lecture, even an inaugural lecture, without wondering what right one has to do so: the institution is there to protect one from that question and the anguish inseparable from the arbitrariness of all new beginnings. As a rite of incorporation and investiture, the inaugural lecture, *inceptio*, is a symbolic enactment of the process of delegation whereby the new master is finally authorized to speak with authority, and which establishes his words as a legitimate discourse, delivered by somebody with the right to speak. The literally magical effectiveness of the ritual rests on the silent and invisible exchange between the new entrant, who makes a public offering of his words, and the gathered scholars who attest by their presence in a body that these words, by being thus accepted by the most eminent masters, become universally acceptable, that is, in the full sense of the word, magisterial. But it is better to avoid taking the inaugural lecture on the inaugural lecture too far: sociology, the science of institutions and of the happy or unhappy relationship one may have with institutions, presupposes and produces a distance that is insurmountable and sometimes intolerable, and not only for the institution; it shakes you out of that state of innocence which enables you to fulfil the expectations of the institution with a sense of satisfaction.

As a parable or a paradigm, the lecture on the lecture, a discourse which reflects itself in the act of discourse, should at least have the virtue of reminding us of one of the most fundamental properties of sociology as I conceive it: all the propositions that this science enunciates can and must be applied to the subject who practises this science. It is when he cannot introduce this objectifying and thus critical distance that the sociologist proves right those who see in him a sort of terrorist inquisitor, available to carry out all the actions required by symbolic policing. One cannot go into sociology without tearing through the adherencies and adhesions by which

Inaugural lecture delivered at the Collège de France on Friday, 23 April 1982.

177

one ordinarily belongs to groups, without abjuring the beliefs that are constitutive of belonging and without disowning every link of affiliation or filiation. In this way, the sociologist whose origins are in what is called the people and who has reached what is called the elite cannot attain the special lucidity which is associated with every kind of social distancing unless he denounces both the populist representation of the people, which deceives nobody except its authors, and the elitist representation of the elite, carefully designed to deceive both those who belong to it and those who don't.

To consider the social integration of the scientist as an insurmountable obstacle to the construction of a scientific sociology is to forget that the sociologist can find weapons against social determinism in the very science which brings them to light, and thus to his conscious awareness. The sociology of sociology, which enables one to mobilize against an emergent science the experience of the science already available, is an indispensable instrument of the sociological method: one practises a science – and especially sociology – *against* one's scientific training as much as *with* one's scientific training. And only history can rid us of history. In this way the social history of social science, so long as it is also considered as a science of the unconscious, in the great tradition of historical epistemology rendered illustrious by Georges Canguilhem and Michel Foucault, is one of the most powerful means of distancing oneself from history, that is from the grip of an incorporated past which survives into the present or of a present which, like that of intellectual fashions, is already out of date the minute it appears. If the sociology of the system of education and the intellectual world seems to me to be fundamental, this is because it also contributes to our knowledge of the subject of cognition by introducing us, more directly than all reflexive analyses, to the unthought categories of thought which limit the thinkable and predetermine what is actually thought: I need merely refer to the universe of prejudice, repression and omission that every successful education makes you accept, and makes you remain unaware of, tracing out that magic circle of powerless complacency in which the elite schools imprison their elect.

Epistemological criticism cannot dispense with social criticism. And to measure what separates us from classical sociology, one need only observe that the author of 'The Primitive Forms of Classification' never considered the social history of the system of education that he proposed in *The Evolution of Educational Thought* to be the genetic sociology of the categories of teachers' understanding for which he none the less provided all the instruments.[1] Perhaps because this same Durkheim, who recommended that the management of public affairs should be handed over to scientists, found it difficult, with regard to his social position as a 'maître à penser', an intellectual master of social thought, to adopt the distance necessary to analyse that role as such. In the same way, no doubt, only a social history of the workers' movement and its relations with its theorists both inside and out would enable us to understand why those who profess to be Marxists have never really submitted Marx's thought and especially the social uses made of it to the test of the sociology of knowledge, which Marx initiated: and yet, without hoping that a historical and sociological critique will ever be able completely to discourage the theological or terrorist use of the canonical writings, one might at least expect it to determine the more lucid and resolute to stir themselves out of their dogmatic slumber and to put into action, in other words, to put to the test, in a scientific practice, theories and concepts which, thanks to the magic of ever-renewed exegesis, are assured of the false eternity of the mausoleum.

Although it evidently owes something to the transformations of the educational institution which authorized the magisterial *certitudo sui* of the past, this critical questioning should not be understood as a concession to the anti-institutional mood which is now in the air. This questioning is indeed the only way of escaping from that systematic principle of error which is the claim to a sovereign overview. When the sociologist arrogates to himself the right, which is sometimes granted him, of determining the limits between classes, regions and nations, and of deciding, with the authority of science, whether or not social classes exist, and if so, how many, or whether this or that social class – proletariat, peasantry or petty bourgeoisie – this or that geographical unit – Brittany, Corsica or Occitania – is a reality or a fiction, then the sociologist assumes or usurps the functions of the *rex* of ancient times, who was invested, according to Benveniste, with the power to *regere fines* and *regere sacra*, to determine frontiers and limits, in other words, the sacred. Latin, which I am also using in homage to Pierre Courcelle, has another word, less prestigious and closer to today's realities, that of *censor*, to designate the man who statutorily held this power of *constitution* which belongs to authorized statements, capable of creating both in

---

1 É. Durkheim, 'The Primitive Forms of Classification', and *The Evolution of Educational Thought: Lectures on the Formation and Development of Secondary Education in France*, tr. P. Collins (London, 1977).

idea and in reality the divisions of the social world: the *censor*, responsible for the technical operation – the *census* – which consisted in classifying citizens by their fortune, is the subject who delivers a judgement closer to that of a judge than to that of a scholar; it consists, that is – and here I quote Georges Dumézil – in 'situating [a man, an act or an opinion, etc.] in his proper hierarchical place, with all the practical consequences of that situation, and this place is determined by a fair public estimation'.

To break free of the ambition, which is that of all mythologies, of grounding in reason the arbitrary divisions of the social order, primarily the division of labour, and thus of providing a logical or cosmological solution to the problem of classifying men and women, sociology must take as its object, instead of letting itself be caught up in it, the struggle for the monopoly of the legitimate representation of the social world, that struggle for classification which is a dimension of every kind of struggle between classes, whether of generation, of gender or of social rank. Anthropological classification is distinguished from zoological or botanical taxonomies in that the objects that it sets – or keeps – in place are themselves classifying subjects. One need only think what would happen if, as in the fables, dogs, foxes and wolves had a vote in how canines were classified and in determining the acceptable limits of variation among the recognized members of the species, and whether the hierarchy of characteristics acknowledged as determining rank in the hierarchy of genera and species were of such a kind as to determine opportunities of access to means of sustenance or to beauty prizes. In short, to the great despair of the philosopher-king who, by assigning an essence to them, claims to enjoin them to be and do what by definition they are meant to be and do, classified and lowly classified men and women may reject the principle of classification which gives them the worst place. In fact, as history shows, it is almost always under the leadership of those seeking a monopoly over the power to judge and to classify, who may themselves quite often be classified, at least from certain points of view, in the dominant classification, that the dominated are able to break out of the grip of the legitimate classification and transform their vision of the world by liberating themselves from those internalized limits that are the social categories of perception of the social world.

Thus, it is one and the same thing to find oneself inevitably involved in the struggle for the construction and imposition of the legitimate taxonomy, and, by raising oneself to the second degree, to take as one's object the science of this struggle, that is, the knowledge of the functioning and functions of the institutions that are involved in it – such as the education system or the great official organizations of census and social statistics. To conceptualize the space of the struggle for classification as it really is – and the position of the sociologist in this space or with respect to it – does not in the least lead to dissolving science in relativism. Doubtless the sociologist is no longer the impartial umpire or divine spectator, who is alone authorized to say where truth resides (or, as common sense would put it, who is right), which comes down to identifying objectivity with an ostentatiously equitable distribution of rights and wrongs. But he is the one who endeavours to tell the truth about struggles which have at stake – among other things – the truth. For example, instead of deciding between those who affirm and those who deny the existence of a class, a region or a nation, he attempts to establish the specific logic of this struggle and to determine, through an analysis of the state of power relations and the mechanics of their transformation, the potential of the different fields. It is his task to construct a true model of the struggles for the imposition of the true representation of reality which contribute to creating reality in the terms in which we are able to record it. It is in this way that Georges Duby proceeds when, instead of accepting it as an indisputable instrument of the historian's work, he takes as the object of historical analysis the model of the three orders, that is, the system of classification through which historical science customarily thinks of feudal society; he thus discovers that this principle of division, which is both the object of conflict and the product of conflict between groups seeking to monopolize the power of constitution, such as bishops and knights, has itself contributed to producing the very reality that it enables us to analyse. In the same way, the report that the sociologist delivers at any given moment, on the properties or opinions of different social classes, and the very criteria of classification which he has to use to draw up this report, are also the product of the whole history of the symbolic struggles which, since they fight over the existence and definition of classes, have in a very real way contributed to *creating* classes: the present result of these past struggles depends, to a far from negligible extent, on the theoretical effect exercised by previous sociologies and especially by those which have contributed to creating the working class, and thereby the other classes, by helping to make it believe that it exists and seems to exist as a revolutionary proletariat. As social science progresses and spreads more widely, sociologists must expect to encounter the social science of the past concretized in the object of their study.

But one need only think of the role that political struggles give to forecasting, or to the ordinary report, to understand that the sociologist most rigorously bent on describing will always be suspected of prescribing or proscribing. In ordinary existence, people hardly ever speak of any state of affairs without adding whether it is in conformity with or contrary to the order of things, normal or abnormal, permitted or forbidden, blessed or cursed. Nouns are supplied with tacit adjectives, verbs with silent adverbs which tend to consecrate or to condemn, to set up as worthy of existing and persisting in being or, on the contrary, to depose, degrade and discredit. So it is no easy task to force scientific discourse to break away from the logic of the trial in which people expect it to function, if only to allow themselves to condemn it. So the scientific description of the relation the most culturally deprived have with high culture has every chance of being understood either as a sly way of condemning the people to ignorance or, on the other hand, as a disguised way of rehabilitating or celebrating lack of education and of demolishing cultural values. And what can be said of the cases in which the effort to find reasons, in which scientific work always consists, risks appearing to be a way of justifying, even of excusing, the existing order? Faced with the servitude of assembly-line labour or the misery of shanty towns, not to mention torture or violence in concentration camps, the 'that's how it is' that Hegel suggests we might utter at the sight of mountains takes on the value of a criminal complicity. And nothing is less neutral, when it comes to the social world, than expressing the way things are with authority, that is, with the power of making people see and believe – a power that is conferred by the recognized capacity to make forecasts; this is why the statements of science inevitably exert a political effect, which may not correspond to the politics which the scientist would like to put into practice.

However, those who deplore the disillusioning pessimism or the demobilizing effects of sociological analysis when it formulates for instance the laws of social reproduction are neither more nor less justified than those who would criticize Galileo for having discouraged the dream of flight by construing the law of falling bodies. To state a social law such as the one which establishes that cultural capital attracts more cultural capital is to offer the possibility of including among the circumstances liable to contribute to the effect which that law predicts – in this particular case, the educational elimination of the children who are most deprived of cultural capital – certain 'modifying elements' as Auguste Comte called them, which, however weak they may be in themselves, can be enough to transform in line with our wishes the result of the relevant mechanisms. By virtue of the fact that knowledge of the mechanisms permits one, here as elsewhere, to determine the conditions and the means of the action designed to master them, the rejection of a sociologism which treats the probable as a destiny is in any case justified; and movements of emancipation are there to prove that a certain dose of utopianism, that magic negation of the real which would elsewhere be called neurotic, may even contribute to creating the political conditions for a practical negation of the realistic view of the facts. But above all, knowledge by itself exercises an effect – one which appears to me to be liberating – every time the mechanisms whose laws of operation it establishes owe part of their effectiveness to miscognition, that is, every time it affects the foundations of symbolic violence. Indeed, this particular form of violence can be practised only on subjects who know, but whose acts of cognition, being partial and mystified, endorse the tacit recognition of domination, which is implied in the miscognition of the true foundations of domination. It is easy to understand why sociology ceaselessly has its scientific status challenged, and first and foremost, of course, by all those who need to carry out their symbolic commerce under cover of the darkness of miscognition.

The necessity of repudiating the temptation to act regally never imposes itself as absolutely as when it is a question of scientifically analysing the scientific world itself or, more generally, the intellectual world. If we have had to rethink the sociology of intellectuals from top to bottom, this is because, by virtue of the importance of the interests at stake and the investments which they consent to make, it is supremely difficult for intellectuals to escape the logic of the struggle in which everyone willingly turns himself into the sociologist – in the most brutally sociologistic sense of the term – of his enemies, at the same time as turning himself into his own ideologue, in accordance with the law of reciprocal blindness and insight which governs all social struggles for truth. It is however only if he apprehends the game as a game, with the stakes, rules or regular sequences that are proper to it, the specific interests created in it and the interests satisfied by it, that he can both *extricate* himself through and for that distancing which grounds theoretical representation, and, simultaneously, discover himself to be *implicated* in the game, in a determined place, with his own determined and determinant stakes and investments. Whatever his scientific pretensions may be, objectification is doomed to remain *partial*, and thus false, for as long as it ignores or refuses to see the viewpoint from which it is stated, and thus view the game as a whole. To construct the game as such, that is, as a space of objective positions which is one of the sources, *inter alia*, of the vision that the holders of each position may have of the other positions and their holders, is to give oneself the means of scientifically objectifying the set of more or less brutally reductive objectifications which agents involved in the struggle indulge in, and of seeing them for what they are, symbolic strategies which aim at imposing the partial truth of a group as the truth of the objective relations between groups. It is to discover in addition that by leaving out the very game that constitutes them as competitors, adversaries become accomplices, agreeing to keep concealed the essential thing, that is, the interests attached to the fact of participating in the game and the objective collusion which results therefrom.

It is all too evident that one must not expect that thinking about limits will enable one to think without limits – which would be tantamount to resuscitating in another form the illusion, formulated by Mannheim, of 'the intelligentsia without attachments or roots', a sort of dream of social flight which is the historical substitute for the ambition of absolute knowledge. The fact remains that each new development in the sociology of science tends to reinforce sociological science by increasing our knowledge of the social determinants of sociological thought, and thus the effectiveness of the critique that each person may bring to bear on the effects of these determinants on his own practice and on that of his rivals. Science is reinforced every time there is a reinforcement in scientific criticism, that is, the scientific quality of the weapons available and, inseparable from this, the necessity, if one is to triumph scientifically, of using the weapons of science and those weapons alone. The scientific field is, indeed, a field of struggles like any other but one in which the critical dispositions aroused by competition have some chance of being satisfied only if they can mobilize the scientific resources accumulated; the more advanced a science is, and thus the more it is endowed with a significant collective experience, the more participation in the scientific struggle depends on the possession of a significant scientific capital. It follows that scientific revolutions are not engineered by the most deprived but by those who are most scientifically rich. These simple laws allow one to understand that transhistorical social products, in other words ones which are relatively independent of their social conditions of production, such as scientific truths, can arise from the historicity of a particular social configuration, that is, from a social field such as that of physics or biology today. In other words, social science can explain the paradoxical progress of a reason that is historical through and through and none the less irreducible to history: if there is a truth, it is that truth is something people struggle over; but this struggle can lead to truth only when it obeys a logic whose terms prevent anyone from triumphing over his adversaries unless he employs against them the weapons of science and thus contributes to the progress of scientific truth.

This logic is also valid for sociology: it would be enough if it were practical to require of all participants and all candidates that they should master the – already immense – experience acquired by the discipline, for there to disappear from its universe certain practices which disqualify the profession. But who, in the social world, has an interest in the existence of an autonomous science of the social world? In any case, it would not be those who are the most scientifically deprived; for they are structurally inclined to seek in an alliance with external powers, of whatever sort, their support or compensation for the constraints and checks that stem from internal competition, and thus they can always find in political denunciation an easy substitute for scientific criticism. Nor are the holders of temporal or spiritual power any more likely to see in a really autonomous social science anything but the most redoubtable of rivals. Especially perhaps when, renouncing the ambition to lay down the law, and thereby, the ambition to institute heteronomy, social science lays claim to a negative and critical authority, one, that is, which is critical of itself, and critical by implication of all the abuses of power committed in the name of science.

It is easy to understand that the existence of sociology as a scientific discipline is constantly under threat. The structural vulnerability which results from the possibility of betraying scientific imperatives by playing the game of politicization means that sociology has almost as much to fear from the powers which expect too much of it as from those who desire its disappearance. Social demands are always accompanied by pressures, injunctions or temptations and the greatest service that can be granted sociology is perhaps that of asking nothing of it. Paul Veyne remarked that 'one can recognize great antiquarians from afar by certain pages that they never write.' What can one say of sociologists who are ceaselessly being invited to pass beyond the limits of their science? It is not so easy to give up the immediate gratifications of playing the part of the daily prophet – all the more since silence, doomed by definition to pass unnoticed, leaves the field free to the hollow trumpeting of false science. In this way certain people, from a failure to repudiate the ambitions of social philosophy and the temptations of essay writing, whose panacea is always ready with its facile answers, can spend their whole life taking up positions on terrains where, given the present state of things, science is defeated in advance. While others, on the other hand, find in these excesses an excuse to justify the abdication often implied by the irreproachable prudence of minute idiographic detail.

Social science can constitute itself only by rejecting the social demand for instruments of legitimatization or manipulation. The sociologist – who may occasionally deplore the fact – has no mandate, no mission, except those which he claims by virtue of the logic of his research. Those who, by what is essentially an abuse of power, feel they have the right or make it their duty to speak for the people, that is, in its favour, but also in its place (even if, as I have had occasion to do, they do so in order to denounce the racism, demagoguery, or populism of those who speak of the people), are still speaking for themselves; or, at least, they are still speaking about themselves, in that they are thus trying, in the best cases – I have in mind Michelet, for example – to allay the suffering caused by social separation by becoming members of the people in their imaginations. But at this point I have to open a parenthesis: when, as I have just done, the sociologist teaches you to relate the most 'pure' acts or discourses, those of the scientist, the artist or the militant, to the social conditions of their production and the specific interests of their producers, far from encouraging the prejudice of reduction and demolition which the sour and the embittered take such delight in, he intends solely to find a way to strip the veil of objective and subjective impeccability away from the rigorism, even the terrorism of envy and resentment; and not least when this is born of the transmutation of a desire for social vengeance into the drive for a compensatory egalitarianism.

Through the sociologist, a historically situated historical agent and a socially determined social subject, history, or rather the society in which the existing remains of history are preserved, turns for a moment back on itself, and reflects on itself; and through the sociologist, all social agents are able to know a little more clearly what they are and what they are doing. But this task is precisely the

186

last that all who have an interest in miscognition, negation, and the refusal to know, and who are ready, in all good faith, to recognize as scientific all the forms of discourse which do not speak of the social world or which discuss it in such a way that they are not really talking about it, are prepared to entrust the sociologist with. This negative demand, with a few, rare exceptions, has no need to declare itself in explicit sanctions: indeed, by virtue of the fact that rigorous science depends on one's decisively breaking away from things that appear self-evident, one need only let the routines of common thinking or the inclinations of bourgeois common sense have their way, in order to obtain the unfalsifiable considerations of all-purpose essay-writing or the half-truths of official science. A good part of what the sociologist strives to reveal is not hidden in the same sense as what the natural sciences aim to bring to light. Numerous realities or relations that it discloses are not invisible, or only in the sense that they 'stare you in the face', in accordance with the paradigm of the purloined letter dear to Lacan: I am thinking for example of the statistical relation which links cultural practices or preferences to the education one has received. The work necessary to bring the truth to light and to enable it to be recognized once it has been disclosed comes up against the collective defence mechanisms which tend to ensure a real 'negation', in Freud's sense of the word. The refusal to recognize a traumatic reality is on the same scale as the interests being defended, and one can thus understand the extreme violence of resistance reactions which are aroused, in those who hold cultural capital, by analyses which disclose the denied conditions of the production and reproduction of culture: to people trained to think of themselves in terms of the unique and the innate, these analyses show only the common and the acquired. In this case, self-knowledge is indeed, as Kant thought, 'a descent into Hell'. Similar to the souls who, in the myth of Er, have to drink the water of the river Ameles, which brings forgetfulness, before returning to earth to live there the lives that they have themselves chosen, cultured people owe their purest cultural pleasures only to the amnesia of the origin which enables them to live their culture as if it were a gift of nature. In this logic, which is well known to psychoanalysis, they will not recoil from contradiction in order to defend the vital error which is their *raison d'être* and to save the integrity of an identity based on the conciliation of opposites: resorting to a form of the faulty logic of the kettle as described by Freud, they will thus be able to reproach scientific objectification both with its absurdity and its self-evidence, and therefore its banality, its vulgarity.

187

Conclusion

The adversaries of sociology have the right to wonder whether an activity which presupposes and produces the negation of a collective denegation must exist; but nothing authorizes them to contest its scientific nature. It is certain that there is not, strictly speaking, any social demand for a total knowledge of the social world. And only the relative autonomy of the scientific field of production and the specific interests generated in it can authorize and encourage the appearance of a supply of scientific – in other words, as often as not, critical – products, which pre-exist any form of demand. In favour of the scientific option, which is more than ever that of the *Aufklärung*, of demystification, one could be content with referring to a text by Descartes which Martial Guéroult liked to quote: 'I cannot at all approve of the fact that people try to deceive themselves by feeding on false imaginings. That is why, seeing that it is a greater perfection to know the truth, even when it is to our disadvantage, than not to know it, I confess that it is better to be less happy and to have more knowledge.' Sociology unmasks self-deception, that collectively en-tertained and encouraged form of lying to oneself which, in every society, is at the basis of the most sacred values and, thereby, of all social existence. It teaches, with Marcel Mauss, that 'society always pays itself in the false coinage of its dreams'. This is to say that this iconoclastic science of ageing societies can at least contribute to making us to some degree masters and possessors of social nature, by enabling progress to be made in the knowledge and awareness of the mechanisms which are at the basis of all forms of fetishism: I am thinking, of course, of what Raymond Aron, who has been such a prestigious practitioner of this teaching, calls the 'secular religion', that state cult which is a worship of the state, with its civil festivals, its civic ceremonies and its national or nationalist myths, always predisposed to arouse or justify contempt or racist violence, and which is not a feature of totalitarian states alone; but I also have in mind the worship of art and science which, as a substitute idol, may work for the legitimatization of a social order which is in part based on the unequal distribution of cultural capital. In any case, one can at least expect from social science that it will keep at bay the temptation of magic, that *hubris* of self-ignorant ignorance – an ignorance which, expelled from one's relation to the natural world, survives in one's relation to the social world. The revenge of the real shows no pity for unenlightened good will or utopian voluntarism; and the tragic destiny of those political endeavours which have appealed to the authority of a presumptuous social science acts as a reminder that the magical ambition of transforming the social world

188

without knowing the mechanisms that drive it exposes itself to the
risk of replacing the 'inert violence' of the mechanisms that its
pretentious ignorance has destroyed with another and sometimes
even more inhuman violence.

Sociology is a science whose peculiar feature is the peculiar
difficulty it has of becoming a science like the others. This is because,
far from opposing each other, the refusal to know and the illusion of
knowing by instinct cohabit perfectly, among researchers as well as
practitioners. And only a rigorously critical disposition can dissolve
the practical certainties that insinuate themselves into scientific
discourse through the presuppositions inscribed in language or the
preconstructions inherent in the routine of daily discourse about
social problems, in short, through the fog of words which ceaselessly
comes between the researcher and the social world. In a general
way, language expresses things more easily than it does relations,
states more easily than processes. To say for example of someone
that he has power, or to wonder who, today, really holds power, is to
think of power as a substance, a thing which certain people hold,
preserve and transmit; it is to ask science to determine 'who governs'
(as the title of a classic of political science puts it) or who decides; by
admitting that power, as substance, is situated somewhere, it is to
wonder whether it comes from above, as common sense thinks, or,
by a paradoxical reversal which actually leaves the doxa untouched,
from below, from the dominated. Far from opposing each other, the
reified illusion and the personalist illusion go together. And there
would be no end to a list of the false problems that are created by the
opposition between the person-individual, as interiority and singularity, and the society-thing, as exteriority: ethico-political debates
between those who grant an absolute value to the individual,
individual attitudes and individualism, and those who grant priority
to society, the social and socialism, form the background of the
ever-renewed theoretical debate between a nominalism which reduces social realities, whether groups or institutions, to theoretical
artefacts without objective reality, and a substantialist realism which
reifies abstractions.

Only the tenacity of the oppositions created by ordinary thought,
reinforced by the full strength of the differences dividing the social
groups which express themselves through them, can explain the
extraordinary difficulty of the work necessary to transcend these
scientifically deadly oppositions; can explain, too, the fact that this
work has constantly to be begun anew, against collective regressions
towards modes of thought that are more common because they are

socially based and encouraged. It is easier to treat social facts as things or as people than as relations. Thus those two decisive breaks with the spontaneous philosophy of history and with the common vision of the social world, namely the analysis, carried out by Fernand Braudel, of 'long-term' historical phenomena, and the application, by Claude Lévi-Strauss, of the structural mode of thinking to objects as resistant as systems of kinship or symbolic systems, led to scholastic discussions of the relations between individual and structure. And above all, the grip of the old alternatives led to everything that old-style history had discussed being rejected into the category of the event and the contingent, in short, relegated beyond the grasp of science, instead of encouraging a transcendence of the antithesis between infrastructural history and the history of dates and events, and of the antithesis between macrosociology and microsociology. At the risk of abandoning to chance or mystery the whole real universe of practices, one must seek, in a structural history of the social spaces in which the dispositions which make 'great men' are generated and fashioned – the field of power, the artistic field, the intellectual field or the scientific field – the means of filling in the gap between the slow and imperceptible movements of the economic or demographic infrastructure and the surface agitation recorded by the day-to-day chronicles of political, literary or artistic history.

The source of historical action, that of the artist, the scientist or the member of government just as much as that of the worker or the petty civil servant, is not an active subject confronting society as if that society were an object constituted externally. This source resides neither in consciousness nor in things but in the relation between two states of the social, that is, between the history objectified in things, in the form of institutions, and the history incarnated in bodies, in the form of that system of enduring dispositions which I call habitus. The body is in the social world but the social world is also in the body. And the incorporation of the social achieved in the learning process is the foundation of that presence to the social world presupposed by socially successful action and the ordinary experience of this world as something entirely natural.

Only a real case analysis, but one which would require to be set out at great length, would be able to show that decisive break with the ordinary vision of the social world which is made by substituting for the naive relation between the individual and society the relation constructed between those two modes of existence of the social, the habitus and the field, history made into a body and history made into a thing. To convince you completely and to constitute in logical chronicle form the chronology of the relations between Monet, Degas and Pissarro or between Lenin, Trotsky, Stalin and Bukharin or again between Sartre, Merleau-Ponty and Camus, one would indeed have to acquire a sufficient knowledge of these two partly independent causal series that are, on the one hand, the social conditions of production of the protagonists or, more precisely, of their enduring dispositions, and, on the other hand, the specific logic of each of the fields of competition in which they bring these dispositions to bear – the artistic field, the political field or the intellectual field, without forgetting, of course, the conjunctural or structural constraints which weigh on these relatively autonomous spaces.

To think of each of these particular universes as a field means acquiring the means of examining their historical singularity in the most singular detail, in the manner of the most painstaking historians, while constructing them in such a way as to see in them a 'particular case of the possible', in Bachelard's phrase, or, more simply, one configuration among others of a structure of relations. And this presupposes, once again, that one pays attention to the pertinent relations, most often invisible or unnoticed at first glance, between directly visible realities, such as individual people, designated by proper names, or collective people, both named and produced by the sign or acronym which constitutes them as juridical personalities. In this way it will be possible to analyse a specifically located and dated polemic between an avant-garde critic and an established professor of literature as a particular form of a relation that can also be seen in the mediaeval opposition between *auctor* and *lector* or the antagonism between prophet and priest. When it is guided by the search for pertinent features which enables data to be constructed for purposes of comparison and generalization, even the reading of the dailies may become a scientific act. Poincaré defined mathematics as 'the art of giving the same name to different things'; in the same way, sociology – mathematicians will forgive me the boldness of this comparison – is the art of conceiving phenomenally different things as being similar in their structure and their functioning, and of transferring what has been established about one constructed object, for example the religious field, to a whole series of new objects, the artistic field, or the political field, and so on. This sort of theoretical induction, which makes it possible to generalize on the basis of the hypothesis of formal invariance in material variation, has nothing in common with induction or with the empirically based intuition with which it is sometimes identified; thanks to the reasoned use of the comparative method on which it confers its full effectiveness, sociology, like the other sciences which, in Leibniz's phrase, 'become more concentrated the more they are extended', can apprehend an increasingly extended number of objects with an increasingly reduced number of concepts and theoretical hypotheses.

Thinking in terms of a field requires a conversion of one's entire usual vision of the social world, a vision which is interested only in those things which are visible: in the individual, the *ens realissimum* to which a sort of fundamental ideological interest attaches us; in the group, which is only apparently defined by the mere relations, temporary or enduring, informal or institutionalized, obtaining between its members; or even in relations understood as *interactions*, that is, as concretely enacted intersubjective relations. In fact, just as the Newtonian theory of gravitation could be developed only by breaking away from Cartesian realism, which refused to recognize any mode of physical action other than shock and direct contact, in the same way, the notion of field presupposes that one break away from the realist representation which leads one to reduce the effect of the milieu to the effect of the direct action that takes place in any interaction. It is the structure of the constitutive relations of the space of the field which determines the forms that can be assumed by the visible relations of interaction and the very content of the experience that agents may have of them.

Paying attention to the space of relations in which agents move implies breaking away radically from the philosophy of history which is inscribed in the ordinary or semi-scientific usage of ordinary language or in the habits of thought associated with the polemics of politics, whereby we seek at all costs to find the people responsible, for the best as for the worst. One could produce an endless list of the mistakes, mystifications or mystiques created by the fact that the words designating institutions or groups, State, Bourgeoisie, Employers, Church, Family and School, can be constituted as subjects of propositions of the form 'the State decides' or 'School rejects' and, thereby, as historical subjects capable of posing and realizing their own aims. Processes whose meaning and purpose are, strictly speaking, neither thought nor posited by anyone (without this making them either blind or random), are thus ordered by reference to an intention which is no longer that of a creator conceived of as a person but that of a group or an institution functioning as a final cause capable of justifying everything, and with the least effort, without ever explaining anything. However, as can be shown, by reference to the celebrated analysis conducted by Norbert Elias, this theologico-political vision is not even justified in the case apparently best designed to conform it, that of a monarchic state which presents to the highest degree, for the monarch himself – 'l'État c'est moi' – the appearance of an 'apparatus': courtly society functions as a gravitational field in which the person holding absolute power is himself held, even when his privileged position allows him to take over the greater part of the energy generated by the balance of forces. The source of the perpetual motion which impels the field does not reside in some immobile prime mover – in this case, the Sun King – but in the tensions which, produced by the structure constitutive of the field (differences in rank between princes, dukes, marquesses, etc.), tend to reproduce this structure. The source resides in the actions and reactions of agents who, unless they exclude themselves from the game, have no other choice than to struggle to maintain or improve their position in the field, thus helping to bring to bear on all the others the weight of the constraints, often experienced as intolerable, which stem from antagonistic coexistence.

By virtue of the position that he occupies in the gravitational field of which he is the sun, the king has no need to want or even to think of the system as such in order to reap the advantages of a universe structured in such a way that everything in it will turn to his advantage. In a general way, both in the intellectual field or in the religious field and in the field of power, the dominant are, far more often than the theological illusion of the prime mover would seem to show, those who express the immanent forces of the field – and this is far from being an insignificant factor – rather than producing them or directing them.

I could also have taken the example of the circus-hippodrome of Constantinople, in the now-classic analysis of Gilbert Dagron. It is doubtless not fortuitous that this paradigmatic realization of the political field is presented in the form of a socially instituted playing area which periodically transforms the people gathered together into a popular assembly, invested with the power to contest or to ritually consecrate the imperial legitimacy. The institutional space, in which all the social agents – the emperor, placed in the position of referee, the senators, the high functionaries, but also the people, in their different factions – have their places assigned to them, *produces* so to speak the properties of those who occupy them, and the relations of competition and conflict which set them against each other: in this closed field, the two camps, the Greens and the Blues, confront each other ritually, in accordance with a logic which is both partly that of a sports competition and that of political struggle; and the autonomy of this social form, a sort of instituted *taxis* which, as such, transcends one or the other camp, *tagma*, which it ceaselessly generates, is demonstrated by the fact that it 'lends itself to the expression of conflicts of every sort', discouraging efforts to find for these antagonisms a precise and constant social or political basis.

As the case of this altogether exemplary social game clearly shows, sociology is not a subdivision of mechanics, and social fields are force-fields but also fields of struggle to transform or preserve these force-fields. And the practical or theoretical relation that agents have with the game is part of the game and may be at the root of its transformation. The most different social fields, court society, the field of political parties, the field of business firms or the academic field, can function only if there are agents who invest in them, in the different senses of this term, who commit their resources to them and pursue their objectives, thus helping, even when hostile, to maintain the structure of the field or, in certain conditions, to transform it.

Because we are always more or less caught up in one of the social games offered us by different fields, it does not occur to us to ask why there is action rather than nothing – which, unless one supposes a natural propensity for action or work, is not at all self-evident. Everyone knows by experience that what gets the senior civil servant going may leave the research scientist cold and that the artist's investments remain unintelligible to the banker. This means that a field can function only if it can find individuals who are socially predisposed to behave as responsible agents, to risk their money, their time, and sometimes their honour or their life, to pursue the objectives and obtain the profits which the field offers and which, seen from another point of view, may appear illusory, as indeed they always are because they rest on that relation of ontological complicity between the habitus and the field which is the basis of entry into the game and commitment to the game, that is, *illusio*.

It is in the relation between the game and the sense of the game that stakes are generated and values constituted which, although they do not exist outside this relation, impose themselves, within it, with an absolute necessity and self-evidence. This originary form of fetishism is at the root of all action. The motor – what is sometimes called motivation – resides neither in the material or symbolic purpose of action, as naive finalists imagine, nor in the constraints of the field, as the mechanistic thinkers suppose. It resides in the relation between the habitus and the field which means that the habitus contributes to determining what determines it. The sacred only exists for those who have a sense of the sacred, who none the less, when faced with the sacred itself, still experience it as fully transcendent. The same is true of every kind of value. *Illusio* in the sense of investment in the game doesn't become illusion, in the originary sense of the art of deceiving myself, of *divertissement* (in Pascal's sense of the term) or of bad faith (in Sartre's sense) until the game is apprehended from outside, from the point of view of the impartial spectator, who invests nothing in the game or in its stakes. This, the point of view of the stranger who does not recognize himself as such, means that one fails to recognize that investments are well-founded illusions. Indeed, through the social games that it proposes, the social world procures for agents many more and very different things than the apparent stakes and manifest ends of action: the hunt counts as much as, if not more than, the capture and there is a profit to be found in action, a profit which exceeds the explicitly pursued profits – salary, prizes, rewards, trophies, titles and function – and which consists in emerging from indifference, and in affirming oneself as an active agent, taken up in the game and engaged in it, an inhabitant of the world who is inhabited by the world, projected towards ends and endowed, objectively and thus subjectively, with a social mission.

Social functions are social fictions. And the rites of institution *create* the person they institute as king, knight, priest or professor by forging his social image, fashioning the representation that he can and must give as a moral person, that is, as a plenipotentiary, representative or spokesman of a group. But they also create him in another sense. By giving him a name, a title, which defines, institutes, and constitutes him, they summon him to become what he is, or rather, what he has to be; they order him to *fulfil* his function, to take his place in the game, in the fiction, to play the game, to act out the function. Confucius was merely expressing the truth of all those rites of institution when he mentioned the principle of the 'justification of names', requiring everyone to conform to his function in society, to live in accordance with his social nature: 'The sovereign should act as a sovereign, the subject as a subject, the father as a father, and the son as a son.' By giving himself body and soul to his function, and, thereby, to the constituted body which confers this function on him – *universitas, collegium, societas, consortium*, as the canonists said – the legitimate heir, the function-ary, or the dignitary contributes to ensuring the eternity of the function which pre-exists him and will survive him – *Dignitas non moritur* – and of the mystic body he incarnates, and in which he participates, thereby participating in its eternity.

Although it has, in order to constitute itself, to reject all the forms of that biologism which always tends to naturalize social differences by reducing them to anthropological invariants, sociology can under-stand the social game in its most essential aspects only if it takes into account certain of the universal characteristics of bodily existence, such as the fact of existing as a separate biological individual, or of being confined to a place and a moment, or even the fact of being and knowing oneself destined for death, so many more than scien-tifically attested properties which never come into the axiomatics of positivist anthropology. Doomed to death, that end which cannot be taken as an end, man is a being without a reason for being. It is society, and society alone, which dispenses, to different degrees, the justifications and reasons for existing; it is society which, by produc-ing the affairs or positions that are said to be 'important', produces the acts and agents that are judged to be 'important', for themselves and for the others – characters objectively and subjectively assured of their value and thus liberated from indifference and insignificance. There is, whatever Marx may say, a philosophy of poverty, which is closer to the desolation of the tramp-like and derisory old men of Beckett than to the voluntarist optimism traditionally associated with progressive thought. Pascal spoke of the 'misery of man without God'. One might rather posit the 'misery of man without mission or social consecration'. Indeed, without going as far as to say, with Durkheim, 'Society is God', I would say: God is never anything other than society. What is expected of God is only ever obtained from society, which alone has the power to justify you, to liberate you from facticity, contingency and absurdity; but – and this is doubtless the fundamental antinomy – only in a differential, distinc-tive way: every form of the sacred has its profane complement, all distinction generates its own vulgarity, and the competition for a social life that will be known and recognized, which will free you from insignificance, is a struggle to the death for symbolic life and death. 'To quote', say the Kabyles, 'is to bring back to life.' The judgement of others is the last judgement; and social exclusion is the concrete form of hell and damnation. It is also because man is a God unto man that man is a wolf unto man.

Especially when they are adepts of an eschatological philosophy of history, sociologists feel socially mandated, and mandated to give meaning, to explain, even to set in order and assign aims and objectives. Thus they are not the best placed to understand the misery of men without social qualities, whether we are talking about the tragic resignation of old people abandoned to the social death of hospitals and hospices, about the silent submission of the unemployed or the desperate violence of those adolescents who seek in action reduced to infraction a means of acceding to a recognized form of social existence. And, doubtless because they, like everyone, have too deep a need for the illusion of having a social mission to confess to themselves what underlies it, they find it difficult to discover the real foundation of the exorbitant power exercised by all the social sanctions of importance – all the symbolic toys, decorations, crosses, medals, palms or ribbons – but also all the social supports of the vital *illusio* – missions, functions and vocations, ministries and magistracies.

But a lucid perception of the truth of all vocations and acclamations condemns us neither to abdication nor to desertion. One can always join the game without illusions, by making a conscious and deliberate resolution. In fact, ordinary institutions do not ask so much. One is reminded of what Merleau-Ponty said of Socrates: 'He gives reasons for obeying the laws, but it is already too much to have reasons for obeying . . . What they expect of him is just what he can't give: assent to the thing itself, without preamble.'[2] If those who are in league with the established order, whatever it might be, have no great liking for sociology, this is because it introduces a freedom from primary adherence which means that even conformity takes on the appearance of heresy or irony.

Such, doubtless, would have been the lesson of an inaugural sociology lecture devoted to the sociology of the inaugural lecture. A discourse which takes itself as its object attracts attention less to the referent, which could be replaced by any other act, than to the operation which consists of referring to what one is in the process of doing and to what distinguishes it from the fact of simply doing what one is doing, of being, as they say, *entirely* absorbed in what one is doing. This reflexive self-examination, when it occurs, as here, in the midst of the situation itself, has something unusual, or even insolent, about it. It breaks the spell cast by the occasion, it disenchants. It draws attention to how simply doing what one is supposed to do enables one to forget and persuade other people to forget as well. It

---

2 M. Merleau-Ponty, *Leçon inaugurale* (Paris, 1953).

lists oratorical or rhetorical effects which, like the fact of reading in the earnest tone of improvisation a text prepared in advance, aims to prove and to make palpable the fact that the orator is altogether present in what he is doing, that he believes in what he is saying and adheres fully to the mission with which he is invested. It thus introduces a distance which threatens to annihilate, both in the orator and in his public, the belief that is the ordinary precondition of the successful functioning of the institution.

But this freedom from the institution is doubtless the only homage worthy of an institution of freedom, which has always been attached, like this one, to defending that freedom from institutions which is the precondition of all science, and first and foremost of a science of institutions. It is also the only way of expressing gratitude worthy of those who have gone out of their way to welcome here a science that is unsure of itself and not well loved: and among whom I would especially like to mention André Miquel. The paradoxical enterprise which consists in using a position of authority to say with authority what saying with authority involves, to give a lecture, a lesson, but a lesson of freedom from all lessons, would be merely inconsistent and even self-destructive, if the very ambition of creating a science of belief did not presuppose a belief in science. Nothing is less cynical, less Machiavellian in any case than these paradoxical statements which announce or denounce the very principle of the power which they exercise. There is no sociologist who would take the risk of destroying the slender veil of faith or bad faith which is the charm of all institutional pieties, if he didn't have faith in the possibility and necessity of universalizing that freedom from institutions which sociology affords; if he didn't believe in the liberating virtues of what is doubtless the least illegitimate of symbolic powers, that of science, especially when it takes the form of a science of the symbolic powers capable of restoring to social subjects the mastery of the false transcendence that miscognition ceaselessly creates and recreates.

Bibliography of the works of Pierre Bourdieu, 1958–1988

Compiled by Yvette Delsaut

1958

Work

1. *Sociologie de l'Algérie*, Paris, PUF, Coll. 'Que Sais-je', no. 802, 1958, new rev. and corr. edn 1961. English trans.: *The Algerians* (tr. A. C. M. Ross), Boston, Mass., Beacon Press, 1962.

1959

Articles

1. 'Tartuffe ou le drame de la foi et de la mauvaise foi', *Revue de la Méditerranée*, no. 4–5 (92–93) (July–October 1959), pp. 453–8.
2. 'La logique interne de la civilisation algérienne traditionnelle', in *Le sous-développement en Algérie*, Algiers, Secrétariat social, 1959, pp. 40–51.
3. 'La choc des civilisations', in *Le sous-développement en Algérie*, Algiers, Secrétariat social, 1959, pp. 52–64.

1960

Article

1. 'Guerre et mutation sociale en Algérie', *Études méditerranéennes*, 7 (Spring 1960), pp. 25–37.

1961

Article

1. 'Révolution dans la révolution', *Esprit*, 1 (January 1961), pp. 27–40.

1962

Articles

1. 'De la guerre révolutionnaire à la révolution', in *L'Algérie de demain*, ed. F. Perroux, Paris, PUF, 1962, pp. 5–13.

Bibliography

2. 'Les relations entre les sexes dans la société paysanne', *Les temps modernes*, 195 (August 1962), pp. 307–31.
3. 'Célibat et condition paysanne', *Études rurales*, 5–6 (April–September 1962), pp. 32–136.
4. 'La hantise du chômage chez l'ouvrier algérien. Prolétariat et système colonial', *Sociologie du travail*, 4 (1962), pp. 313–31.
5. 'Les sous-prolétaires algériens', *Les temps modernes*, 199 (December 1962), pp. 1030–51. English trans.: 'The Algerian Subproletariat', in *Man, State and Society in the Contemporary Maghrib*, ed. I. W. Zartman, London, Pall Mall Press, 1973.

1963

Work

1. *Travail et travailleurs en Algérie*, Paris and The Hague, Mouton, 1963 (with A. Darbel, J. P. Rivet and C. Seibel).

Articles

2. 'La société traditionnelle. Attitude à l'égard du temps et conduite économique', *Sociologie du travail*, 1 (January–March 1963), pp. 24–44.
3. 'Sociologues des mythologies et mythologies de sociologues', *Les temps modernes*, 211 (December 1963), pp. 998–1021 (with J. C. Passeron).

1964

Works

1. *Le déracinement, la crise de l'agriculture traditionnelle en Algérie*, Paris, Éd. de Minuit, 1964 (with A. Sayad).
2. *Les héritiers, les étudiants et la culture*, Paris, Éd. de Minuit, 1964, new augm. edn, 1966 (with J. C. Passeron). English trans.: *The Inheritors: French Students and their Relation to Culture* (tr. R. Nice), with a new Epilogue 1979, Chicago and London, University of Chicago Press, 1979.
3. *Les étudiants et leurs études*, Paris and The Hague, Mouton, Cahiers du Centre de sociologie européenne, 1, 1964 (with J. C. Passeron).

Articles

4. 'The attitude of the Algerian peasant toward time' (tr. G. E. Williams), in *Mediterranean Countrymen*, ed. J. Pitt-Rivers, Paris and The Hague, Mouton, 1964, pp. 55–72.
5. 'Paysans déracinés, bouleversements morphologiques et changements culturels en Algérie', *Études rurales*, 12 (January–March 1964), pp. 56–94 (with A. Sayad).
6. 'Les musées et leurs publics', *L'expansion de la recherche scientifique*, 21 (December 1964), pp. 26–8.

1965

Work

1. *Un art moyen, essai sur les usages sociaux de la photographie*, Paris, Éd. de Minuit, 1965, new rev. edn 1970 (with L. Boltanski, R. Castel and J. C. Chamboredon).

Bibliography

Articles

2. 'Le paysan et la photographie', *Revue française de sociologie*, 6, no. 2 (April–June 1965), pp. 164–74 (with M. C. Bourdieu).
3. 'Le musée et son public', *L'information d'histoire de l'art*, 3 (May–June 1965), pp. 120–2.
4. 'The Sentiment of Honour in Kabyle Society' (tr. P. Sherrard), in *Honour and Shame. The Values of Mediterranean Society*, ed. J. G. Peristiany, London, Weidenfeld & Nicolson, 1965, pp. 191–241.
5. 'Langage et rapport au langage dans la situation pédagogique' (with J. C. Passeron), in *Rapport pédagogique et communication*, ed. P. Bourdieu, J. C. Passeron and M. de Saint Martin, Paris and The Hague, Éd. Mouton, Cahiers du Centre de sociologie européenne, 2, 1965, pp. 9–36; also, *Les temps modernes*, 232 (September 1965), pp. 435–66. English trans.: 'Language and Pedagogical Situation' (tr. R. Teese), *Melbourne Working Papers 1980*, ed. D. McCallum and U. Ozolins, Melbourne, University of Melbourne, Department of Education, 1980, pp. 36–77.
6. 'Les étudiants et la langue d'enseignement' (with J. C. Passeron et M. de Saint Martin), in *Rapport pédagogique et communication*, ed. P. Bourdieu, J. C. Passeron and M. de Saint Martin, Paris and The Hague, Éd. Mouton, Cahiers du Centre de sociologie européenne, 2, 1965, pp. 37–69. English trans.: 'Students and the Language of Teaching' (tr. R. Teese), *Melbourne Working Papers 1980*, ed. D. McCallum and U. Ozolins, Melbourne, University of Melbourne, Department of Education, 1980, pp. 78–124.
7. 'Les utilisateurs de la bibliothèque universitaire de Lille' (with M. de Saint Martin), in *Rapport pédagogique et communication*, ed. P. Bourdieu, J. C. Passeron and M. de Saint Martin, Paris and The Hague, Éd. Mouton, Cahiers du Centre de sociologie européenne, 2, 1965, pp. 109–20.

1966

Work

1. *L'amour de l'art, les musées d'art et leur public*, Paris, Éd. de Minuit, 1966, new augm. edn, *L'amour de l'art, les musées d'art européens et leur public*, 1969 (with A. Darbel and D. Schnapper).

Articles

2. 'Différences et distinctions', in Darras, *Le partage des bénéfices, expansion et inégalités en France*, Paris, Éd. de Minuit, 1966, pp. 117–29.
3. 'La fin d'un malthusianisme?', in Darras, *Le partage des bénéfices, expansion et inégalités en France*, Paris, Éd. de Minuit, 1966, pp. 135–54 (with A. Darbel).
4. 'La transmission de l'héritage culturel', in Darras, *Le partage des bénéfices, expansion et inégalités en France*, Paris, Ed. de Minuit, 1966, pp. 383–420.
5. 'Comment la culture vient aux paysans?', *Paysans*, 62 (October–November 1966), pp. 6–20.
6. 'Une étude sociologique d'actualité: les étudiants en sciences', *Revue de l'enseignement supérieur*, 4 (1966), pp. 199–208 (with L. Boltanski, R. Castel, M. Lemaire and M. de Saint Martin).
7. 'Condition de classe et position de classe', *Archives européennes de sociologie*, 7, no. 2 (1966), pp. 201–23.

Bibliography

8. 'L'école conservatrice, les inégalités devant l'école et devant la culture', *Revue française de sociologie*, 7, no. 3 (July–September 1966), pp. 325–47. English trans.: 'The school as a conservative force: scholastic and cultural inequalities' (tr. J. C. Whitehouse), in *Contemporary Research in the Sociology of Education*, ed. John Eggleston, London, Methuen, 1974, pp. 32–46; also in *Schooling and Capitalism, A Sociological Reader*, ed. R. Dale *et al.*, London, Routledge & Kegan Paul/The Open University Press, 1976, pp. 192–200.

9. 'Une sociologie de l'action est-elle possible?', *Revue française de sociologie*, 7, no. 4 (October–December 1966), pp. 508–17 (with J. D. Reynaud). English trans.: 'Is a Sociology of Action Possible?', in *Positivism and Sociology*, ed. A. Giddens, London, Heinemann Educational Books, 1974.

10. 'Champ intellectuel et projet créateur', *Les temps modernes*, Problèmes du structuralisme, 246 (November 1966), pp. 865–906. English trans.: 'Intellectual field and creative project' (tr. S. France), *Social Science Information*, 8, no. 2 (April 1969), pp. 89–119; also in *Knowledge and Control: New Directions for the Sociology of Education*, ed. Michael F. D. Young, London, Collier-Macmillan, 1971, pp. 161–88.

Oral presentation

11. 'L'idéologie jacobine', Communication à la Semaine de la pensée marxiste (9–15 March 1966) in *Démocratie et liberté*, Paris, Éditions sociales, 1966, pp. 167–73.

Interview

12. 'Pour une pédagogie rationnelle', *Lambda*, November 1966, pp. 3–5.

1967

Articles

1. 'Les paradoxes de l'automate', *Coopération technique*, 51–52–53 (April 1967), pp. 101–4.

2. 'La communication entre professeurs et étudiants', *Travail social*, Communications humaines, Paris, Fédération française des travailleurs sociaux, 1966–7, pp. 133–6.

3. 'La comparabilité des systèmes d'enseignement', in *Education, développement et démocratie*, ed. R. Castel and J. C. Passeron, Paris and The Hague, Mouton, Cahiers du Centre de sociologie européenne, 4, 1967, pp. 21–58 (with J. C. Passeron).

4. 'Sociology and Philosophy in France since 1945: Death and Resurrection of a Philosophy without Subject', *Social Research*, 34, no. 1 (Spring 1967), pp. 162–212 (with J. C. Passeron).

5. 'L'image de l'image', *L'Année 66*, Catalogue de l'exposition Bernard Rancillac, Paris, Galerie Blumenthal-Mommaton, February 1967.

Afterword

6. Afterword to E. Panofsky, *Architecture gothique et pensée scolastique*, tr. P. Bourdieu, Paris, Éd. de Minuit, 1967, new augm. edn, 1970, pp. 133–67.

Oral presentations

7. 'Systèmes d'enseignement et systèmes de pensée', Communication to the VIe Congrès mondial de la sociologie (Evian, September 1966), *Revue interna-*

Bibliography

tionale des sciences sociales, Fonctions sociales de l'éducation, 19, no. 3 (1967), pp. 367–88. English trans.: 'Systems of Education and Systems of Thought', *International Social Science Journal*, 19, no. 3 (1967), pp. 338–58; also in *Readings in the Theory of Educational System*, ed. Earl Hopper, London, Hutchinson, 1971, pp. 159–83; also in *Knowledge and Control: New Directions for the Sociology of Education*, ed. Michael F. D. Young, London, Collier–Macmillan, 1971, pp. 189–207; also in *Schooling and Capitalism, A sociological reader*, ed. Roger Dale *et al.*, London, Routledge & Kegan Paul/The Open University Press, 1976, pp. 192–200.

8. *Émissions de philosophie 1966–1967*, consacrées au langage, Paris, Institut pédagogique national, Dossiers pédagogiques de la radiotélévision scolaire, 1967.

1968

Work

1. *Le métier de sociologue*, Paris, Mouton-Bordas, 1968 (with J. C. Chamboredon and J. C. Passeron).

Articles

2. 'Neutralità della sociologia?', *Libri nuovi*, September 1968, p. 2.
3. 'L'examen d'une illusion', *Revue française de sociologie*, 9, special number, Sociologie de l'éducation II, 1968, pp. 227–53 (with J. C. Passeron).
4. 'Éléments d'une théorie sociologique de la perception artistique', *Revue internationale des sciences sociales*, Les arts dans la société, 20, no. 4 (1968), pp. 640–64; also, *Noroit*, no. 134 (January 1969), pp. 3–14; no. 135 (February 1969), pp. 5–14. English trans.: 'Outline of a sociological theory of art perception', *International Social Science Journal*, 20 (Winter 1968), pp. 589–612.
5. 'Structuralism and Theory of Sociological Knowledge' (tr. A. Zanotti-Karp), *Social Research*, 35, no. 4 (Winter 1968), pp. 681–706.

Oral presentation

6. 'Introduction à la sociologie', *Émissions de philosophie 1967–1968*, Paris, Ministère de l'Éducation nationale, 1968 (with J. C. Passeron).

1969

Articles

1. 'Le système des fonctions du système d'enseignement', in *Education in Europe*, ed. M. A. Mattÿssen and C. E. Vervoort, The Hague, Mouton, 1969, pp. 181–9.
2. 'Sociologie de la perception esthétique', in *Les sciences humaines et l'oeuvre d'art*, Brussels, La connaissance S. A., 1969, pp. 161–76, 251–4.

Oral presentation

3. 'Système et innovation', Communication au Colloque national d'Amiens (1968), in *Pour une école nouvelle. Formation des maîtres et recherches en éducation*, Paris, Dunod, 1969, pp. 347–50.

Bibliography

1970

Works

1. *La réproduction. Éléments pour une théorie du système d'enseignement*, Paris, Éd. de Minuit, 1970 (with J. C. Passeron). English trans.: *Reproduction in Education, Society and Culture* (tr. R. Nice), London and Beverly Hills, Calif., Sage Publications, 1977.

Articles

2. 'La maison kabyle ou le monde renversé', in *Échanges et communications. Mélanges offerts à Claude Lévi-Strauss à l'occasion de son 60ème anniversaire*, ed. J. Pouillon and P. Maranda, Paris and The Hague, Mouton, 1970, pp. 739–58. English trans.: 'The Berber House or the World Reversed', *Social Science Information*, 9, no. 2 (April 1970), pp. 151–70; also 'The Berber House', in *Rules and Meanings. The Anthropology of Everyday Knowledge. Selected Readings*, ed. M. Douglas, Harmondsworth, Penguin, 1973, pp. 98–110.

3. 'L'excellence scolaire et les valeurs du système d'enseignement français', *Annales*, 25, no. 1 (January–February 1970), pp. 147–75 (with M. de Saint Martin). English trans.: 'Scholastic Excellence and the Values of the Educational System' (tr. J. C. Whitehouse), in *Contemporary Research in the Sociology of Education*, ed. J. Eggleston, London, Methuen, 1974, pp. 338–71.

Interview

4. 'La théorie' (with O. Hahn), *VH 101*, 2 (Summer 1970), pp. 12–21.

1971

Articles

1. 'Champ du pouvoir, champ intellectuel et habitus de classe', *Scolies*, Cahiers de recherches de l'École normale supérieure, 1 (1971), pp. 7–26.

2. 'Une interprétation de la théorie de la religion selon Max Weber', *Archives européennes de sociologie*, 12, no. 1 (1971), pp. 3–21. English trans. (new rev. and modif. version): 'Legitimation and Structured Interests in Weber's Sociology of Religion' (tr. C. Turner), in *Max Weber, Rationality and Modernity*, ed. S. Whimster and S. Lash, London, Allen & Unwin, 1987, pp. 119–36.

3. 'Genèse et structure du champ relgieux', *Revue française de sociologie*, 12, no. 3 (1971), pp. 295–334.

4. 'Disposition esthétique et compétence artistique', *Les temps modernes*, 295 (February 1971), pp. 1345–78.

5. 'Formes et degrés de la conscience du chômage dans l'Algérie coloniale', *Manpower and Unemployment Research in Africa*, 4, no. 1 (April 1971), pp. 36–44.

6. 'Le marché des biens symboliques', *L'année sociologique*, 22 (1971), pp. 49–126. English trans.: 'The Market of Symbolic Goods' (tr. R. Swyer), *Poetics* (Amsterdam), 14, no. 1/2 (April 1985), pp. 13–44.

7. 'La défense du corps', *Information sur les sciences sociales*, 10, no. 4 (August 1971), pp. 45–86 (with L. Boltanski and P. Maldidier).

8. 'The Thinkable and the Unthinkable', *The Times Literary Supplement*, 15 October 1971, pp. 1255–6.

Bibliography

Oral presentation

9. 'Reproduction culturelle et reproduction sociale' (Communication to the Colloquium at Durham, April 1970), *Information sur les sciences sociales*, 10, no. 2 (April 1971), pp. 45–99. English trans.: 'Cultural Reproduction and Social Reproduction', in *Knowledge, Education, and Cultural Change*, ed. R. Brown, London, Tavistock, 1973, pp. 71–112; also in *Power and Ideology in Education*, ed. J. Karabel and A. H. Halsey, New York, Oxford University Press, 1977, pp. 487–511.

10. 'L'opinion publique n'existe pas', Conference (Arras, Noroit, 155, January 1971), *Noroit*, 155 (February 1971); debate, *Noroit*, 156 (March 1971); also, *Les temps modernes*, 318 (January 1973), pp. 1292–309; also in P. Bourdieu, *Questions de sociologie*, Paris, Éd. de Minuit, 1989, pp. 222–35. English trans.: 'Public Opinion Does Not Exist' (tr. M. C. Axtmann), in *Communication and Class Struggle*, ed. A. Mattelart and S. Siegelaub, New York/Bagnolet, International General/IMMRC, 1979, vol. I, 'Capitalism, Imperialism', pp. 124–30.

1972

Work

1. *Esquisse d'une théorie de la pratique, précédé de trois études d'ethnologie kabyle*, Geneva, Droz, 1972. English trans.: pp. 162–89, 'The Three Forms of Theoretical Knowledge', *Social Science Information*, 12, no. 1, 1973, pp. 53–80; also, *Outline of a Theory of Practice* (tr. R. Nice), Cambridge, Cambridge University Press, 1977; also, pp. 3–9, 72–3, 'Structures, Strategies, and the Habitus', in *French Sociology, Rupture and Renewal Since 1968*, ed. C. C. Lemert, New York, Columbia University Press, 1981, pp. 86–96.

Articles

2. 'Composition sociale de la population étudiante et chances d'accès à l'enseignement supérieur', *Orientations*, 41 (January 1972), pp. 89–102 (with C. Grignon and J. C. Passeron).

3. 'Die Museumskonservatoren' (tr. C. Weber and W. M. Sprondel), in *Berufssoziologie*, ed. Thomas Luckmann and Walter Michael Sprondel, Cologne, Kiepenheuer & Witsch, 1972, pp. 148–53.

4. 'Les doxosophes', *Minuit*, 1 (November 1972), pp. 26–45.

5. 'Les stratégies matrimoniales dans le système de reproduction', *Annales*, 4–5 (July–October 1972), pp. 1105–27. English trans.: 'Marriage Strategies as Strategies of Social Reproduction' (tr. E. Forster), in *Family and Society*, Selections from the Annales, ed. R. Forster and O. Ranum, Baltimore, Md and London, John S. Hopkins University Press, 1976, pp. 117–44.

Oral presentation

6. Compte-rendu of Group I, in *Vie active et formation universitaire*, Actes du Colloque d'Orléans (November 1970), Paris, Dunod, 1972, pp. 109–13.

1973

Articles

1. 'Classes et classement', *Minuit*, 5 (September 1973), pp. 22–4.

2. 'Les stratégies de reconversion. Les classes sociales et le système

Bibliography

d'enseignement', *Information sur les sciences sociales*, 12, no. 5 (October 1973), pp. 61–113 (with L. Boltanski and M. de Saint Martin). English trans.: 'Changes in social structure and changes in the demand for education', in *Contemporary Europe. Social Structures and Cultural Patterns*, ed. S. Giner and M. Scotford-Archer, London, Routledge & Kegan Paul, 1977, pp. 197–227 (with L. Boltanski).

1974

Articles

1. 'Avenir de classe et causalité du probable', *Revue française de sociologie*, 15, no. 1 (January–March 1974), pp. 3–42.
2. 'Les fractions de la classe dominante et les modes d'appropriation des oeuvres d'art', *Information sur les sciences sociales*, 13, no. 3 (June 1974), pp. 7–32.

Oral presentation

3. 'Haute couture et haute culture', *Noroit*, 192 (November 1974), pp. 1–2, 7–17; debate, *Noroit*, 193–194 (December 1974–January 1975), pp. 2–11; also in P. Bourdieu, *Questions de sociologie*, Paris, Éd. de Minuit, 1980, 196–206.

1975

Articles

1. 'Méthode scientifique et hiérarchie sociale des objets', *Actes de la recherche en sciences sociales*, 1 (January 1975), pp. 4–6.
2. 'Le couturier et sa griffe. Contribution à une théorie de la magie', *Actes de la recherche en sciences sociales*, 1 (January 1975), pp. 7–36 (with Y. Delsaut).
3. 'L'invention de la vie d'artiste', *Actes de la recherche en sciences sociales*, 2 (March 1975), pp. 67–94. English trans.: 'The Invention of the Artist's Life' (tr. E. R. Koch), *Yale French Studies*, 73 (1987), pp. 75–103.
4. 'Les catégories de l'entendement professoral', *Actes de la recherche en sciences sociales*, 3 (May 1975), pp. 68–93 (with M. de Saint Martin). English trans.: 'The Categories of Professorial Judgement' (tr. P. Collier), in P. Bourdieu, *Homo academicus*, Cambridge, Polity Press, 1988, pp. 194–225.
5. 'La spécificité du champ scientifique et les conditions sociales du progrès de la raison', *Sociologie et sociétés* (Montréal), 7, no. 1 (May 1975), pp. 91–118; also, 'Le champ scientifique', *Actes de la recherche en sciences sociales*, 2–3 (June 1976), pp. 88–104. English trans.: 'The specificity of the scientific field and the social conditions of the progress of reason' (tr. R. Nice), *Social Science Information*, 14, no. 6 (December 1975), pp. 19–47; also in *French Sociology, Rupture and Renewal Since 1968*, ed. C. C. Lemert, New York, Columbia University Press, 1981, pp. 257–92.
6. 'Le titre et le poste. Rapports entre le système de production et le système de reproduction', *Actes de la recherche en sciences sociales*, 2 (March 1975), pp. 95–107 (with L. Boltanski). English trans.: 'Formal Qualifications and Occupational Hierarchies: the Relationship Between the Production System and the Reproduction System' (tr. R. Nice), in *Reorganizing Education*, Sage Annual Review, Social and Educational Change, vol. I, 1977, pp. 61–9; also, 'The Educational System and the Economy: Titles and Jobs', in *French*

206

Bibliography

Sociology, Rupture and Renewal Since 1968, ed. C. C. Lemert, New York, Columbia University Press, 1981, pp. 141–51.

7.   'Le fétichisme de la langue', *Actes de la recherche en sciences sociales*, 4 (July 1975), pp. 2–32 (with L. Boltanski).

8.   'La critique du discours lettré', *Actes de la recherche en sciences sociales*, 5–6 (November 1975), pp. 4–8.

9.   'L'ontologie politique de Martin Heidegger', *Actes de la recherche en sciences sociales*, 5–6 (November 1975), pp. 109–56; also, *L'ontologie politique de Martin Heidegger*, Paris, Éd. de Minuit, 1988.

10.   'Le langage autorisé. Note sur les conditions sociales de l'efficacité du discours rituel', *Actes de la recherche en sciences sociales*, 5–6 (November 1975), pp. 183–90.

11.   'La lecture de Marx: quelques remarques critiques à propos de "Quelques remarques critiques à propos de *Lire le Capital*"', *Actes de la recherche en sciences sociales*, 5–6 (November 1975), pp. 65–79.

Interview

12.   'Les intellectuels dans le champ de la lutte des classes' (with A. Casanova and M. Simon), *La nouvelle critique*, 87 (October 1975), pp. 20–6.

1976

Articles

1.   'Le sens pratique', *Actes de la recherche en sciences sociales*, 1 (February 1976), pp. 43–86.

2.   'Les modes de domination', *Actes de la recherche en sciences sociales*, 2–3 (June 1976), pp. 122–32.

3.   'La production de l'idéologie dominante', *Actes de la recherche en sciences sociales*, 2–3 (June 1976), pp. 3–73 (with L. Boltanski).

4.   'Un jeu chinois. Notes pour une critique sociale du jugement', *Actes de la recherche en sciences sociales*, 4 (August 1976), pp. 91–101.

5.   'Anatomie du goût', *Actes de la recherche en sciences sociales*, 5 (October 1976), pp. 2–112 (with M. de Saint Martin).

Oral presentation

6.   'Les conditions sociales de la production sociologique: sociologie coloniale et décolonisation de la sociologie', Intervention au Colloque sur 'Ethnologie et politique au Maghreb' (Paris, June 1975), in *Le mal de voir*, Paris, Union générale d'éditions (UGE), coll.10/18, Cahiers Jussieu 2, 1976, pp. 416–27; also, 'Pour une sociologie des sociologues', in P. Bourdieu, *Questions de sociologie*, Paris, Éd. de Minuit, 1980, pp. 79–85.

1977

Work

1.   *Algérie 60, structures économiques et structures temporelles*, Paris, Éd. de Minuit, 1977. English trans.: *Algeria 1960* (tr. R. Nice), Cambridge and Paris, Cambridge University Press/Éd. de la Maison des sciences de l'homme, 1979, pp. 1–94.

Bibliography

Articles

2. 'Questions de politique', *Actes de la recherche en sciences sociales*, 16 (September 1977), pp. 55–89.
3. 'Une classe objet', *Actes de la recherche en sciences sociales*, 17–18 (November 1977), pp. 1–5.
4. 'La production de la croyance: contribution à une économie des biens symboliques', *Actes de la recherche en sciences sociales*, 13 (February 1977), pp. 3–43. English trans.: 'The production of belief: contribution to an economy of symbolic goods' (tr. R. Nice), *Media, Culture and Society*, 2, no. 3 (July 1980), pp. 261–93; also in *Media, Culture and Society, A Critical Reader*, London, Sage Publications, 1986, pp. 131–63.
5. 'Remarques provisoires sur la perception sociale du corps', *Actes de la recherche en sciences sociales*, 14 (April 1977), pp. 51–4.

Oral presentations

6. 'Sur le pouvoir symbolique', Conference (Harvard University, 1973), *Annales*, 3 (May–June 1977), pp. 405–11. English trans.: 'Symbolic Power' (tr. C. Wringe), in *Identity and Structure: Issues in the Sociology of Education*, ed. D. Gleeson, Driffield, Nafferton Books, 1977, pp. 112–19; also *Critique of Anthropology* (tr. R. Nice), 4, no. 13–14 (Summer 1979), pp. 77–85.
7. 'L'économie des échanges linguistiques', Seminar (Paris, EHESS, 25 November 1976), *Langue française*, 34 (May 1977), pp. 17–34. English trans.: 'The economics of linguistic exchanges' (tr. R. Nice), *Social Science Information*, 16, no. 6 (December 1977), pp. 645–68.
8. Participation à la Table ronde, 'Linguistique et sociologie du langage' (Paris, Maison des sciences de l'homme, October 1976), *Langue française*, 34 (May 1977), pp. 35–51 (with J. C. Chevalier, S. Delesalle, P. Encrevé, G. Fauconnier, J. C. Milner and A. Rey).
9. 'La censure', Intervention au Colloque sur la science des oeuvres (Lille, May 1974), *Information sur les sciences sociales*, 16, no. 3/4 (1977), pp. 385–8; also in P. Bourdieu, *Questions de sociologie*, Paris, Éd. de Minuit, 1980, pp. 138–42.
10. 'Le paradoxe du sociologue', Conference (Arras, Noroit, October 1977), *Noroit*, 222 (November 1977); debate, *Noroit*, 223 (December 1977); also, *Sociologie et sociétés* (Montréal), 11, no. 1 (April 1979), pp. 85–94; also in P. Bourdieu, *Questions de sociologie*, Paris, Éd. de Minuit, 1980, pp. 86–94.

Interview

11. 'Le droit à la parole' (with P. Viansson-Ponté), *Le Monde*, Les grilles du temps (11 October 1977), pp. 1–2; sequel, 'La culture, pour qui et pourquoi?', *Le Monde*, Les grilles du temps (12 October 1977), p. 2.

1978

Articles

1. 'Capital symbolique et classes sociales', *L'arc*, Georges Duby, 72 (1978), pp. 13–19.
2. 'Le patronat', *Actes de la recherche en sciences sociales*, 20–21 (March–April 1978), pp. 3–82 (with M. de Saint Martin).
3. 'Sur l'objectivation participante. Réponses à quelques objections', *Actes de*

Bibliography

la recherche en sciences sociales, 23 (September 1978), pp. 67–9.

4. 'Dialogue sur la poésie orale', *Actes de la recherche en sciences sociales*, 23 (September 1978), pp. 51–66 (with M. Mammeri).

5. 'Titres et quartiers de noblesse culturelle. Éléments d'une critique sociale du jugement esthétique', *Ethnologie française*, 8, no. 2–3 (March–September 1978), pp. 107–44 (with M. de Saint Martin).

6. 'Classement, déclassement, reclassement', *Actes de la recherche en sciences sociales*, 24 (November 1978), pp. 2–22. English trans.: Epilogue (tr. R. Nice), in P. Bourdieu, *The Inheritors, French Students and Their Relation to Culture*, Chicago and London, University of Chicago Press, 1979, pp. 77–97.

Oral presentations

7. 'Pratiques sportives et pratiques sociales', Conférence inaugurale au Congrès international de l'HISPA (Paris, INSEP, 28 March–2 April 1978), *Actes du VIIe Congrès international*, Paris, INSEP, 1978, tome 1, pp. 17–37; also, 'Comment peut-on être sportif?', in P. Bourdieu, *Questions de sociologie*, Paris, Éd. de Minuit, 1980, pp. 173–95. English trans.: 'Sport and social class' (tr. R. Nice), *Social Science Information*, 17, no. 6 (1978), pp. 819–40.

8. 'Savoir ce que parler veut dire', Intervention au Congrès de l'AFEF (Limoges, 30 October 1977), *Le français aujourd'hui*, 41 (March 1978), pp. 4–20 (debate, 'Questions à Pierre Bourdieu', *Le français aujourd'hui*, Supplement to no. 41, March 1978, pp. 51–7); also in P. Bourdieu, *Questions de sociologie*, Paris, Éd. de Minuit, 1980, pp. 95–112.

9. 'Le racisme de l'intelligence', *Cahiers Droit et liberté* (Races, sociétés et aptitudes: apports et limites de la science, Colloque de l'UNESCO, 27 May 1978), Supplement to no. 382, 1978, pp. 67–71; also, *Réforme*, 1 December 1979, pp. 6–7; also in P. Bourdieu, *Questions de sociologie*, Paris, Éd. de Minuit, 1980, pp. 264–68; also in Jean Belkhir, *L'intellectuel: l'intelligentsia et les manuels*, Paris, Éd. Anthropos, 1983, pp. 187–94; also, 'Tout racisme est un essentialisme', *Différences*, no. 24–25 (June–July 1983), p. 44.

Interviews

10. 'Les intellectuels sont-ils hors jeu?' (with F. Hincker), *La nouvelle critique*, 111–112 (February–March 1978), pp. 56–61; also in P. Bourdieu, *Questions de sociologie*, Paris, Éd. de Minuit, 1980, pp. 61–6.

11. 'Deux doigts de Ravel sec' (with C. Huvé), *Le Monde de la musique*, 6 (December 1978), pp. 30–1; also, 'L'origine et l'évolution des espèces de mélomanes', in P. Bourdieu, *Questions de sociologie*, Paris, Éd. de Minuit, 1980, pp. 155–60.

12. Interview (with A. M. Métailié), in *Les jeunes et le premier emploi*, Paris, Association des âges, 1978, pp. 520–30; also, 'La jeunesse n'est qu'un mot', in P. Bourdieu, *Questions de sociologie*, Paris, Éd. de Minuit, 1980, pp. 143–54.

13. 'Tra struttura e libertà' (with M. d'Eramo), in P. Bourdieu, *Campo del potere e campo intellettuale*, Cosenza, Lerici, 1978, pp. 41–58.

1979

Work

1. *La distinction. Critique sociale du jugement*, Paris, Éd. de Minuit, 1979; new edn. augm. with an introduction, 1982. English trans.: prepublications (tr.

Bibliography

R. Nice), pp. 9–61, 'The Aristocracy of Culture', *Media, Culture and Society*, 2, no. 3 (July 1980), pp. 225–54; also in *Media, Culture and Society, A Critical Reader*, London, Sage Publications, 1986, pp. 164–93; pp. 139–44, 'A diagram of social position and life-style', *Media, Culture and Society*, 2, no. 3 (July 1980), pp. 255–59; complete publication, *Distinction. A Social Critique of the Judgement of Taste* (tr. R. Nice), Cambridge, Mass. Harvard University Press, 1984; paperback edition, London and New York, Routledge & Kegan Paul, 1986.

Article

2. 'Les trois états du capital culturel', *Actes de la recherche en sciences sociales*, 30 (November 1979), pp. 3–6.

Oral presentation

3. 'Numerus clausus', Intervention aux Assises de l'enseignement de l'architecture (May 1978), *Pré-livre blanc*, 1979; also, 'Débat: numerus clausus ou débouchés?', *BIP*, 94 (29 October 1980), p. 3.

Interview

4. 'Des goûts artistiques et des classes sociales' (with D. Eribon), *Libération*, 3–4 November 1979, pp. 12–13; also, 'L'art de résister aux paroles', in P. Bourdieu, *Questions de sociologie*, Paris, Éd. de Minuit, 1980, pp. 10–18.

1980

Works

1. *Le sens pratique*, Paris, Éd. de Minuit, 1980.
2. *Questions de sociologie*, Paris, Éd. de Minuit, 1980.
3. *Travaux et projets*, Paris, Centre de sociologie européenne, 1980.

Articles

4. 'Le capital social. Notes provisoires', *Actes de la recherche en sciences sociales*, 31 (January 1980), pp. 2–3.
5. 'Lettre à Paolo Fossati à propos de la *Storia dell'arte italiana*', *Actes de la recherche en sciences sociales*, 31 (January 1980), pp. 90–2.
6. 'Le mort saisit le vif. Les relations entre l'histoire réifiée et l'histoire incorporée', *Actes de la recherche en sciences sociales*, 32–33 (April–June 1980), pp. 3–14.
7. 'Et si on parlait de l'Afghanistan?' (with Pierre and Micheline Centlivres), *Actes de la recherche en sciences sociales*, 34 (September 1980), pp. 2–16.
8. 'Le Nord et le Midi. Contribution à une analyse de l'effet Montesquieu', *Actes de la recherche en sciences sociales*, 35 (November 1980), pp. 21–5.
9. 'L'identité et la représentation. Éléments pour une réflexion critique sur l'idée de région', *Actes de la recherche en sciences sociales*, 35 (November 1980), pp. 63–72.
10. 'Où sont les terroristes?', *Esprit*, 11–12 (November–December 1980), pp. 253–8.
11. 'Sartre' (tr. R. Nice), *London Review of Books*, 2, no. 22 (20 November–3 December 1980), pp. 11–12. Pub. in French, 'Sartre, l'invention de l'intellectuel total', *Liberation*, 31 March 1983, pp. 20–21.

210

Bibliography

Oral presentation

12. 'La fin des intellectuels?', Conference (Arras, Noroit, October 1980), *Noroit*, 253 (November 1980), pp. 2–8, 17–23; debate, *Noroit*, 254 (December 1980).

Interviews

13. 'Des contradictions linguistiques léguées par le colonisateur' (with D. Eribon), *Libération*, 19–20 (April 1980), p. 13.
14. 'La grande illusion des intellectuels' (with D. Eribon), *Le Monde Dimanche*, 4 May 1980, pp. i and xvii; also, 'Comment libérer les intellectuels libres?', in P. Bourdieu, *Questions de sociologie*, Paris, Éd. de Minuit, 1980, pp. 67–78.
15. 'La sociologie est-elle une science?' (with P. Thuillier), *La recherche*, 112 (June 1980), pp. 738–43; also, 'Une science qui dérange', in P. Bourdieu, *Questions de sociologie*, Paris, Éd. de Minuit, 1980, pp. 19–36.

1981

Articles

1. 'La représentation politique. Éléments pour une théorie du champ politique', *Actes de la recherche en sciences sociales*, 36–37 (February–March 1981), pp. 3–24.
2. 'Décrire et prescrire. Note sur les conditions de possibilité et les limites de l'efficacité politique', *Actes de la recherche en sciences sociales*, 38 (May 1981), pp. 69–73.
3. 'Épreuve scolaire et consécration sociale. Les classes préparatoires aux Grandes écoles', *Actes de la recherche en sciences sociales*, 39 (September 1981), pp. 3–70.
4. 'Pour une sociologie de la perception', *Actes de la recherche en sciences sociales*, 40 (November 1981), pp. 3–9 (with Y. Delsaut).
5. 'Men and Machines', in *Advances in Social Theory and Methodology. Toward an Integration of Micro- and Macrosociologies*, ed. K. Knorr-Cetina and A. V. Cicourel, Boston, Mass., London and Henley, Routledge & Kegan Paul, 1981, pp. 304–17.

Prefaces

6. Preface, in *Le français chassé des sciences*, Actes du Colloque d'Orsay, Paris, CIREEL (Centre d'Information et de Recherche pour l'Enseignement et l'Emploi des Langues), 1981, pp. 9–10.
7. Preface, in P. Lazarsfeld, M. Jahoda and H. Zeisel, *Les chômeurs de Marienthal*, Paris, Éd. de Minuit, 1981, pp. 7–12.
8. Introduction, in *Le grand livre du rugby français 1981–1982*, Belleville (Rhône), FMT Editions S.A., 1981, p. 7.

Oral presentations

9. 'Mais qui a créé les créateurs?', Conference (Paris, ENSAD, 1980), in *Art: Sur 10 ans, aujourd'hui, 1981*, Paris, Ministère de la Culture, 1981, pp. 71–84; also in P. Bourdieu, *Questions de sociologie*, Paris, Éd. de Minuit, 1980, pp. 207–21.

Bibliography

10. 'Lecture, lecteurs, lettres, littérature', Conference (Grenoble, 1981), in *Recherches sur la philosophie et le langage*, Grenoble, Université des sciences sociales, Cahier du Groupe de recherches sur la philosophie et le langage, 1981, pp. 5–16; also in P. Bourdieu, *Choses dites*, Paris, Éd. de Minuit, 1987, pp. 132–43.

Interview
11. 'Retrouver la tradition libertaire de la gauche' (with R. Pierre and D. Eribon, concerning Poland), *Libération*, 23 December 1981, pp. 8–9; also, *Libération*, special issue, 'Pologne, 500 jours de libertés qui ébranlèrent le communisme', January–February 1982, pp. 209–10.

1982

Works
1. *Leçon sur la leçon*, Paris, Éd. de Minuit, 1982; *Leçon inaugurale*, no. 90, Paris, Collège de France, 1982.
2. *Ce que parler veut dire. L'économie des échanges linguistiques*, Paris, Fayard, 1982.

Article
3. 'La sainte famille. L'épiscopat français dans le champ du pouvoir', *Actes de la recherche en sciences sociales*, 44–45 (November 1982), pp. 2–53 (with M. de Saint Martin).

Book reviews, Tributes
4. 'Zaslawsky, contre la magie des mots', *Libération*, 7 December 1982, p. 21.
5. 'Erving Goffman est mort', *Libération*, 2 December 1982, p. 23.
6. 'Goffman, le découvreur de l'infiniment petit', *Le Monde*, 4 December 1982, pp. 1 and 30. English trans.: 'Erving Goffman, Discoverer of the Infinitely Small' (tr. R. Nice), *Theory, Culture and Society*, 2, no. 1 (1983), pp. 112–13.

Oral presentations
7. 'Les rites d'institution' (Neuchâtel, October 1981), *Actes de la recherche en sciences sociales*, 43 (June 1982), pp. 58–63; also, 'Les rites comme actes d'institution', in *Les rites de passage aujourd'hui*, ed. P. Centlivres and J. Hainard, Actes du Colloque de Neuchâtel 1981, Lausanne, Éditions L'Age d'Homme, 1986, pp. 206–15.
8. Résumé des cours et travaux, *Annuaire du Collège de France 1981–1982*, Paris, Collège de France, 1982, pp. 473–6.

Interview
9. 'Dévoiler les ressorts du pouvoir' (with D. Eribon), *Libération*, 19 October 1982, p. 28.

1983

Articles
1. 'The Philosophical Establishment' (tr. K. McLaughlin), in *Philosophy in France Today*, ed. A. Montefiore, Cambridge, Cambridge University Press, 1983, pp. 1–8.
2. 'Le changement linguistique' (with William Labov and Pierre Encrevé),

Bibliography

Actes de la recherche en sciences sociales, 46 (March 1983), pp. 67–71.
3. 'Vous avez dit "populaire"?' *Actes de la recherche en sciences sociales*, 46 (March 1983), pp. 98–105.
4. 'Mai 68', *Lire*, 93 (May 1983), p. 22.
5. 'La discipline', *Contact*, special number, 'Exercer l'autorité aujourd'hui', no. 25 (June 1983), pp. 25–6.
6. 'Les sciences sociales et la philosophie', *Actes de la recherche en sciences sociales*, 47–48 (June 1983), pp. 45–52.
7. 'The Field of Cultural Production or: the Economic World Reversed' (tr. R. Nice), *Poetics* (Amsterdam), 12, no. 4–5 (November 1983), pp. 331–56.
8. 'Ökonomisches Kapital, kulturelles Kapital, soziales Kapital' (tr. R. Kreckel), *Soziale Welt* (Göttingen), special number, 'Soziale Ungleichheiten', ed. R. Kreckel, Sonderheft 2, 1983, pp. 183–98. English trans.: 'The Forms of Capital' (tr. R. Nice), in *Handbook of Theory and Research for the Sociology of Education*, ed. J. G. Richardson, New York, Westport Conn. and London, Greenwood Press, 1986, pp. 241–58.

Oral presentations
9. Intervention, Convegno Internazionale di Studi, (Florence, September 1982), *Gli Uffizi, Quattro secoli di una galleria*, ed. P. Barocchi and R. Ragionieri, Florence, Leo S. Olschki Editore, 1983, vol. II, pp. 584–6, 630–3.
10. Résumé des cours et travaux, *Annuaire du Collège de France 1982–1983*, Paris, Collège de France, 1983, pp. 519–24.

Interviews
11. 'Die Worte und die Wahrheit' (with J. Altwegg and A. Schmidt), *Basler Magazin*, 10 (March 1983), pp. 3–7.
12. 'Interview met Pierre Bourdieu' (with J. Heilbron and B. Maso), *Sociologisch Tijdschrift* (Amsterdam), 10, no. 2 (October 1983), pp. 307–34. Published in French, 'Repères', in P. Bourdieu, *Choses dites*, Paris, Éd. de Minuit, 1987, pp. 47–71.
13. 'Pierre Bourdieu haastattelu' (with J. P. Roos, J. Heilbron and B. Maso), *Sosiologia* (Helsinki), 4 (1983), pp. 319–29.
14. 'Die feinen Unterschiede, oder: Die Abhängigkeit aller Lebensäusserungen vom sozialen Status' (with H. D. Zimmerman, tr. B. Schwibs), *L'80* (Cologne), 28 (November 1983), pp. 131–43; German television, 11 April 1983 (abridged version), 3 November 1983 (complete version).

1984

Work

1. *Homo academicus*, Paris, Éd. de Minuit, 1984. English trans.: *Homo academicus* (tr. P. Collier), with a preface to the English Edition (pp. xi–xxvi), Cambridge, Polity Press, 1988.

Articles
2. 'La perception du monde social: une question de mots?', *Actes de la recherche en sciences sociales*, 52–53 (June 1984), pp. 13–14.
3. 'La représentation de la position sociale', *Actes de la recherche en sciences sociales*, 52–53 (June 1984), pp. 14–15.
4. 'Le hit-parade des intellectuels français, ou qui sera juge de la légitimité des

juges?', *Actes de la recherche en sciences sociales*, 52–53 (June 1984), pp. 95–100.
5. 'Le champ littéraire. Préalables critiques et principes de méthode', *Lende-mains* (Berlin and Cologne), 9, no. 36 (1984), pp. 5–20.
6. 'Capital et marché linguistiques', *Linguistische Berichte* (Constance), no. 90 (1984), pp. 3–24.
7. 'La dernière instance', in *Le siècle de Kafka*, Paris, Centre Georges Pompidou, 1984, pp. 268–70.
8. 'Consommation culturelle', in *Encyclopaedia Universalis*, new edn, 1984, tome 2, 'Art', pp. 779–82.

Preface, tributes
9. Preface, in Anna Boschetti, *L'impresa intellettuale. Sartre e 'Les Temps Modernes'*, Bari, Edizioni Dedalo, 1984, pp. 5–6.
10. 'Le plaisir de savoir' (about Michel Foucault), *Le Monde*, 27 June 1984, pp. 1 and 10.
11. 'Non chiedetemi chi sono. Un profilo di Michel Foucault', *L'indice* (Rome), no. 1 (October 1984), pp. 4–5.

Oral presentations
12. 'Espace social et genèse des "classes"' (University of Frankfurt, February 1984), *Actes de la recherche en sciences sociales*, 52–53 (June 1984), pp. 3–12. English trans.: 'The Social Space and the Genesis of Groups' (tr. R. Nice), *Social Science Information*, 24, no. 2 (1985), pp. 195–220; also, *Theory and Society*, 14 (1985), pp. 723–44.
13. 'Pour une critique de la lecture' (Strasbourg, Centre de documentation en histoire de la philosophie, 1984), *La lecture II*, Cahiers du Séminaire de philosophie, 2, 1984, pp. 13–17.
14. 'La délégation et le fétichisme politique' (Paris, Association des étudiants protestants, June 1983), *Actes de la recherche en sciences sociales*, 52–53 (June, 1984), pp. 49–55; also in P. Bourdieu, *Choses dites*, Paris, Éd. de Minuit, 1987, pp. 185–202. English trans.: 'Delegation and Political Fetishism' (tr. K. Robin-son), *Thesis Eleven*, 10–11 (November 1984–March 1985), pp. 56–70.
15. 'Réponse aux économistes' (Paris, Colloquium on 'Le modèle économique dans les sciences sociales', Université de Paris-I, April 1981), *Économies et sociétés*, 18, no. 10 (October 1984), pp. 23–32; also, 'L'intérêt du sociologue', in P. Bourdieu, *Choses dites*, Paris, Éd. de Minuit, 1987, pp. 124–31.
16. Conférence introductive (VIIIe Symposium de l'ICSS, Paris, July 1983), in *Sports et sociétés contemporaines*, Paris, Société française de sociologie du sport, 1984, pp. 323–31.
17. Résumé des cours et travaux, *Annuaire du Collège de France 1983–1984*, Paris, Collège de France, 1984, pp. 551–3.

Interviews
18. 'Université: les rois sont nus' (with D. Eribon), *Le nouvel observateur*, 2–8 November 1984, pp. 86–90.
19. Interview (with A. Rényi), *Valóság* (Budapest), 7 (1984), pp. 93–8.

Bibliography

1985

Articles

1. 'Remarques à propos de la valeur scientifique et des effets politiques des enquêtes d'opinion', *Pouvoirs*, 'Les sondages', 33 (April 1985), pp. 131–9; also, 'Le sondage, une "science" sans savant', in P. Bourdieu, *Choses dites*, Paris, Éd. de Minuit, 1987, pp. 217–24.

2. 'Quand les Canaques prennent la parole', *Actes de la recherche en sciences sociales*, 56 (March 1985), pp. 69–83 (with A. Bensa).

3. 'Effet de champ et effet de corps', *Actes de la recherche en sciences sociales*, 59 (September 1985), p. 73.

4. 'Dialogue à propos de l'histoire culturelle' (with R. Chartier and R. Darnton), *Actes de la recherche en sciences sociales*, 59 (September 1985), pp. 86–93.

5. 'Existe-t-il une littérature belge? Limites d'un champ et frontières politiques', *Études de lettres* (Lausanne), 4 (October–December 1985), pp. 3–6.

6. 'The Genesis of the Concepts of Habitus and Field' (tr. Ch. Newman), *Sociocriticism* (Pittsburgh, Pa and Montpellier), Theories and Perspectives II, no. 2, December 1985, pp. 11–24.

Tributes

7. 'Les intellectuels et les pouvoirs', in *Michel Foucault, une histoire de la vérité*, Paris, Syros, 1985, pp. 93–4.

8. 'A Free Thinker: "Do not ask me who I am"' (tr. R. Nice), *Paragraph* (London), 5 (March 1985), pp. 80–7.

Oral presentations

9. 'Le champ religieux dans le champ de production symbolique' (Strasbourg, October 1982), Afterword, in *Les nouveaux clercs*, Geneva, Labor et fides, 1985, pp. 255–61; also, 'La dissolution du religieux', in P. Bourdieu, *Choses dites*, Paris, Éd. de Minuit, 1987, pp. 117–23.

10. 'Les professeurs de l'Université de Paris à la veille de Mai 68' (Paris, Colloque organisé par l'Institut d'histoire moderne et contemporaine et l'EHESS, June 1984), in *Le personnel de l'enseignement supérieur en France aux XIXe et XXe siècles*, Paris, Éd. du CNRS, 1985, pp. 177–84.

11. Résumé des cours et travaux, *Annuaire du Collège de France 1984–1985*, Paris, Collège de France, 1985, pp. 559–62.

Interviews

12. 'La lecture: une pratique culturelle' (with R. Chartier), in *Pratiques de la lecture*, Paris, Rivages, 1985, pp. 218–39.

13. 'De la règle aux stratégies' (with P. Lamaison), *Terrains*, 4 (March 1985), pp. 93–100; also in P. Bourdieu, *Choses dites*, Paris, Éd. de Minuit, 1987, pp. 75–93. English trans.: 'From Rules to Strategies' (tr. R. Hurley), *Cultural Anthropology*, 1, no. 1 (February 1986), pp. 110–20.

14. 'Du bon usage de l'ethnologie' (with M. Mammeri), *Awal*, Cahiers d'études berbères, no. 1, 1985, pp. 7–29.

15. 'Vernunft ist eine historische Errungenschaft, wie die Sozialversicherung' (with B. Schwibs), *Neue Sammlung* (Stuttgart), 3 (1985), pp. 376–94.

16. 'Le rapport du Collège de France: Pierre Bourdieu s'explique' (with J. P. Salgas), *La Quinzaine Littéraire*, 445 (1–31 August 1985), pp. 8–10.

Bibliography

17. '"Den socialistiska kulturpolitiken: Frankrike har bara lagt ut rökridaer"' (with G. Wirén), *Dagens Nyheter* (Stockholm), 21 October 1985, p. 4.

1986

Articles

1. 'La science et l'actualité', *Actes de la recherche en sciences sociales*, 61 (March 1986), pp. 2–3.
2. 'L'illusion biographique', *Actes de la recherche en sciences sociales*, 62–63 (June 1986), pp. 69–72. English trans.: 'The Biographical Illusion' (tr. Y. Winkin and W. Leeds-Hurwitz), *Working Papers and Proceedings of the Center for Psychosocial Studies* (Chicago), 14 (1987), pp. 1–7.
3. 'Nécessiter', *L'Herne*, Cahier Francis Ponge, Paris, Éditions de l'Herne, June 1986, pp. 434–7.
4. 'La force du droit. Éléments pour une sociologie du champ juridique', *Actes de la recherche en sciences sociales*, 64 (September 1986), pp. 5–19. English trans.: 'The Force of Law: Toward a Sociology of the Juridical Field' (tr. R. Terdiman), *Hastings Law Journal*, 38, no. 5 (July 1987), pp. 814–53.
5. 'Les mésaventures de l'amateur', in *Éclats/Boulez*, ed. R. Samuel, Paris, Éditions du Centre Georges Pompidou, 1986, pp. 74–5.
6. 'An Antinomy in the Notion of Collective Protest', in *Development, Democracy, and the Art of Trespassing: Essays in Honor of Albert O. Hirschman*, ed. A. Foxley, M. S. McPherson and G. O'Donnell, Notre Dame, Ind., University of Notre Dame Press, 1986, paperback edition, 1988, pp. 301–2.

Oral presentations

7. 'Habitus, code et codification', Conference (Neuchâtel, May 1983), *Actes de la recherche en sciences sociales*, 64 (September 1986), pp. 40–4; also, 'La codification', in P. Bourdieu, *Choses dites*, Paris, Éd. de Minuit, 1987, pp. 94–105.
8. 'De quoi parle-t-on quand on parle du "problème de la jeunesse"?' (Paris, Colloque organisé par le Programme mobilisateur Technologie, Emploi, Travail, du Ministère de la recherche et de la technologie, December 1985), in *Les jeunes et les autres. Contributions des sciences de l'homme à la question des jeunes*, Vaucresson, CRIV (Centre de recherche interdisciplinaire de Vaucresson), 1986, tome II, pp. 229–34.
9. Résumé des cours et travaux, *Annuaire du Collège de France 1985–1986*, Paris, Collège de France, 1986, pp. 555–60.

Interviews

10. 'Der Kampf um die symbolische Ordnung' (with A. Honneth, H. Kocyba and B. Schwibs; tr. B. Schwibs), *Ästhetik und Kommunikation* (Frankfurt), 16, no. 61–62 (1986), pp. 142–63. Pub. in French, '"Fieldwork in philosophy"', in P. Bourdieu, *Choses dites*, Paris, Éd. de Minuit, 1987, pp. 13–46; English trans.: 'The Struggle for Symbolic Order' (tr. J. Bleicher), *Theory, Culture & Society*, 3, no. 3 (1986), pp. 35–51.
11. 'D'abord défendre les intellectuels' (with D. Eribon), *Le nouvel observateur*, 12–18 September 1986, p. 82.
12. 'A quand un lycée Bernard Tapie?' (with A. de Gaudemar), *Libération*, 4 December 1986, p. 4; also, *Libération*, special issue, 'La nouvelle vague',

Bibliography

January 1987, pp. 106–7. English trans.: 'Revolt of the Spirit' (tr. Ch. Turner), *New Socialist*, 46 (February 1987), pp. 9–11.

1987

Work
1. *Choses dites*, Paris, Éd. de Minuit, 1987.

Articles
2. 'L'institutionnalisation de l'anomie', *Les Cahiers du Musée national d'art moderne*, 19–20 (June 1987), pp. 6–19.
3. 'Für eine Realpolitik der Vernunft' (tr. B. Schwibs), in *Das Bildungswesen der Zukunft*, ed. S. Müller-Rolli, Stuttgart, Ernst Klett, 1987, pp. 229–34.
4. 'Agrégation et ségrégation. Le champ des grandes écoles et le champ du pouvoir', *Actes de la recherche en sciences sociales*, 69 (September 1987), pp. 2–50 (with M. de Saint Martin).
5. 'Variations et invariants. Éléments pour une histoire structurale du champ des grandes écoles', *Actes de la recherche en sciences sociales*, 70 (November 1987), pp. 3–30.
6. 'The Historical Genesis of a Pure Aesthetic' (tr. Ch. Newman), *The Journal of Aesthetics and Art Criticism*, 46, special issue, 1987, pp. 201–10; also in *Analytic Aesthetics*, ed. R. Shusterman, Oxford and New York, Basil Blackwell, 1989.

Tribute
7. 'L'assassinat de Maurice Halbwachs', *La liberté de l'esprit*, Visages de la Résistance, 16 (Autumn 1987), pp. 161–8.

Oral presentations
8. 'Sociologues de la croyance et croyances de sociologues' (Paris, Congrès de l'Association française de sociologie religieuse, December 1982), *Archives de sciences sociales des religions*, 63, no. 1 (January–March, 1987), pp. 155–61; also in P. Bourdieu, *Choses dites*, Paris, Éd. de Minuit, 1987, pp. 106–11.
9. 'La révolution impressionniste' (Arras, Noroit, January 1987), *Noroit*, 303 (September–October 1987), pp. 3–18.
10. 'What Makes a Social Class? On The Theoretical and Practical Existence Of Groups' (Chicago, The University of Chicago, April 1987; tr. L. J. D. Wacquant and D. Young), *Berkeley Journal of Sociology*, 32 (1987), pp. 1–17.

Interviews
11. 'Professore o commerciante?' (with S. Ottolenghi), *Panorama* (Milan), 18 October 1987, p. 145.
12. 'Esquisse d'un projet intellectuel: un entretien avec Pierre Bourdieu' (with C. Duverlie), *The French Review*, 61, no. 2 (December 1987), pp. 194–205.

1988

Articles
1. 'Flaubert's Point of View' (tr. P. Parkhurst Ferguson), *Critical Inquiry*, 14 (Spring 1988), pp. 539–62.

Bibliography

2. 'Penser la politique', *Actes de la recherche en sciences sociales*, 71–72 (March 1988), pp. 2–3.

3. 'La vertu civile', *Le monde*, 16 September 1988, pp. 1–2.

Prefaces, book reviews.

4. Preface, in P. Rabinow, *Un ethnologue au Maroc*, Paris, Hachette, 1988, pp. 11–14.

5. Preface, in B. Mazon, *Aux origines de l'Ecole des hautes études en sciences sociales. Le rôle du mécénat américain*, Paris, Éd. du cerf, 1988, pp. i–v.

6. Preface, in T. Yacine Titouh, *L'Izli ou l'amour chanté en kabyle*, Paris, Éd. de la Maison des sciences de l'homme, 1988, pp. 11–12.

7. 'A long trend of change' (concerning M. Lewin, *The Gorbachev Phenomenon: A historical interpretation*), *The Times Literary Supplement*, 12–18 August 1988, pp. 875–6.

Oral presentations

8. 'On Interest and the Relative Autonomy of Symbolic Power: A Rejoinder to Some Objections' (Düsseldorf, February 1987; tr. L. J. D. Wacquant and M. Lawson), *Working Papers and Proceedings of the Center for Psychosocial Studies* (Chicago), 20 (1988), pp. 1–11.

9. 'The Crumbling of Orthodoxy and its Legacy' (University of Chicago, April 1987; tr. L. J. D. Wacquant), *Theory and Society*, 17 (1988), pp. 773–87.

10. Résumé des cours et travaux, *Annuaire du Collège de France 1987–1988*, Paris, Collège de France, 1988, pp. 483–92.

Interviews

11. 'Heidegger par Pierre Bourdieu: le krach de la philosophie' (with R. Maggiori), *Libération*, 10 March 1988, Supplément Livres, pp. vi–vii.

12. '"... ich glaube, ich wäre sein bester Verteidiger", Ein Gespräch mit Pierre Bourdieu über die Heidegger-Kontroverse' (with H. Woetzel), *Das Argument* (Berlin), 171 (October 1988), pp. 723–6.

Index

Algeria, 23
Althusser, Louis, 4, 9, 17
anachronism, in attitude to culture,
    104–5
Aron, Raymond, 188
art, 7
artistic field, and interest, 110
Athenaeus, 99
auctor, 94–5
Austin, J. L., 28–9

Bachelard, Gaston, 3
Bakhtin, Mikhail, 95
Bateson, G., *Naven*, 72
Béarn region, 8, 59, 63, 68, 71
Bendix, Richard, 125
Bensa, Alban, 72
Berger, Bennett, 125
bilingualism, 91
biologism, 196
Bollack, Jean, 96–7, 103
Boltanski, Luc, 65
Bourdieu, Pierre
    Un art moyen, 23
    'The Categories of Professional
        Judgement', 124
    Distinction, 17, 23, 42, 107, 113–14,
        117, 119, 123, 126–7
    'The Field of Cultural Production
        or: the Economic World
        Reversed', 110 n.
    Homo academicus, 19
    *The Inheritors (Les héritiers, les
        étudiants et la culture)*, 4
    *The Logic of Practice (Le sens
        pratique)*, 8, 12, 13

'The Peculiar History of Scientific
    Reason', 111
*Rapport pédagogique et
    communication*, 124
*Reproduction in Education, Society
    and Culture (La reproduction)*,
    123–4
'Structuralism and Theory of Social
    Knowledge', 18
'Symbolic Power' ('Sur le pouvoir
    symbolique'), 115 n.
'Systems of Education and Systems
    of Thought' ('Systèmes
    d'enseignement et systèmes de
    pensée'), 24
'What Makes a Social Class?',
    118 n.
Braudel, Fernand, 190
Bürger, Peter, 142–3

Canguilhem, Georges, 3, 4
capital, symbolic, 22, 35, 93, 111–12,
    128, 182–3
    legitimized by state, 135–7
Cassirer, Ernst, 39, 40, 47, 126
change, 118–19
Chomsky, Noam, 9, 13
Cicourel, Aaron, 136
Cladel, Léon, 151
class, 49–50, 75, 117–18, 128–9, 138–9,
    181–2
classification, 24, 25, 28, 65–6, 73, 131–
    2, 180
    struggles over, 180–1
Clément, Jean-Paul, 157–160

Index

codification, 65, 66, 67
and formalization, 82–5
and normalization of practice, 80
and writing, 81–2
Cohn-Bendit, Daniel, 46
condescension, strategies of, 127
Confucius, 195
consensus, conflict and, 41
Constantinople, circus-hippodrome
at, 143–4
Critique, 4
cultural capital/*see* capital, symbolic
cultural production, field of
autonomy of, 145
position in field of power, 144–6
culture, 29
anachronism in attitude to, 104–5
custom, 67

Dabit, Eugène, 151
Dagron, Gilbert, 193
dance, 98–9, 165, 166
Davy, Georges, 5 n.
Descartes, René, 83, 188
determinations, social, 15
distance, social, 127–8
distinction, 11, 133, 188–9
domination, 24, 41, 112, 183
Duby, Georges, 181
Dumézil, Georges, 180
Durkheim, Emile, 6, 24, 38, 103, 125,
126, 178–9

Ecole normale, 3, 5
economic field, 73–4, 110–11
and interest, 88–9
economic strategies, 90–3
economics
and education system, 44
and sociology, 46–8
economy, principle of, 92–3
education, 23–4, 39, 42–5, 124, 178–9
Elias, Norbert, 193
Elster, Jon, 10, 11, 12, 107, 108
Empedocles, 97, 101
Episcopate, in France, 116
Esprit, 5
ethnology, 6, 7, 70
classification in, 72, 73

and objectification of practice, 98–
101
situation of observer in, 59–60
sociology *v.*, 66
existentialism, 3, 4–5

family, reproduction of the, 68–9
Fanon, Frantz, 7
Feuerbach, Ludwig, 13
Fichte, Johann, 13
field, 14, 72, 87–8, 107–8, 191–2
form, symbolic force of, 85
formalization
and codification, 82–5
and law, 84
Foucault, Michel, 4, 6
freedom, 14–16
Friedmann, Georges, 5

gift, ideology of, 109
Goffman, Erving, 134
Goldmann, Lucien, 13
Goodman, Nelson, 137, 138
Gouhier, Henri, 3
grammar, 79–80
Gramsci, Antonio, 27–8
groups, 75, 118, 137–9
and symbolic power, 192–3
Guéroult, Martial, 3

habitus, 9, 10, 11–12, 14–15, 61, 62,
63, 64, 73, 74, 76, 77–8, 90, 107–
9, 112–13, 116, 130–1, 190–1, 195
Havelock, E., 98
Hegel, G. W. F., 12
Heidegger, Martin, 5, 10
Hesiod, 99, 104
history, 41–2, 46, 190
Homer, *Odyssey*, 98, 102–5
homogamy, 71
honour, 22
Hüsserl, Edmund, 3, 4, 5, 10, 12, 109

illusio, 195
informational models, 79
institution, rites of, 195–6
institutions, 192–3
interactionism, 127, 130
interest, 48, 87, 106, 108–11

220

Joly, Henri, 99

Kabylia
  matrimonial strategies, 63, 66, 69,
    70, 77, 94, 134
  poets, 96–7
Kafka, Franz, 136
Kant, Immanuel, 6, 12, 24, 43
kinship
  relations, 96
  rules, 8, 9
  studies, 74
knowledge, 111–12
Koyré, Alexander, 3, 4
Kuhn, Thomas, 37

Lancelot, Alain, 172
language
  and codification, 80
  popular, 154–5
law, and formalization, 67, 84
Lazarsfeld, Paul, 19, 37
lector, 94–5
legalism, 76, 86
Leibniz, Gottfried, 83
Lemonier, Louis, 151
Lévi-Strauss, Claude, 6, 7, 9, 10, 20,
    23, 60–2, 71, 190
literary field, 150
  autonomy of, 144–5
  power relations in, 141, 143–4
  symbolic capital in, 141
  see also literature
literature
  populist, 151
  study of, 146–8
  see also literary field; text,
    interpretation of; writing
Locke, John, 47

Mammeri, Mouloud, 96
Manet, Edouard, 148–9
marriage
  and codification, 78
  see also matrimonial strategies
Marx, Karl, and Weber, 35–6
Marxism, 3, 7, 16–17, 27–8, 35–6,
    48–50, 118, 129, 179
materialism, 13
mathematical models, 47–8

matrimonial strategies, 9, 10, 63–4,
    67–71
Mauss, Marcel, 12
May '68 movement, 45–6
meanings, conflict over, 55, 96–7, 134–
    5
Merleau-Ponty, Maurice, 3, 5, 10, 197
Merton, Robert, 37
mimesis, 81, 98, 166–7
models, 47–8, 60–1, 79
monarchy, 193
myth, reinterpretation of, 99–105

naming, 55, 134
norms, universal, 31–2

objectification of practice, 79, 99–101
objectivism, 129–30
  v. subjectivism, 124–6
official discourse, 136
official nomination, 135–6
open concepts, 40–1
opinion polls, 168–74

Panofsky, Erwin, 12–13
Parsons, Talcott, 37
peasants, 21, 153–4
perception of social reality, 130–5
  symbolic struggle over, 134–5
phenomenology, 3, 10
philology, 95–8
philosophy, 5–6, 39–40
  changes in social meaning of, 162–3
Plato, 81, 98, 100
poetry, 143
politics, 24–5, 119, 150
  and populism, 152–3
Ponton, Rémy, 151
popular language, 154–5
populism
  politics and, 152–3
  writers and, 150–5
Poulaille, Henri, 151
power, field of, 127
  cultural producers and, 146
  and literary field, 144–5
power, symbolic, 115, 134–9
  basis of, 137–8
praxis, 22
preference, systems of, 91

principles, behaviour-guiding, 78–9
professionals, 151
project, 109–10
protension, 109
Proust, Marcel, 51
publication, 82

qualifications, educational, 135–6

Raphael, Max, 7
Rational Action Theory, 47
rationalization, 85
reading, 94–105
reason, 31–2, 108
regularity in social practice, 64–5
religion, 36, 150, 151
representation, 53–4, 134
reproduction, strategies of, 68–9, 74–5
ritual, 8, 10, 65–6, 73, 98–100
rules, 60–1, 64–5, 66, 76

Saint-Martin, Monique de, 69
Sartre, Jean-Paul, 3, 12, 49
Saussure, Ferdinand de, 6, 13, 82, 83,
    95, 96
schemata, 99
scholastic fallacy, 112
scholè, 21, 95, 112
Schütz, A., 125
science, 14, 32, 40–1
    and interest, 110–11
    positivist philosophy of, 19–20
    sociology of, 183–4
slang, 154–5
social functions, 195–6
social space, and symbolic space, 113–
    14
social world, perception of the, 130–5
society, and meaningful existence, 196
sociology, 5–6
    autonomy of, 185
    comparative method in, 191–2
    and creation of social reality, 17–18,
        181–2
    'crisis of', 37
    demand for, 50–1
    and economics, 46–8
    objectivism *v*. subjectivism in, 124–6
    oppositions in, 31, 34–5, 189
    political pressures on, 182, 185–6

reactions against, 187–8
    role of, 188
    as a science, 189
    specialization in, 39
    style of writing in, 51–5
sport
    amateur/professional divide in, 165
    and authoritarian regimes, 167
    and bodily communication, 166–7
    changes in practice of, 158
    changes in social meaning of, 163
    and social appropriation, 161, 164
    and social space, 157–8
    sociology of, 156
    structure of, 158–61
    supply and demand and, 161–2
Stalinism, 3
state, the, and symbolic capital, 136,
    137
Stoetzel, Jean, 5
strategy, 61–4
structuralism, 6, 8, 9–10, 18–22, 60,
    61, 62, 68, 71–2, 123–4
structure *v*. interaction, 127
structures, social, 132–3
    and mental structures, 14, 130–1
    and symbolic structures, 17–18, 53–
        4
subjectivism *v*. objectivism, 124–6
substantialism, 126

taxonomies, practical, 73
text, interpretation of, 94–105
theory, 30–1
Thérive, André, 151
Thompson, E. P., 129
Tiresias, 102
truth, 32

universal norms, 31–2
utilitarian theories, 108, 109

value, 89–90
Veblen, Thorstein, 11, 109, 133
violence, symbolic, 84–5, 135, 136,
    137, 183
Vuillemin, Jules, 4

Weber, Max, 21, 28, 45, 46, 49, 84, 85,
    106–7

and Marx, 35–6
Weil, Eric, 3, 4
Wittgenstein, Ludwig, 9, 28, 40, 73
working-class discourse, 154

writers/*see* literary field; literature; texts; writing
writing, codification and, 81–2